Sergei Prokofiev

SERGEI PROKOFIEV

SERGEI PROKOFIEV

His Musical Life

BY

ISRAEL V. NESTYEV

Translated from the Russian by ROSE PROKOFIEVA

Introduction by SERGEI EISENSTEIN

ALFRED A. KNOPF : NEW YORK

1946

Manufactured in the United States of America

FIRST AMERICAN EDITION

Preface

IN writing this brief review of the life and work of Sergei Prokofiev, I have set myself the task not so much of making an exhaustive analysis of his music as of briefly reviewing the most significant of his works and of making a few cursory remarks concerning the principal features of his style.

The bulk of this book was written in 1941 to mark Prokofiev's fiftieth birthday. After spending a year at the front I returned to Moscow on leave. During the time I spent in Moscow I was able to make a few additions dealing with Prokofiev's work during the war.

I have freely drawn on the composer's *Autobiography*, written in 1941 for *Sovietskaya Muzyka*, on my own personal meetings with him, and on a large number of reviews published both in Russia and abroad. My acknowledgments are due to Nikolai Miaskovsky, Boris Asafyev (Igor Glebov), Konstantin S. Saradzhev, V. V. Derzhanovsky, V. M. Morolev, L. V. Nikolayev, N. E. Dobychina, Reinhold Glière, and Abraham Spivakovsky, who have assisted me on a number of points of information. My thanks are also due to Grigori Shneerson, who has helped me in going through the foreign press, and N. P. Shastin, who has provided me with some unpublished materials.

I. V. N.

Contents

P-R-K-F-V

"YOU'LL have the music by noon."

We leave the small projection-room. Although it is now midnight, I feel quite calm. At exactly 11.55 a.m. a small, dark blue automobile will come through the gate of the film studio.

Sergei Prokofiev will emerge from the car.

In his hands will be the necessary piece of music.

At night we look at the new sequence of film.

By morning the new sequence of music will be ready for it.

This is what happened recently when we worked on *Alexander Nevsky*.

And this happens now, as we work together on *Ivan the Terrible*.

1.

Prokofiev works like a clock.

This clock neither gains nor loses time.

Like a sniper, it hits the very heart of punctuality. Prokofiev's punctuality is not a matter of business pedantry.

His exactness in time is a by-product of creative exactness.

Of absolute exactness in musical imagery.

Of absolute exactness in transposing this imagery into a mathematically exact means of expression, which Prokofiev has harnessed behind a bridle of hard steel.

This is the exactness of Stendhal's laconic style translated into music.

In crystal purity of expressive language Prokofiev is equaled only by Stendhal.

Clarity of idea and purity of image, however, are not always sufficient to achieve the popular accessibility of a worn penny.

A century ago Stendhal said: *"Je mets un billet dans une loterie dont le gros lot se réduit à ceci: être lu en 1935"*; although it is hard for us now to believe that there was once an

ix

age that did not understand the transparency of Stendhal's style.

Prokofiev is luckier.

His works are not obliged to wait a hundred years.

For many years he was not understood.

Then he was accepted — as a curiosity.

And only recently have they ceased to look askance at him.

Now, both at home and abroad, Prokofiev has moved onto the broadest road of popular recognition.

This process has been speeded by his contact with the cinema. Not merely because this contact popularized his creative work through the subjects, the large number of prints, or the wide accessibility of the screen.

But because Prokofiev's being consists in something below the surface appearance of the film medium — something similar to that which an event must undergo in being broken up for its passage through the film process.

First, the event must pass through the lens, in order that, in the aspect of a film image, pierced by the blinding beam of the projection-machine, it may begin to lead a new and magic life of its own on the white surface of the screen.

2.

One can see the early Prokofiev in the pictures produced by the most extreme tendencies of modern painting.

Occasionally he reminds one of the elegantly audacious Matisse.

More often — of the early Picasso's harsh arrogance.

Less often — of Rouault's frank coarseness.

At the same time there is often something in him resembling the sculptured texture of a bas-relief.

Fugitive Visions. Sarcasms. The Buffoon.

Here, a jagged edge of tin; there, the oily coating on the lacquer of asphalt; here, the agonizing twists of a spiral, bouncing like a spring toward the observer.

In their own various ways the "modern" painters sought,

not a reflection of events, but a bared solution for the riddle of the structure of phenomena.

They had to pay for their solution — with the sacrifice of the perceptible likeness of the object: all anecdotal quality in the object and all "integrated fact" gave way to the elements and their component parts, made tangible.

The "city theme" is no longer an impressionist weaving of street sensations — now it becomes a conglomerate of city elements: iron, a newspaper page, black letters, glass.

And this was young Prokofiev's road.

It was in vain that Henri Monnet in *Cahiers d'art* waxed ironical over the music of *Le Pas d'acier*: "It evokes thunder with thunder, a hammer-blow with a hammer-blow: fine stylization!"

It was the very lies of stylization from which Prokofiev was consciously fleeing, as he sought the objectivity of actual sounds.

But alongside that irony, in the same issue of *Cahiers d'art* (1927, No. 6), there is this comment on Picasso: "For Picasso painting is the skull of Yorick. He revolves it constantly in his hands, with intent curiosity" (Christian Zervos).

Isn't Prokofiev doing the same thing? Though perhaps with this difference, that in his long hands he revolves, with no less curiosity, not the form of music, but its object.

Not a skull, but a living face.

At first, simple objects — "things" — looked at from the viewpoints of their texture, material, materiality, structure.

These become faces, which can be identified by their eyelids, cheek-bones, crania.

Later these grow into human images, composed of emotions (*Romeo and Juliet*), and, finally, they develop into images that embody pages of history, images of phenomena, of social systems — collective images of the people.

Thus the hoof-beats of the Teutonic knights in *Alexander Nevsky* do not merely "hammer for the sake of hammering," but out of this "hammer for hammer" and "gallop for gallop" there is evolved a universal image, galloping across the thirteenth century to the twentieth — toward the unmasking of fascism.

In this inner revelation of the spirit and nature of fascism, in this objectivization via fixed elements of tonal imagery, there is something akin to that period of modern painting when painters searched for the way to reveal the actuality of phenomena, through the physical composition of their materials — glass, wire, tin, or cardboard.

This is another level. A difference in degree. In theme.

For these solutions are no longer possible without social aim or without passion.

3.

The Prokofiev of our time is a man of the screen.

And he is related to the young Prokofiev very much as the motion-picture screen is related to the extreme searches of modern painting.

One of those extreme seekers said cleverly: "Modern art has finally achieved *suprematism* — a black square and a white quadrangle." All that remained was for the quadrangle to become a screen. And racing across this screen is the optical phenomenon of cinematic chiaroscuro.

The new Prokofiev can be sensed through the screen.

Prokofiev is a man of the screen in that special sense which makes it possible for the screen to reveal not only the appearance and substance of objects, but also, and particularly, their peculiar inner structure.

The logic of their existence. The dynamics of their development.

We have seen how for decades the "modern" experiments in painting sought, at an immeasurable cost in effort, to resolve those difficulties which the screen has solved with the ease of a child. Dynamics, movement, chiaroscuro, transitions from form to form, rhythm, plastic repetition, etc., etc.

Unable to achieve this to perfection, the painters nevertheless paid for their search at the cost of the representation and objectivity of the imaged thing.

Among all the plastic arts the cinema alone, with no loss of expressive objectivity, and with complete ease, resolves all these problems of painting, but at the same time the cinema is able to communicate much more. It alone is able to reconstruct so profoundly and fully the inner movement of phenomena, as we see it on the screen.

The camera-angle reveals the innermost being of nature. . . .

The juxtaposition of various camera viewpoints reveals the artist's viewpoint on the phenomenon.

Montage structure unites the objective existence of the phenomenon with the artist's subjective relation to it.

None of the severe standards set for itself by modern painting are relinquished. At the same time everything lives with the full vitality of the phenomenon.

It is in this particular sense that Prokofiev's music is amazingly plastic. It is never content to remain an illustration, but everywhere, gleaming with triumphant imagery, it wonderfully reveals the inner movement of the phenomenon and its dynamic structure, in which is embodied the emotion and meaning of the event.

Whether it be the March from the fantastic *Love for Three Oranges*, the duel between Mercutio and Tybalt, the gallop of the Teutonic knights in *Alexander Nevsky*, or the entrance of Kutuzov in the finale of *War and Peace* — everywhere, in the very nature of phenomena, Prokofiev grasps the structural secret that, before all else, conveys the broad meaning of the phenomenon.

Having grasped this structural secret of all phenomena, he clothes it in the tonal camera-angles of instrumentation, compelling it to gleam with shifts in timbre, and forces the whole inflexible structure to blossom into the emotional fullness of orchestration.

The moving graphic outlines of his musical images, which

xiii

thus rise, are thrown by him onto our consciousness just as, through the blinding beam of the projector, moving images are flung onto the white plane of the screen.

This is not an engraved impression in paint of a phenomenon, but a light that pierces the phenomenon by means of tonal chiaroscuro.

4.

I am not speaking of Prokofiev's musical technique, or of his method of composition.

Nor do I speak of the path toward the achievement of this impression, but of the nature of the achieved sensation.

And in the nature of Prokofiev's expressive speech the first thing I notice is the "steel step" of drumming consonants, which, above all, beat out the clarity of thought in those places where many others would have been tempted to use indistinctly modulated nuances, equivalent to the candied fluency of the vowel elements.

The frenzied conscience of Rimbaud, carried in his *"bateau ivre"* along the flowing lava of diffuse and drunken images, dictated to him that litany of praise to the vowels — *Le Sonnet des voyelles.*

If Prokofiev had written this sonnet, he would have dedicated it to the sensible supports of language — to the Consonants.

In the same way that he writes operas, leaning not on the melody of rhymes, but on the bony angularity of unrhythmic prose.

. . . He would have written his sonnet to the Consonants. . . .

But stop — what's this?

Under the cunning clauses of contracts — in the polite inscriptions on photographs for friends and admirers — in the upper right-hand corner of the music-paper of a new piece —
— we see, always — the harsh tap-dance of consonants:

—P—R—K—F—V—

This is the usual signature of the composer!
He even spells his name with nothing but consonants!

5.

Once Bach found a divine melodic pattern in the very outlines of the letters in his name.

Read as notes, these letters — B A C H — arranged themselves in a musical line, which became the melodic base for one of his works.

The consonants with which Prokofiev signs his name could be read as a symbol of the undeviating consistency of his entire talent.

From the composer's creative work — as from his signature — everything unstable, transient, accidental, or capricious has been expelled.

This is how they wrote on ancient icons:

Gospod (Lord) was written "Gd," and Tzar "Tzr,"

and "Rzhstvo Btzy" stood for *Rozhdestvo Bogoroditzy* (Birth of the Mother of God).

The strict spirit of the old Slavonic canon is reflected in these eliminations of everything accidental, transient, mundane.

In teaching, the canon leaned on the eternal, over the transient.

In painting — on the existent, rather than on the ephemeral.

In inscriptions — on the consonants, apparently symbols of the eternal, as opposed to the accidental.

This is what we find in the ascetic drum-beat of those five consonants — P, R, K, F, V — sensed through the dazzling radiation of Prokofiev's musical chiaroscuro.

And it is thus that the black-lacquered letters flash over the rhythmic conflict of sharp-edged planes on the canvases of Picasso.

And thus the gold letters burn dimly on the frescoes of Spaso-Nereditzkaya.

Or they echo with the abbot's stern call through the floods

of sepia and the celestial azure of cobalt in the murals of Feofan the Greek on the vaults of the Fyodor Stratilat Church in Novgorod.

Equal to the inflexible severity of Prokofiev's writing is the magnificence of his lyricism, which blossoms in that miracle of Prokofiev orchestration — the "Aaron's rod" of his structural logic.

6.

Prokofiev is profoundly nationalistic.

But not in the *kvas* and *shchi* manner of the conventionally Russian pseudo-realists.

Nor is he nationalistic in the "holy water" detail and genre of Perov's or Repin's brush.

Prokofiev is nationalistic in the severely traditional sense that dates back to the savage Scythian and the unsurpassed perfection of the thirteenth-century stone carvings on the cathedrals of Vladimir and Suzdal.

His nationalism springs from the very sources that shaped the national consciousness of the Russian people, the source that is reflected in the folk-wisdom of our old frescoes or the icon-craftsmanship of Rublev.

That is why antiquity resounds so wonderfully in Prokofiev's music — not by archaic or stylized means, but by the most extreme and hazardous twists of ultra-modern musical composition.

Here, within Prokofiev himself, we find the same paradoxical synchronization as when we juxtapose an icon with a cubist painting — Piscasso with the frescoes of Spaso-Nereditzkaya.

Through this true (in a Hegelian sense) originality, through this "firstness" of his, Prokofiev is, at the same time, both profoundly national — and international.

Just as international and ultra-modern as an icon painted on sandalwood hanging among the canvases of a New York art gallery.

xvi

7.

But it is not only in this way that Prokofiev is international.
He also is international in the active variety of his expressive
speech.

In this the canon of his musical mentality is again similar to
a canon of antiquity, but in this case to the canon of Byzantine
tradition, which has the faculty of shining through any environment it finds itself in, ever fresh and unexpected.

On Italian soil it shines through the Madonnas of Cim-
abue.

On Spanish soil — through the works of Domenikos Theo-
tokopoulos, called El Greco.

In the state of Novgorod — through the murals of anony-
mous masters, murals barbarically trampled underfoot by the
brutish hordes of invading Teutons. . . .

Thus the art of Prokofiev can be fired by more than purely
national, historical, or patriotic themes, such as the heroic
events of the nineteenth, sixteenth, or thirteenth centuries
(the triad of *War and Peace*, *Ivan the Terrible*, and *Alexander
Nevsky*).

The pungent talent of Prokofiev, attracted by the passionate
environment of Shakespearean Italy of the Renaissance, flares
up in a ballet on the theme of that great dramatist's most lyrical tragedy.

In the magic environment of Gozzi's phantasmagoria, from
Prokofiev there issues forth an amazing cascade of fantasy, a
quintessence of Italy at the end of the eighteenth century.

In the nursery — the scrawny neck of Andersen's *Ugly Duckling* or *Peter and the Wolf*.

In the environment of the bestialities of the thirteenth century — the unforgettable image of the blunted iron "wedge"
of Teutonic knights, galloping forward with the same "irre-
sistibility" as did the tank columns of their loathsome descend-
ants.

8.

Everywhere — search: severe, methodical. This makes Prokofiev kin to the masters of the early Renaissance, when a painter — simultaneously philosopher and sculptor — would inevitably be a mathematician as well.

Everywhere freedom from an impressionistic "generality," from the mask of "approximation," and from the smeared color of "blobs."

In his hands one senses not an arbitrary brush, but a responsible camera-lens.

Once in an article on Degas, Paul Valéry wrote about the art of the future. Far from the mess of paint-pots, the smell of glue and kerosene and turpentine, from dirty brushes and dusty easels, Paul Valéry displays for us not a studio, but something closer to a laboratory — something between an operating-room and a dynamo station. Among the exact movements of people clad in sanitary gowns, in rubber gloves, amid the steely glitter of the prepared instruments — new works of painting would be born.

Valéry's dream came true — by the end of Degas's life the cinema had appeared.

The ideal in painting, in Valéry's view, is embodied in music, it seems to me, in the work of Prokofiev.

And that is why his work is so brilliantly organic especially amid the microphones, flashing photo-elements, celluloid spirals of film, the faultless accuracy of meshing sprockets in the motion-picture camera, the millimetric exactness of synchronization, and the mathematical calculations of length in film montage. . . .

The blinding beam of the projection-machine is shut off.

The ceiling lights of the projection-room are turned on.

Prokofiev wraps his scarf around him.

I may sleep calmly.

At exactly 11.55 a.m. tomorrow morning his small blue automobile will come through the gate of the film studio.

Five minutes later the score will lie on my desk.
On it will be the symbolic letters:
P–R–K–F–V.
Nothing ephemeral, nothing accidental.
All is distinct, exact, perfect.

That is why Prokofiev is not only one of the greatest composers of our time, but also, in my opinion, the most wonderful film composer.

SERGEI EISENSTEIN [1]

ALMA ATA, November 1942
Moscow, November 1944

---

[1] Translated by Jay Leyda.

Introduction

SERGEI PROKOFIEV is well known throughout the world as one of the leading and most distinguished of modern composers. Few composers in either hemisphere can rival the power and originality of his talent, his wide popularity, or the scope and fertility of his genius.

All that he has written during the long years of his career, and especially his music for the piano, has long since won a lasting place for itself in the repertory of Soviet and foreign musicians. With more than thirty years of independent activity behind him, Prokofiev has preserved all his indefatigable creative energy, his keen imagination and ingenuity, and his inexhaustible vitality. He is a stranger to academic complacency, to the smug self-satisfaction of those who have achieved a certain professional mastery, to saccharine prettiness, and to petty self-adulation. He is always striving for perfection, renewing the range of his artistic media, and absorbing the new trends in the ever changing life around him. Yet he has remained true to himself.

It is edifying to observe how tirelessly Prokofiev fights for his artistic principles, never succumbing to the inertia of the stereotyped. This was true of him thirty years ago, when he threw down the gauntlet to the academic musical world of pre-Revolutionary Russia. It was true of him during his wanderings through America and Europe, when he hungrily pursued his quest of the new, notwithstanding the furious attacks of the critics. It is still true of him at the present day. During the past decade Sergei Prokofiev has been living and working with us as one of the most interesting masters of Soviet music. Soviet reality is exercising a more and more tangible and beneficent influence on his work: after *Romeo and Juliet, Alexander Nevsky, Zdravitsa,* and *Semyon Kotko* one can speak quite definitely of a *new phase* in Prokofiev's music, what one might term the creative synthesis of the whole of his thirty-five years of mature work as a composer. His brilliant inventiveness and inexhaustible virtuosity have been directed more and more confidently toward the solution of the social problems facing Soviet art. It is precisely with this phase that the social trend of his art has become more clearly defined, more conscious and purposeful.

A diligent and systematic worker, Prokofiev never allows himself to be guided by the whims of inspiration. There is nothing of the egocentric manner of the romantics in his method. He works at times like a talented architect capable of placing the whole of his knowledge and artistic ability at the service of one or another productive task. And when a productive task is not warmed by the breath of poetic feeling, when it is not touched by the inner world of the artist and is not in harmony with his sharply individual style, the music is bound to seem cold, superficial, and artificial.

A passion for exploring new pastures, the enthusiasm of the experimenter, the avidity of the traveler, a constant striving to discover new musical fields, have been Prokofiev's outstanding traits since his student days in the Conservatory. New methods of orchestration, original harmonies, new, unexplored dramatic situations in opera, unique unorthodox uses of the libretto — all these have attracted Prokofiev from his very childhood. It is not surprising that not all of his discoveries have withstood the test of time, that not all of them are comprehensible to the average concert-goer or suitable for further development.

But whenever a new discovery retains its ties with the musical past, when it is destined to unfold some page of living truth, when it reveals the keen and sensitive eye of the observer, the humor of the narrator, the skill of the virtuoso, then the experiment crosses the boundary into the realm of living art and becomes a true expression of the epoch.

Need it be pointed out that innovation and the restless search for new modes of expression are precisely the qualities most in keeping with the spirit of our times? Without them Soviet music could not advance. Even when innovation is limited to the sphere of laboratory experimentation, it is far more valuable than placid unimaginative composition along the beaten track.

However conflicting Prokofiev's searchings of recent years may be, whatever the effect on them of rational, cold-blooded experimentation, of that regrettable abuse of the primitive, that artificial simplicity, one thing is quite clear: Prokofiev is undoubtedly approaching that summit of true art which has beckoned to him from the earliest years of his career as a composer.

Sergei Prokofiev's advent in the world of Russian music coincided with a grave crisis in Russian art. Those were the troublous times that preceded the First World War and the October Revolution, when the decay and inevitable collapse of the culture of the Russian bourgeoisie and nobility became most apparent. Fashions in art in that period changed with fantastic rapidity: imperialist Russia, keeping pace with the West, produced an ever increasing number of new and extreme schools and trends in art, each of which denounced the art of its predecessors. In the domain of painting, for instance, the exquisite stylization and decorative retrospection of the World of Art [1] were replaced by the rude earthiness, solid color effects, and formalistic objectivism of the Russian Cézanne school ("Jack of Diamonds"). In their turn, the young futurist groupings ("Ass's Tail" and "Target") rebelled against the French orientation of the "Jack of Diamonds," proclaimed the cult of the primitive and simplified, and pointed the way to abstract, subjectless, "black square" designs.

In poetry the shortlived domination of symbolism had ended. The archæology and mysticism of the older generation of symbolists already sounded old-fashioned. The cleverest of the symbolist poets, such as Alexander Blok, themselves admitted that the school had collapsed. Onto the poetic arena

---

[1] See p. xxv, note 3.

emerged the acmeists or Adamists, with their cult of the concrete, their material, mundane system of symbols and affected Scythianism. "The band of Adams with partings in their hair," Mayakovsky aptly christened them. And in the midst of the group of ultra-Lefts, the anarchistic and rebellious Moscow cubo-futurists, alongside the out-and-out formalists of the nihilist variety, rose the young Mayakovsky, who flayed with equal passion the "castrated psychology" of the naturalists, the passive æstheticism of the symbolists, and the "perfumed pornography" of Igor Severyanin.

The very same process of feverish change of different, sometimes mutually exclusive schools and trends was taking place in Russian music. The representatives of the great tradition of Russian music, the direct proponents of Five and Tchaikovsky schools, were still living and occupying a leading position in the musical life of the country. But in modernist circles these traditions were already considered as shamefully out of date as the realistic traditions of the *Peredvizhniki* [2] in the circles of the young painters. A conscious anti-Tchaikovskyism became the credo of the modern musicians. Serge Rachmaninoff and Nikolai Medtner, so recently associated with modernistic trends, found themselves in the second decade of the twentieth century in the camp of the moderate Rights. Amazingly rapid was the evolution of the brilliant Scriabin from Chopinism and neo-romantic sympathies to extremely subjective, expressionist art, to the assertion of his super-individualistic aspirations in forms that grew more and more complex, more and more remote from accepted musical genres and standards.

Similarly rapid were the rise and decline of trends emulating French impressionism. Vladimir Rebikov, the first Russian impressionist, faded into obscurity before his grandiose projects were realized; the experiments of Nikolai Tcherepnin and the young Sergei Vassilenko, followers of the World of Art

---

[2] *Peredvizhniki* — the name given to a group of painters of a decidedly realistic and democratic trend in the last quarter of the nineteenth century.

school, the effective stylization of the Diaghilev [3] ballet (*Scheherazade, The Firebird*) were ousted by the cubist barbarism of Stravinsky's *Le Sacre du printemps*. Analogous processes were at work in the Russian theater: from the symbolist experiments of the Moscow Art Theater and the Komissarzhevskaya Theater, through the leanings toward the grotesque and the masque, the tendency ran toward the purely formalistic futurist extravaganzas of Meyerhold; and alongside it was the repudiation in principle of all operatic art as having allegedly outlived its purpose, and the striving to replace it with a semi-acrobatic pantomime.

All branches of art in this period passed from the elaborate beauty of symbolism and impressionism to crude simplification and cynical primitivization: to cubism and absence of subject in painting, to a studied abracadabra and verbal cacophony in poetry, to a constructivism devoid of both meaning and emotion in music, and in the theater to the "stunts" and arbitrary eccentricities of the producer.

And, of course, Lenin, Plekhanov, Gorky, and Tolstoy were right when they voiced so many sharp protests against the decadence of art, against its deliberate negation of the idea. They correctly pointed out that the exalted ideal of great art which could "sear the hearts of men with a word" does not tolerate the worship of form *per se*.

However much we may value the outstanding examples of Russian modernism, however highly we may appraise its vividness of form, its culture, taste, inventiveness, and originality, it is quite clear to us today that the World of Art group, Balmont, the young Stravinsky, the masters of the "Jack of Diamonds," and the Diaghilev troupe, all represented an ivory-tower art that shut itself off from Russian life on the eve of the

---

[3] Sergei Pavlovich Diaghilev (1872–1929), distinguished Russian art scholar, musician, and lawyer by education. In the late nineties of last century led the struggle of the young Russian innovators against academism and the followers of the *Peredvizhniki*. Organizer of the World of Art group, which rallied around the magazine of the same name. From 1909 organized the Russian modernist ballet abroad. While in Paris Diaghilev produced most of the ballets of Stravinsky, Prokofiev, Debussy, Ravel, Poulenc, Milhaud, and Auric.

Revolution, displaying a total indifference to the vital interests and passions of the world around them.

It was only in spite of principles of modernism, as a repudiation of these principles, that artists who were sensitive to the pulse of the Russia of their day rose from the morass of decadence. Such were Blok and Bryusov in symbolist poetry, and Scriabin and Miaskovsky in the new Russian music. Blok, Bryusov, and Miaskovsky were subsequently among the first to embrace in their own way the October Revolution.

The music of the young Prokofiev had a dual quality. On the one hand it cannot be considered apart from the kaleidoscopic change of styles and schools occurring in all spheres of Russian art at that time. Prokofiev is undoubtedly a genuine product of Russian modernism. His talent was inspired and nurtured by the proponents of the new modernistic trends with Diaghilev at their head. Their credo was originality, invention, formal novelty at all costs; the meaning of art, they held, lay in the inimitable personality of the artist himself. The social struggle, great human ideals — all this was no concern of the artist.[4] A product of modernism, bound to it by a thousand threads and to a considerable extent infected by many of its prejudices, the young Prokofiev at the same time rebelled against conventional, academic art and decadent symbolist art. Like Mayakovsky in poetry, he swept the outmoded rubbish and the rotten scum of decadence out of the Augean stables of Russian music, directing music along the road of simplicity, concreteness, and accessibility.

As Mayakovsky wrote in his *Order of the Day for the Army of Art:*

> Drag the pianos into the street,
> fish the drums out of the window.
> Piano the drums
> and drum on the pianos to beat
> the band, till they lighten
> and thunder.

---

[4] "An artist should love beauty alone," wrote Diaghilev. "The reactions of art to worldly cares and worries are unworthy of this smile of the divinity." (Quoted by N. Sokolova in *The World of Art.*)

The fierce nihilism of the rebel musician, notwithstanding his revolutionary tendencies, was fraught with danger; his very rebellion, unless there were positive ideals to counterbalance it, might have degenerated into something akin to the "ultra-Left" variety of modernism. In that case the spirit of rebellion would have led Prokofiev to a negation of the very foundations of art and to an anarchic repudiation of all its standards and canons, as in the case of the "Left" painters, or to a cold "impasse of perversion," as with Stravinsky and Schönberg. Then Prokofiev would have perished for us in the bog of formalism. But fortunately his rebellion was always combined with an intuitive striving toward exalted human ideals, with positive artistic aspirations. And if he did not reach out toward his own truth in art as clearly and confidently as did the young Mayakovsky, that truth has triumphed for him too in the final analysis and returned him to the fold of Soviet art. In the present review of his artistic development I shall endeavor to trace the path by which, after overcoming many obstacles, the composer arrived at the realization of his true goal.

I. N.

Sergei Prokofiev

Book I

Early Years

1 : Childhood

SERGEI SERGEYEVICH PROKOFIEV was born on April 23, 1891 in the village of Sontsovka, near what is now the town of Stalino in the Donbas. His father, Sergei Alexeyevich Prokofiev (1846–1910), managed the estate of Sontsov, a local landowner, for thirty years. A first-class agronomist, a graduate of the Petrovsko-Razumovskoye Agricultural Academy in Moscow, the composer's father built up in Sontsovka a model economy complete with imported machinery, a stud farm, and so on.

In his youth Sergei Alexeyevich, who came from a family of Moscow commoners, participated in student disturbances and paid the price of his convictions. Although he subsequently retired from politics, he preserved his progressive views to the end of his life and devoted much time and effort to organizing schools in the district and helping the peasants with their farming. In his home at Sontsovka he possessed a large library, to which he was always adding. Faith in the progress of human culture was the foundation of Sergei Alexeyevich's liberal outlook.

The mother of the future composer, Marya Grigoryevna Zhitkova (1855–1924), was born in St. Petersburg in a middle-

3

class family. She was an excellent pianist and an intelligent teacher. Together with her husband she took an active part in the life of the village, teaching in the local school.

When, after the death of two small daughters, a son was born to the Prokofievs, it was perhaps natural that he should become the object of particular love and attention. The parents took great pains with his education. They did not send him to school, but taught him themselves, "torturing" him, as Prokofiev now recalls, for six hours a day.

It is to his mother that he owes his early musical training. From the first years of his life little Seryozha heard classical music, chiefly Beethoven and Chopin, as played by his mother. She introduced the boy to music with infinite pedagogical tact. At first she allowed him to describe his own impressions of the music he heard; then, on his own initiative, to "help" her play scales and exercises, tapping out his own baby version in the upper register until gradually he began to pick out the melody by himself. At the age of five and a half he composed his first piece of music, a *Hindu Gallop*, the result of his impressions after listening to stories about the Hindus. The piece, which was written down by his mother, was in F major, but without the B flat, for the budding composer still fought shy of the black notes.

At the age of six he had already written a waltz, a march, and a rondo, and at seven, a march for four hands. His mother led him imperceptibly into the world of music, gradually enriching his knowledge and striving to develop his independent judgment and a sincere love for music.

In Sontsovka, Seryozha spent much time in the society of the village children. One of their favorite pastimes was to stage improvised versions of stories heard or read. The scenarios for these juvenile *commedie dell'arte* were usually composed by the young Prokofiev himself.

Ukrainian and Russian folk-melodies were often sung in the village, and though Seryozha had little taste for any but serious music, there can nevertheless be little doubt that his

feeling for Russian national melody can be traced to his childhood years in the village.

In the year 1899, when Seryozha was eight, his parents took
him with them on a visit to Moscow. The trip made a lasting
impression on the lad. He was taken to the Grand Opera to
see *The Sleeping Beauty*, and heard *Faust* and *Prince Igor* at
the Solodovnikov Theater. This served as the stimulus for his
first independent attempts at opera. In June of the following
year he had completed a three-act opera, *The Giant*, written in
a piano arrangement without the vocal parts.[1] Then came another opera, *Desert Islands*, based on a plot of thrilling adventure complete with storms and shipwrecks. "The story didn't
hang together very well," Prokofiev recalls, "but there were
definite attempts to depict the elements — rain and storm."

In the summer of 1901, when the young composer was visiting at the estate of the Rayevskys, wealthy relatives of his
mother (Marya Prokofieva's sister was married to the landowner Rayevsky, a descendant of Pushkin's friends of the
same name), *The Giant* was performed [2] under the author's
own direction with great success. His uncle was delighted.
"When your operas are produced in an imperial theater," he
said jovially, "don't forget that the first performance of your
work was given in my house."

The following year Seryozha was taken to Moscow again,
where Y. Pomerantsev, who later became conductor of the
Moscow Grand Opera, introduced him to Sergei Taneyev.
After hearing the overture to *Desert Islands*, Taneyev formed
a high opinion of the boy's talent. He advised the mother to
"cherish the boy's gifts," and recommended his pupil Pomerantsev as a tutor for the lad. But the traditional studies in
harmony frightened and repelled Seryozha. "I wanted to compose operas with marches, storms and blood-curdling scenes
and instead they saddled me with tiresome exercises." [3]

---

[1] The text was inserted above the treble-clef part. — *Editor.*
[2] With a cast made up of the boy's relatives. — *Editor.*
[3] This quotation, like all others given subsequently without reference to the
source, is taken from Prokofiev's *Autobiography*, the first section of which was

SERGEI PROKOFIEV

Pomerantsev was succeeded by Reinhold Glière, who, at
the invitation of the Prokofievs, spent the summers of 1902
and 1903 at Sontsovka, teaching the boy the rudiments of
harmony, analysis of form, and instrumentation. Study of the
three-part song form resulted in pianoforte pieces that the
young composer called *Ditties*, of which he composed whole
series in the years that followed. Glière, who proved to be a
pedagogue of unusual ability and intelligence, found the correct approach to the psychology of the talented lad. Lessons
in instrumentation and composition were followed by a game
of croquet or chess. The elements of form and instrumentation were taught, not abstractly, but on the basis of a concrete
analysis of familiar works. Glière had the greatest respect for
the strictly regulated regimen of work that existed in the Prokofiev household. Each day had to bring some tangible sign
of progress in Seryozha's studies. Every year the mother would
bring from Moscow heaps of studies and exercises for the
piano, which the boy zealously practiced. This habit of regu-
lar and organized work, inculcated in him by his parents, has
remained. In contrast to the bohemian lack of discipline of so
many musicians, his regimen is always exact, assiduous, and
systematic.

Many of the *Ditties* composed under Glière's guidance have
remained in Prokofiev's files to this day. They afford an insight into the musical predilections of the eleven-year-old
composer. In them one can catch echoes of Schubert's *Erl-
könig*, Schumann's syncopated rhythms, melodies in the spirit
of Bellini and Verdi, side by side with specimens of more
common genres — marches, waltzes, and mazurkas. There is
among them a most amusing sentimental waltz written "for
Aunt Tanechka's birthday."

Nevertheless, the individuality of the composer was already
asserting itself in these childish pieces with their sharply ac-
cented rhythms, their predilection for dance measures, their

published in *Sovietskaya Muzyka*, No. 4 (1941), while the rest remains in
manuscript.

6

Examples

1. Ditty No. 10, 1st Series. Dedicated to Aunt Tanechka, December 25 (O.S.), 1902.

striving after hyperboles and unexpectedness (for example, *Ditty* No. 7, 1st series, with the *forte-forte-fortissimo* climax and the peculiar chord accompaniment in the recapitulation).

By the end of the summer of 1902, Prokofiev's studies with Glière culminated in the composition of a four-movement Symphony in G major for full orchestra. This score has also been preserved. The opening *presto* bears traces of the author's leanings toward the classics, with certain echoes of the Italian operatic overture. In November the symphony was shown to Taneyev, who indiscreetly laughed at its "crude" harmony. Prokofiev was wounded to the quick by Taneyev's criticism, which nevertheless had the effect of inducing him to experiment in harmony.[4]

Following a violin sonata (the main theme of which was used by Prokofiev ten years later for his cello *Ballad*, Op. 15) the young composer tried his hand at opera once more. This

---

[4] Eight years later the same Taneyev, on hearing the *Études*, Op. 2, which abounded in "false notes," as he put it, was much put out at the thought that it was he who had been responsible for launching Prokofiev "on such a slippery path."

was during Glière's second visit to Sontsovka, in the summer of 1903. Based on the text of Pushkin's *Feast during the Plague*, the opera was quite a professional job, complete with vocal parts and orchestral score. True, the Overture was disproportionately long, comprising almost half of the opera. Nevertheless, the young composer was inordinately proud of his opera, and even compared it to one on the same subject by César Cui that appeared about the same time. Six years later, when graduating from the composition department of the Conservatory, Prokofiev returned to the *Feast during the Plague* and rewrote it completely.

Early in 1904 Seryozha was introduced to Glazunov, who advised sending him at once to the St. Petersburg Conservatory. "There is every chance of his becoming a real artist," said Glazunov.

2 : Years of Study

> The last duckling was very ugly. It had no feathers, and its legs were long and gawky. "What if it's a turkey!" exclaimed the mother duck in horror.
>
> ANDERSEN: *The Ugly Duckling*

IN the autumn of 1904, after a Sontsovka summer spent in composing the first act of a new opera, *Undine* (after La Motte-Fouqué and Zhukovsky), Prokofiev, now turned thirteen, entered the St. Petersburg Conservatory. His mother moved with him to St. Petersburg, while his father remained in Sontsovka. The young composer came to the entrance examinations armed with his four operas, two sonatas, a symphony, and a number of pieces for the piano. The examining board, which included such eminent musicians as Rimsky-Korsakov, Glazunov, and Anatoly Lyadov, was impressed.

Rimsky-Korsakov was delighted with the lad's talent. "Here is a pupil after my own heart," he said.

Thus began Prokofiev's ten years in the St. Petersburg Conservatory, ten years of rapid development of his original talent, ten years of ceaseless, stubborn struggle with his professors for the assertion of his own individual style.

The trouble began almost at once in Lyadov's class; the dry, traditional methods of training irked the young composer. Although a fine and intelligent musician himself, Lyadov had never liked the teaching profession and took little interest in the creative aspirations of his pupils. *Undine* remained unfinished and no one in the Conservatory appeared interested in the work. On the other hand, Lyadov laid particular emphasis on purity in voice-leading and on strict observance of the rules in harmony exercises. Prokofiev frequently failed to measure up to these requirements, and his notebooks were often criss-crossed with the nervous lines drawn by the pen of his infuriated professor.

Then came the 1905 Revolution, with its student meetings and disturbances, the disgraceful dismissal of Rimsky-Korsakov, and the resignation of Lyadov and Glazunov. The young Prokofiev was caught up in the vortex of events without understanding what was happening. "I also signed a protest in which we threatened to leave the Conservatory, much to the horror of my father." With Lyadov's departure the harmony lessons were suspended. Prokofiev spent the 1905–6 school year studying the piano with Alexander Winkler and working with Lyadov at the latter's home on the second act of *Undine* and some pieces for the piano.

His summers were invariably spent at Sontsovka, where the earnest young Conservatory student from St. Petersburg became a happy carefree boy again, full of fun and mischief. His daily quota of piano practice over, he would run outside to romp and play with the village lads. During these summer visits home Prokofiev met a sincere admirer of his gifts, V. M. Morolev, a young veterinary surgeon. Morolev took a great

interest in the lad's compositions and often played duets with
him on the piano, treating him as though he were his equal in
years. Later Prokofiev dedicated to Morolev his First Sonata,
Op. 1, his March in F minor, Op. 12, and several unpublished
pieces for the piano, including *Reproach*.

2. *Reproach*, unpublished piano piece, January 1907.

The year 1906–7 saw the beginning of the molding of Prokofiev's talent as a composer. Lyadov and Rimsky-Korsakov
had returned to the Conservatory, and the classes in the composition department were resumed. A number of talented
young men who later rose to prominence — Boris Asafyev,
Nikolai Miaskovsky, Y. Akimenko-Stepovy, and Lazare Samin-
sky — were studying counterpoint under Lyadov during this
period. Prokofiev's lifelong friendship with Miaskovsky began
at this time. They seemed an ill-assorted pair, sixteen-year-old
Seryozha Prokofiev, who often tried the patience of Lyadov
and Rimsky-Korsakov with his mischievous taunting, and
serious-minded, level-headed Nikolai Miaskovsky, a sapper offi-
cer with definite views on most subjects. But this friendship
with Miaskovsky served to broaden Prokofiev's musical outlook and prompted him to take a more serious interest in new

music. Gradually his preference for Grieg, Rimsky-Korsakov, and Wagner gave way to an avid interest in Richard Strauss, Reger, and Debussy. These latter were, of course, regarded in the Conservatory as forbidden fruit. When Lyadov lectured his pupils for taking liberties with harmony, he would say indignantly: "I don't understand why you study with me. Why don't you go to Richard Strauss or to Debussy?"

Max Reger's visit to St. Petersburg in 1907 marked the beginning of Prokofiev's systematic study of the new music of the West. A closer intimacy with Miaskovsky on the grounds of joint music-making began with Reger's Serenade in G major for four hands. Later the two were joined by the pianist B. Zakharov. They played four-hand arrangements of Strauss (*Don Juan, Till Eulenspiegel, Also sprach Zarathustra, Tod und Verklärung*), Reger, and Schumann. They spent many enjoyable evenings discussing, arguing, and demonstrating their own compositions. They sometimes held impromptu composition contests; a group of young composers would undertake to write songs on one and the same text, or someone would conceive the idea of depicting snow in musical images (Miaskovsky wrote the music of a "most disagreeable storm," Prokofiev's snow was "soft and gentle, falling in large flakes"). Prokofiev's passion for Reger (the violin sonatas in C major and F-sharp minor, *From a Diary*, Variations on a Bach Theme) suggested many harmonic novelties to Prokofiev (complicated discords and transition chords) and a tendency to restless, agitated melody. At the same time Prokofiev was intensely interested in the music of Scriabin, whose Third Symphony impressed him profoundly. He was very proud of a two-hand pianoforte arrangement of the first movement of the *Divine Poem* that he had written, and intended to show it to Scriabin.

A lively correspondence sprang up between Miaskovsky and Prokofiev during the latter's stay at Sontsovka in the summers of 1907 and 1908. In their letters they discussed their compositions in detail and offered each other advice. Prokofiev's Symphony in E minor (not included in his catalogued works) was composed in this way in 1908, as was Miaskovsky's First Symphony, in C minor, Op. 3. "I derived much more benefit from this correspondence than from Lyadov's dry lessons," notes Prokofiev himself. During the 1906–7 and 1907–8 school years he worked hard in the classes of Lyadov and Rimsky-Korsakov, but his studies satisfied neither himself nor his teachers. His exercises in counterpoint, a subject in which he was intensely interested, were too original and unusual to be appreciated by Lyadov, who considered them harsh and crude. Lyadov was inclined to lose his temper on such occasions. Rimsky-Korsakov, on the other hand, was coldly ironic, and often ridiculed what he considered to be the unevenness and incoherence of his pupil's exercises in instrumentation.

Besides his class work Prokofiev was required to bring some small piano pieces in the simplest forms to Lyadov's lessons. The G minor Gavotte (subsequently included in Op. 12), the Scherzo of the future Second Sonata, and other piano miniatures came into being in this manner. At the same time he independently undertook a number of larger works, among them the initial versions of his future First, Third, and Fourth Piano Sonatas. Some of them (for example, the Third Sonata, 1907) already bore the stamp of real genius.

Although Prokofiev is to this day rather skeptical of the pedagogical tact of his distinguished teachers, he nevertheless unconsciously learned a great deal from their works. Each new opera by Rimsky-Korsakov, for example, aroused his eager interest (*Kitezh, The Golden Cockerel*). He made a point of acquiring and making a detailed study of every new piano score of Rimsky's operas with the enthusiasm he had applied to the study of all four operas of *Der Ring des Nibelungen* and their complex system of leitmotivs. In October 1908 he first heard his own orchestral music played when, through the offices of Glazunov, the E minor Symphony was performed at a private rehearsal of the court orchestra conducted by Hugo Warlich. "The orchestration of the symphony was rather poor," Prokofiev now recalls, "and the general impression was rather hazy." Glazunov was actually shocked by some of the harmonic liberties (for example, parallel seconds) the composer had taken. Prokofiev kept the symphony in his archives, using its *Andante* later on for the middle part of his Fourth Piano Sonata.

An important role in the molding of Prokofiev's talent as a composer was played by the Evenings of Modern Music, a society he joined in 1908. He was introduced to the society by Mikhail Tchernov, pianist and composer, who taught at the Conservatory. His visits to the Evenings, where the latest Russian and western European music was played, developed Prokofiev's taste for novel musical trends.

The Evenings of Modern Music, held in the first decade of the twentieth century, constituted the backbone of Russian modernism in music. Beginning as an offshoot of the World of Art group, and constituting a sort of musical branch of that society, the Evenings played in the history of Russian music of that period a role that is worth a special study in itself. While coming out in opposition to the dreary professionalism of the followers of the Five and Tchaikovsky, the group of musical innovators banded together in the Evenings of Modern Music at the same time upheld many of the modernistic principles of the bourgeois æsthetes. Two of the active members of the Evenings, Alfred Nurok and Walter Nuvel,[1] were the ideologists of the World of Art group and supporters of the Diaghilev school of thought. Diaghilev's art principles, an orientation toward the modern West (the French impressionists and Reger), emphasis on original and non-repetitive forms, and a rejection of the social and educational implica-

---

[1] Alfred Pavlovich Nurok, admiralty official and art critic, wrote for the *World of Art* magazine under the pen-name of Silenus. Walter Fedorovich Nuvel, official of the Russian Foreign Office, lover of music and painting, was a close friend of K. Somov and other World of Art artists. Nurok and Nuvel subsequently played a significant role in the life of Prokofiev (his acquaintance with Diaghilev, the order for the ballet *Ala and Lolli*, etc.). The Diaghilev influence on Prokofiev's work can be traced directly to both these men.

tions of art — such were the leading principles of this group. Tchaikovsky's music was regarded by them as banal, philistine, and hopelessly out of date. On the other hand, everything interesting and fresh produced by the young musicians was sought out and encouraged. Before every concert hundreds of new works received from abroad or composed in Russia were tried out. Due credit must be given to the organizers of the Evenings for their tremendous enthusiasm and their sincere devotion to their art. The soul of the Evenings, their ardent champion and inspirer, was Vyacheslav Gavrilovich Karatygin (1875–1925). The name of this eminent and intelligent musician, critic, and distinguished scholar, who later invested no little effort in building up Soviet musical culture as well, deserves to take its place beside the classics of Russian musical criticism. Other prominent members of the Evenings society were Ignatz Kryzhanovsky, composer and physician (one of Miaskovsky's first teachers), A. D. Medem, pianist and composer, who taught at the Conservatory, and I. V. Pokrovsky, pianist and closest friend of the young Stravinsky.

The programs of the Evenings included the chamber music of Debussy, Dukas, Fauré, Chausson, Roussel, d'Indy, Schönberg, Reger, Wolf, Richard Strauss, and the modern Russian composers — Scriabin, Stravinsky, Medtner, Rachmaninoff, Rebikov, Senilov, Tcherepnin, Gnessin, and Steinberg. Of works by the established Russian composers, only the freshest and most attractive from the standpoint of modernistic tastes (*Mlada* by Rimsky-Korsakov, *Sunless* by Mussorgsky) were chosen. The leading vocalists and pianists of the day — the singers I. Alchevsky, M. Lunacharsky, N. Zabela, A. Zherebtsova, and the pianists L. Nikolayev, M. Barinova, and S. Polotskaya-Yemtsova — performed willingly and, of course, gratis at the Evenings. The society barely maintained itself on the modest membership fees and the negligible entrance fee. Nevertheless the Evenings were invariably noted by the critics and amply supplied with programs, posters, and the like. Alexander Benois, K. Somov, E. Lanceré and M. Dobuzhinsky of the World of Art rendered every assistance in the organization of the Evenings. Beginning in 1901–2, the Evenings continued until 1912 in the form of monthly chamber concerts held usually in the period between October and April in various concert halls of St. Petersburg.

It was from this circle that the most distinguished representatives of the musical modernism of the post-Scriabin generation — Stravinsky and Prokofiev — sprang. Miaskovsky, too, received his first solid support from the society.

In December 1908 the young Prokofiev made his first public appearance at a public concert arranged by the Evenings of Modern Music (Miaskovsky also made his debut that evening with four songs). Prokofiev played seven pieces for the piano: *Story, Snowflakes, Reminiscence, Élan, Prayer, Despair,* and *Diabolic Suggestions.* The last piece impressed the

3. *Diabolic Suggestions,* Opus 4, No. 4.

audience profoundly by its powerful, irrepressible dynamism. "The whole hall seemed suddenly to be filled with sound," wrote V. M. Morolev, who was present at the concert. " 'Now that is real music!' was the comment heard on all sides." Prokofiev's first appearance was mentioned in the St. Petersburg press (*Slovo, Rech, Peterburgsky Listok,* and the *Zolotoye Runo* chronicle).

In the meantime Prokofiev was finishing the composition course at the Conservatory. His studies under Joseph Wihtol (Vitols), while rather less turbulent than those with Lyadov, had been dull and uninteresting. At this period Prokofiev took a great interest in piano-playing and had studied with Winkler Rubinstein's extremely difficult C major Étude.[2] Encouraged by the modernists, Prokofiev had been bringing to Wihtol's class compositions of an increasingly audacious nature (the Sixth Sonata, subsequently lost,[3] and scenes from his new version of the music for the *Feast during the Plague*). Wihtol did not discourage the bold departures made by his pupil from the established canons, with the result that when the final examinations came round in the spring of 1909, the examiners were scandalized. What shocked them most was a scene from the *Feast during the Plague*: the monologue of the priest who sternly upbraids the drunken revelers was written in a free and harsh-sounding recitative with extremely vivid and dramatic use of the chorus. Lyadov especially was deeply shocked by the musical audacity of Prokofiev. "They are all trying to ape Scriabin," he said bitterly.

Nevertheless, at the age of eighteen Prokofiev was granted the title of Free Artist,[4] though his ratings were far from brilliant (4-plus out of 5 for analysis of form, 4-plus for fugue composition, and 4 for instrumentation). The Conservatory professors were evidently only too glad to be rid of such a restless and troublesome pupil. Thus ended Prokofiev's education in composition.

---

[2] This étude, as well as Schumann's C major *Toccata* at a somewhat later date, evidently served as the point of departure for some of the finger-work passages in Prokofiev's music for the piano (viz., the First and Third Concertos).

[3] Of the six sonatas written during the Conservatory period, the First, Fourth, and Sixth have been lost; the Second was used partly for the First Sonata, Op. 1, the Third formed the basis of the Third Sonata, Op. 28, and the Fifth was incorporated in part in the Fourth Sonata, Op. 29.

[4] Free Artist was a title formerly granted to a graduate of a conservatory.

His friends Miaskovsky and Zakharov urged him to continue his pianoforte studies by enrolling in the class of Annette Essipova, the leading piano tutor in the Conservatory. Under the tutelage of Winkler, who was somewhat dry and pedantic, Prokofiev's performance on the piano was beginning to lose color. Essipova was glad to accept a pupil already famous for his own compositions and endowed with unusual pianistic talents (the performance of Rubinstein's C major Étude had not passed unnoticed). At the same time Prokofiev began to study conducting under Nikolai Nikolayevich Tcherepnin.

The five years between 1909 and 1914 passed in diligent study combined with unceasing and by now completely independent composition. Incidentally, while at Sontsovka in the summer of 1909 he composed his remarkable Études, Op. 2 (D minor, E minor, C minor, C minor), fruits of a rich and perfectly mature pianistic manner. Only in the E minor Étude is the influence of Medtner strongly evident.

Before he had studied many months in Essipova's class, Prokofiev was rebelling again. He refused to conform to the standards set by his distinguished tutor. Nevertheless, Essipova, who had inherited the brilliant traditions of the Leschetizky school, undoubtedly had a very strong influence on Prokofiev's playing, giving it an exceptional freedom of wrist movement and purity of finger technique. It was under her tutelage that he learned to play Schumann (Sonata in F-sharp minor and *Toccata* in C major) and Liszt (Sonata in B minor, a transcription from *Tannhäuser*), Medtner's *Fairy-tales*, Glazunov's Sonata in E minor, and pieces by Tchaikovsky, Rachmaninoff, and Chopin.

In this period, however, Prokofiev, deeply imbued with ultra-modernistic ideals, was strongly opposed to classical and romantic music. He scoffed at the prevailing idea that no piano recital program was complete without Chopin. "I shall prove that one can do quite well without Chopin," he said. His attitude to Mozart was similarly scornful ("What harmony — the tonic, fourth, and fifth!"). Essipova made her pupils play

17

Mozart, Schubert, and Chopin and demanded accurate and finely polished execution. But Prokofiev did not want to give up his grand, careless manner of playing and his fondness for taking liberties with the score.[5] This was the cause of constant friction between him and his tutor, which lasted throughout his Conservatory career.

His relations with Tcherepnin were much better. Tcherepnin proved to be the most influential and tactful of all the Conservatory professors with whom Prokofiev had come in contact. This may have been due to the fact that Tcherepnin was the most modern of the academic group of St. Petersburg composers. The encouragement he gave to the modernistic tastes of his pupils could not fail to win Prokofiev's respect. Besides learning orchestration in Tcherepnin's class, he received encouragement and valuable advice in his experiments in composition. "I have great faith in your talent as a composer," Tcherepnin assured him on more than one occasion. And though he did not have the same high regard for his pupil's ability as a conductor, he nevertheless directed his studies with much intelligence and tact. By 1913 Prokofiev conducted five out of eight symphony numbers at a Conservatory recital. Thanks to Tcherepnin, Prokofiev conducted a great deal in the opera class of Paleček, with the result that he was able in March 1914 to conduct a public performance of Mozart's *Le Nozze di Figaro* and a fragment of Verdi's *Aïda*. Prokofiev's conducting was the subject of wide comment (mostly unfavorable) in the St. Petersburg press.

While supporting his pupil's predilection for the new in music, Tcherepnin at the same time succeeded in imbuing him with respect for the classic tradition, for old operatic culture, and for the music of Haydn and Mozart. These, for Prokofiev, new "neo-classical" tendencies made themselves felt

---

[5] V. M. Morolev placed at my disposal a copy of *Scherzo à la russe* by Tchaikovsky, with notes in Prokofiev's handwriting. The young pianist mercilessly scored out "superfluous" notes, added octaves in the bass, introduced *staccatos* and *accelerandos*, and went so far as to introduce difficult leaps by transposing chords to a higher octave.

partly in his *Sinfonietta*, Op. 5, and some pieces of Op. 12, and with particular force in his *Classical Symphony*, Op. 25.

Study under Tcherepnin stimulated Prokofiev's waning interest in symphonic music. His unsuccessful E minor Symphony was followed in 1909 by a five-part *Sinfonietta* in A major dedicated to Tcherepnin, and in 1910 by two orchestral pieces, *Dreams* and *Autumnal Sketch*. *Dreams*, dedicated to Scriabin, was, with Tcherepnin's aid, performed at a student symphony recital (November 22, 1910) and conducted by Prokofiev himself. Two pieces for female chorus with orchestra written the same year to Balmont's poems *Swan* and *Wave* were also performed at a private Conservatory rehearsal because the choruses were difficult and the Conservatory singers were unable to master them for public performance. The composer himself considers these works immature, mentioning the rather flaccid passiveness of *Dreams* and the marked Rachmaninoff influence in the *Autumnal Sketch*, which echoes the latter's *Isle of the Dead* and Second Symphony.[6] Evidently the decadent cult of symbolism with its passive contemplation and morbid revelations had an influence on the young Prokofiev. This made itself felt also in his interest in Balmont, the whole mood and style of whose poetry might have been expected to be utterly alien to the healthy, realistic outlook of Prokofiev. Yet for a long while Prokofiev was enchanted by the musical quality of Balmont's language and by certain cosmic and barbarously exotic images. This "illicit liaison" with poetry of a trend so foreign to his nature was undoubtedly one manifestation of the conflicting tendencies in Prokofiev's musical development.[7]

---

[6] Nevertheless, Prokofiev returned to his early symphonic works more than once. He revised the *Sinfonietta* on two occasions — in 1914 and in 1929, on the latter occasion in the form of a new opus — Op. 48. In 1930 the *Autumnal Sketch* was reorchestrated.

[7] Balmont's poetry inspired, in addition to Op. 7, one of the songs in Op. 9 (*There Are Other Planets*), one of the songs in Op. 23 (*In My Garden*), the cantata *Seven, They Are Seven*, and five poems, Op. 36. From Balmont he borrowed the title of his piano cycle *Fugitive Visions*:

In February 1910, Moscow musicians heard Prokofiev for the first time when he played his First Sonata in F minor and four *Études*, Op. 2, at one of the musical recitals arranged regularly by the singer M. Deisha-Sionitskaya (February 21, thirteenth recital). The composer was accorded a warm reception by the distinguished Nikolai Kashkin, who mentioned his "giftedness and his earnest attitude to his work" and "youthful courage" (*Russkoye Slovo*, February 23).

Prokofiev continued to appear at the concerts of the St. Petersburg Evenings of Modern Music; during the 1910–11 season he played his *Études*, Op. 2, and some pieces from Op. 3, and in a concert held on March 28, 1911 gave the first performance in Russia of piano works by Schönberg (*Klavierstücke*, Op. 11).

In the period up to 1911 Prokofiev may be said to have been bracing himself for the large and unexpected leap toward the full unfolding of his artistic individuality. Some of his compositions relating to this period still bore the imprint of immaturity and imitativeness. Such was the First Sonata in F minor, written in 1907 and revised in 1909, when the *Adagio* and *Finale* were deleted and only the *Allegro* remained. Hackneyed figuration, pathetic minor themes in the spirit of Rachmaninoff and Medtner, touches reminiscent of Schumann (subordinate theme, reminiscent of one of the themes of the F-sharp minor Sonata) clearly dominated in this sonata over the few flashes of Prokofiev's own personality. The same respectful tribute to his older contemporaries was felt also in his first symphonic works, in which the author himself detects echoes of Rachmaninoff.

Nevertheless, even his early piano miniatures of 1907–9 reveal the restless, inquiring mind of the young composer, ever in quest of new harmonies and rhythms. His pieces for the

----

In every fugitive vision I see worlds,
Full of the changing play of rainbow hues.

In his turn Balmont wrote several verses in Prokofiev's honor in 1921 (*Create Thou Sounds*, Third Concerto). Prokofiev's Third Piano Concerto is dedicated to Balmont.

piano were to Prokofiev the same "laboratory" of new musical images as were, let us say, the *Fantasiestücke* for Schumann and the piano preludes for Chopin, Scriabin, and Shostakovich. Apart from the early versions of the Third (1907) and Fourth (1908) Sonatas, mention should be made here of such compositions as the *Études*, Op. 2, Four Pieces, Op. 3 (*Story, Badinage, March,* and *Phantom*), and especially of the Four Pieces, Op. 4 (*Reminiscence, Élan, Despair,* and *Diabolic Suggestions*).

In these small sketches for future large canvases the artistic individuality of Prokofiev revealed itself to the full: his fondness for pensive day-dreaming and romantic narrative (*Story, Reminiscence,* Etude in E minor), his loud boyish laughter (*Badinage,* the middle of the D minor Étude), his tense theatrical dramatism (Étude No. 4, *Phantom, Despair*). Such pieces as *Diabolic Suggestions* or the Etudes Nos. 4 and 1 might to this day serve as a perfect test of the artistic and technical maturity of a pianist. The highly expressive polytonal complexities and the refreshing harmonic discoveries of *Diabolic Suggestions,* the original polyrhythmic passages in the D minor Étude, the characteristic *ostinato* effects (continually recurring figures) in *Phantom* and *Despair* — all these were for Prokofiev bright flashes of insight into the future.

In 1910 the composer's father died at the age of sixty-four. The visits to Sontsovka ceased. But his mother, who had profound faith in her son's talent, possessed the means and the energy to provide him with the wherewithal to continue his studies.

3 : Recognition

> And suddenly he grew a lion's mane,
> A lion's pointed claw,
> And skittishly the art did demonstrate
> Of touching with one's paw.
>
> V. KHLEBNIKOV

THE year 1911 was an important landmark in the life of Prokofiev. That year he appeared for the first time on the program of a large public symphony concert, his work began to be published, and he wrote his First Piano Concerto, a major composition that crowned his youthful efforts.

The first two events took place in Moscow. It was Konstantin Solomonovich Saradzhev, a progressive Moscow conductor, then chairman of the society of orchestra musicians, who introduced Prokofiev (and, incidentally, Miaskovsky) to Moscow through the medium of the concerts given in the Sokolniki Park in the summer of 1911. Closely associated with Moscow's modernistic circles, Saradzhev was an enthusiastic admirer of the new music. It was thanks to him that, beginning in 1908, all the latest achievements of the French school of composition were played at the Sokolniki concerts. It was here that the works of Debussy, Ravel, Satie, Dukas, Florent Schmitt, as well as the modern Russian composers Vassilenko, Yurasovsky, Krein, Glière, Senilov, and others, were first performed. Here, too, young and as yet unrecognized performers, such as Samuel Feinberg, Alexander Borovsky, N. Orlov, and Nina Koshetz, made their debuts.

When Saradzhev went to St. Petersburg to find new works by young modern composers to add to his programs, I. I. Kryzhanovsky introduced him to two promising young authors — Miaskovsky and Prokofiev. Both were received with interest into Moscow's musical circles and before long Miaskovsky's

Silence and Prokofiev's *Dreams* and *Autumnal Sketch* were given their first hearing from the Sokolniki concert stage. True, neither of Prokofiev's pieces made much of an impression on the critics. As a matter of fact, it was in Moscow that Prokofiev found his bitterest opponent — Leonid Sabaneyev, an ardent admirer of Scriabin and a confirmed modernist theoretician. "It seems to me," Sabaneyev wrote in *Golos Moskvy*, "that this callow musical fledgling is receiving far too much attention. In scope Mr. Prokofiev's talent approximates that of Kalinnikov; I believe he would write in much the same vein were he as sincere as Borodin and other St. Petersburgites. But he is too affected, too anxious to be modern at all costs, although modernism becomes him ill."

Incidentally, while criticizing the young Prokofiev from his ultra-subjective Scriabinist standpoint, Sabaneyev nevertheless described the real, earthy foundation of the composer's art, utterly unshackled by morbid, unhealthy mysticism. "It seems to me," Sabaneyev wrote about *Dreams* (*Golos Moskvy*, July 3, 1911), "that his 'modernism' is far too obvious. He is not at all 'modernistic' at heart, he has none of that intensity of emotion, nothing of the 'exposed nerves' required by the æsthetics of discordant harmonies. I would say that his soul is foreign to the hyperæsthetic ecstasy, the nightmarish horror, love of suffering, and everything else upon which the spirit of modernism is based. He swims benignly upon the physical surface of things. . . ."

But what Sabaneyev the æsthete regarded as a defect in Prokofiev's music was in reality its greatest virtue, that fundamentally healthy quality which distinguished it from the decadent tendencies of his time.

In July 1911 Prokofiev made his debut in St. Petersburg as a symphonic composer when his *Dreams* was included in the program of a concert conducted by A. Kankarovich at the Pavlovsk Vauxhall.

For a long time Prokofiev had been endeavoring unsuccessfully to have his first compositions published. In 1910 two of

his early works had been rejected by the Russian Musical Publishers. His efforts to persuade Bessel and Jurgenson to publish
any of his works likewise ended in failure, notwithstanding
Taneyev's recommendations. At last, after he had applied to
Jurgenson a second time armed with a long and insistent letter
from A. V. Ossovsky, his first four *opera* were accepted for
publication on extremely unfavorable terms for the author
(one hundred rubles for a sonata and twelve pieces for the
piano, or, as Prokofiev put it in one of his letters, "a kopeck a
bushel"). The year 1911 marked the beginning of a long and
furious struggle with a crafty and excessively cautious publisher, a struggle from which the composer in most cases
emerged the victor.[1]

In the autumn of 1911 Prokofiev completed a new one-act
opera, *Magdalene*, after the text by Baroness Lieven. According to the critics, the opera was "akin to Richard Strauss in
intensity of style, but minus the 'banal lyricism' of the latter"
(*Muzyka*, November 1, 1911, No. 44. Notes). The text of
Magdalene possesses no great poetical merit. Its main interest
for the composer lay in its wealth of action and dramatic effects, as well as its guignol plot borrowed from the epoch of
the *risorgimento*. It was the story of a Venetian beauty, Magdalene, and her two lovers, Gennaro and Stenio, who meet in
the home of their perfidious mistress and slay each other in
mortal combat to the accompaniment of ominous flashes of
lightning. The text was written in the cheapest decadent style,
and supplies another instance — after Balmont — of the effect
of the modernist environment on the young composer. Prokofiev, however, was not much interested in the "profound"
philosophy of Baroness Lieven's play. To him *Magdalene* was
no more than an experiment in recitative-writing, a test for
his pen, a sketch for future operatic compositions. The whole
opera was based on harsh, tense, declamatory singing, with a

---

[1] For confirmation see Prokofiev's letters (1913–16) preserved in Jurgenson's files. In 1916 Prokofiev broke with Jurgenson and found another publisher (Russian Musical Publishers, managed by Serge Koussevitzky).

single melodious episode at the end (chorus of boatmen off-stage). Prokofiev added *Magdalene* to his list of works as Op. 13, but did not succeed in having it produced either in the opera class of the Conservatory, for which it had originally been intended, or in K. Marzhanov's Free Theater, where, with the assistance of Saradzhev, it was heard out with considerable interest in the summer of 1913. After a few changes made in 1913 *Magdalene* remained both unproduced and unpublished.

Magdalene was followed by the First Piano Concerto in D-flat major, originally conceived as a concertino. This was the composer's first mature work, something in the nature of a declaration of his coming of age. It was the performance of this concerto in Moscow and St. Petersburg [2] that brought real fame to Prokofiev and revealed his original artistic personality. The power and originality of Prokofiev's pianistic conceptions were demonstrated to the full for the first time in this composition constructed on the lines of Liszt's symphonic poems in one movement. For the first time the sharply contrasting forms typical of Prokofiev's music were united in a single dramatic conception — the athletic suppleness and the stiffness of the motor and dance themes (introduction and main theme), pure, pensive lyricism (central episode in G-sharp minor), and nervous, tragic, tense statement (subordinate theme).

The performance of the First Concerto gave rise to a heated controversy in the press. Criticism was divided into two sharply opposing camps, one wildly enthusiastic, the other definitely hostile. "This energetic, rhythmic, harsh, coarse, primitive cacophony hardly deserves to be called music," cried Sabaneyev in *Golos Moskvy*. "In his desperate search for 'novelty' utterly foreign to his nature the author has definitely overreached himself. Such things do not happen with real talent." Sabaneyev was echoed in the *Peterburgskaya Gazeta* by the second-

---

[2] July 25, 1912, in the Moscow People's House (conducted by Saradzhev) and August 3, 1912, in Pavlovsk (conducted by Aslanov).

rate critic N. Bernstein, who suggested that what Prokofiev needed was a strait-jacket.

On the other hand Karatygin in *Rech* and Florestan (Derzhanovsky) in *Utro Rossii* paid glowing tribute to the composer's talent. They spoke of the brilliance, the humor, the wit, and the rich imagination of Prokofiev's music, its "freedom from the mildew of decadence" (*Vecherneye Vremya*, August 4, 1912). One reviewer went so far as to speak — albeit hesitantly and naïvely — of the historic role of Prokofiev's music: "Prokofiev might even mark a stage in Russian musical development, Glinka and Rubinstein being the first, Tchaikovsky and Rimsky-Korsakov the second, Glazunov and Arensky the third, and Scriabin and Prokofiev the fourth. Why not?" (*Peterburgsky Listok*, No. 213, August 5, 1912).

Most symptomatic was the fact that, despite the malicious hissing of the retrogrades and æsthetic snobs, Prokofiev's appearances were invariably a success as far as the general public was concerned. The convincing power of his graphic piano music could only have a direct appeal for the concert audience. "He played . . . with amazing assurance and freedom," remarked one reviewer. "Under his fingers the piano does not so much sing and vibrate as speak in the stern and convincing tone of a percussion instrument, the tone of the old-fashioned harpsichord. Yet it was precisely this convincing freedom of execution and these clear-cut rhythms that won the author such enthusiastic applause from the public" (*Russkiye Vedomosti*, No. 173, 1912).

In Moscow Prokofiev gained reliable public support in the magazine *Muzyka*, organ of the Moscow modernist circles. The magazine's following (Derzhanovsky, Saradzhev, Belyayev, Miaskovsky, and subsequently Igor Glebov [3]) held the same creed as the St. Petersburg Evenings of Modern Music society. Orientation toward progressive trends in the West and a certain narrow exclusiveness and aloofness from the big social problems of art were combined here with a courageous

[3] Pseudonym of Boris Asafyev. — *Editor.*

defense of everything new and fresh and with genuine lack of self-interest on the part of the organizers and contributors to the magazine. (None of the contributors was paid for his work. V. Derzhanovsky, editor and publisher, barely managed to make both ends meet by taking paid advertisements and by occasional donations from wealthy patrons.) Miaskovsky's brief but extremely fruitful career as music critic began in *Muzyka* in 1911. He was one of the first to discern in Prokofiev the new and healthy quality that distinguished his art in principle from bourgeois decadence. "What pleasure and surprise," he wrote, "it affords one to come across this vivid and wholesome phenomenon amid the morass of effeminacy, spinelessness, and anemia of today!" (*Muzyka*, No. 94, September 8, 1912, review of *Four Études*, Op. 2, signed "M."). Prokofiev's music "by its freshness and power . . . and its unusual robustness should enliven the flaccid and often stagnant atmosphere of our concert life," Miaskovsky wrote in another review (*Muzyka*, No. 151, September 12, 1913, bibliographical note signed "N. M.").

Two or three years later this idea was developed in the columns of the same magazine by the discerning Igor Glebov, another bold and tireless proponent of Prokofiev's music: "Can it be our life, our times that are reflected in his music?" wrote Glebov. "We are so much obsessed, on the one hand, by a hysterical fear of the malignant power of destiny, and, on the other hand, have attuned ourselves to such an extent to languid delicacy and fragility — that is, to an art of shrinking violets" (*Muzyka*, No. 249, 1916, article entitled "Recent Impressions"). "It seems to me," he maintained, "that Prokofiev has the right not only to dislike but actually to loathe the old culture. . . . Let him appear a wild and terrible creature to those who tremble for their 'ancient' beauty, to which they cling in mortal fear lest it should die, lest some new world outlook should come and take its place" (*Muzyka*, December 27, 1914).

The struggle waged by the progressive elements of *Muzyka*

(Miaskovsky, Glebov) for public recognition of Prokofiev's talent and against the fading culture of the decadence was an expression of the militant outpost of the new Russian art, blazing the trail, however intuitively and gropingly, toward the æsthetics of our day. The bold polemics and active, aggressive policy pursued by these progressive men recall the most illustrious pages in the militant past of Russian music — namely, the struggle waged by Stasov and Cui for the recognition of the young musicians of the Five. From this standpoint the persistent efforts of Miaskovsky in the columns of *Muzyka* to secure the inclusion of Prokofiev's works in the programs of the big symphony concerts (the Belyayev and Siloti concerts) is extremely symptomatic (*Muzyka*, No. 125, 1913, and No. 178, April 19, 1914).

Particularly impressive was an article by Miaskovsky (published under a pseudonym) entitled "St. Petersburg Fogs." This ridiculed Siloti and charged him with conservatism and indifference to the fate of the new generation of composers.[4] This struggle ended with the complete victory of Prokofiev and his comrades-in-arms and the defeat of the over-cautious leaders of the concert life of the time.

The editor of *Muzyka* tried to persuade Prokofiev to try his hand at music reviews and criticism, but after a few minor bibliographical items on the chamber music of Stanchinsky, Miaskovsky, and Stravinsky and one or two analyses of his own early works he abandoned his attempts at journalism.

Encouraged by the success of his First Concerto and the recognition of his experiments in new fields, Prokofiev produced in 1912 and 1913 music that was still more audacious and vivid in idiom. In 1912 he wrote his *Toccata*, Op. 11, with its swift machine-like rhythm and its curious polytonal and constructivist effects. In August of the same year he completed his Second Sonata, Op. 14, a remarkable piece of music built on

---

4 Siloti refused to include Prokofiev's music in the programs of his symphony concerts on the grounds that Prokofiev "had not yet found himself" (this was after his Second Concerto for the piano).

sharply contrasting moods, shifting with startling suddenness from romantic yearning to malicious satire. His *Ballad* for the cello, Op. 15, written at the request of the wealthy amateur cellist N. P. Ruzsky, the dynamic Scherzo in A minor, Op. 12, and the first of the pieces later to be called *Sarcasms* relate to the same period.

Even more "Left" in musical language was his output in 1913 (the Second Piano Concerto, second and third *Sarcasms*, *Scherzo* for four bassoons). In the Second, G minor, Concerto for the piano, begun in the latter part of 1912, the composer strove for greater depth of content in contrast to the somewhat superficial bravura or "football" touch in the D-flat major Concerto that immediately preceded it.[5]

The same touch of seriousness and restrained lyricism made itself felt in some of the pieces of Op. 12 written that year (*Legend, Caprice, Allemande*). Here, too (Prelude in C major for harp or piano), there were flashes of that neo-classicism which was to declare itself four years later in the *Classical Symphony*.

The pianoforte cycle, Op. 12, was a collection of compositions of different periods and styles, partly revised.[6] Some of them bore traces of the young Prokofiev's predilection, subsequently pointed out by Lunacharsky, for the "nursery." It is curious to note the youthful circle of friends and acquaintances reflected in the numerous dedications of this opus. Here we find Tcherepnin and "Kolyechka [Nikolai] Miaskovsky," "Vasyusha [Vassili] Morolev," his old Sontsovo chum, V. Deshevov and M. Schmithof, his Conservatory friends, and Eleonora Damskaya, the harpist, side by side with quaint

---

[5] The athletic, "football" quality of the First Concerto had been mentioned more than once by hostile critics. Curiously enough, the young composer actually did take an interest in sports at that period. He attended gymnastic drill in an athletic society, and even wrote a sports march that was published by the society.

[6] A comparison between the original version of the march composed in Sontsovka in 1906 and the final version written in 1913 will reveal the interesting development of harmonic modernization and tone color this simple childish piece underwent.

childish nicknames such as "Boryusya" (Boris Zakharov) and others. The young composer's circle of acquaintances was extremely wide. It included half-starved Conservatory students as well as mature and adult musicians, old friends from his native village, and fashionable young men of the world.[7]

Prokofiev at that time was a curious combination of the diligent, hard-working musician and the spoiled, capricious child. Many of his ill-wishers could not forgive him for what they termed his impudent behavior. He had no respect for authority and did not hesitate to voice his opinions, however extreme. His first meeting with the already famous Igor Stravinsky was marred in this way. After hearing the author play his *Firebird* in piano arrangement at one of the modernist concerts, Prokofiev bluntly told him that he didn't like the music: "Nothing interesting, rather like *Sadko*!" Stravinsky was deeply offended. True, this lack of understanding changed later to a keen interest and respect for the work of this legislator of new musical tastes.

In the summer of 1913 Prokofiev went abroad for the first time, visiting Paris and London and spending part of his summer vacationing in the Auvergne.

That same summer his name resounded once again in the musical world of St. Petersburg. On August 23 his Second Piano Concerto was performed for the first time at Pavlovsk under the baton of Aslanov. This time the young composer won the attention of the general public.

"The debut of this pianoforte cubist and futurist has aroused universal interest," said the *Peterburgskaya Gazeta*. "Already in the train to Pavlovsk one heard on all sides 'Prokofiev, Prokofiev, Prokofiev.' A new piano star!"

"On the platform appears a lad with the face of a Peterschule[8] student. It is Sergei Prokofiev," one newspaper feature

---

[7] One of his best friends at that period was Maximilian Schmithof, the pianist with whom he had studied at the Conservatory. Schmithof subsequently committed suicide. The Second Sonata, Second Piano Concerto, Fourth Sonata, and *Allemande* from Op. 12 are dedicated to him.

[8] An exclusive German school in St. Petersburg.

writer glibly described the event. "He takes his seat at the piano and appears to be either dusting the keys or trying out the notes with a sharp, dry touch. The audience does not know what to make of it. Some indignant murmurs are audible. One couple gets up and runs toward the exit. 'Such music is enough to drive you crazy!' is the general comment. The hall empties. The young artist ends his concerto with a relentlessly discordant combination of brasses. The audience is scandalized. The majority hisses. With a mocking bow Prokofiev resumes his seat and plays an encore. The audience flies, with exclamations of: 'To the devil with all this futurist music! We came here for enjoyment. The cats on our roof make better music than this!' " (*Peterburgskaya Gazeta*, August 25, 1913).

Most of the critics could not find words to express the full measure of their indignation at this gross violation of musical dogma. Y. Kurdyumov referred to the concerto as a "babel of insane sounds without form or harmony heaped one upon another" (*Peterburgsky Listok*, August 24, 1913). N. Bernstein called it "a cacophony of sounds having nothing whatever in common with genuine music. . . . Prokofiev's cadenzas, for example, are unbearable; they are such a musical mess that one might think them the result of an inkwell spilt on the paper" (*Peterburgskaya Gazeta*, August 25, 1913). Not far behind in vituperative criticism was M. Ivanov of the Black Hundred *Novoye Vremya*.

What a bold challenge to this malignant chorus were the prophetic words uttered by V. G. Karatygin, the only critic who took up the cudgels in unreserved defense of Prokofiev's new concerto! "The fact that the public hissed means nothing," he wrote. "Ten years from now it will atone for last night's catcalls by unanimous applause for this new composer with a European reputation" (*Rech*, March 25, 1913).

Curiously enough, Prokofiev's sensational appearance in Pavlovsk almost coincided in time with the famous tour of Russian cities made by the Russian futurists — Mayakovsky, Kamensky, and Burlyuk. The audacious, shocking utterances of the young Mayakovsky and his friends evoked exactly the same reaction from the public and the critics as Prokofiev's piano performances. It is not surprising that three years later one of the critics, in an effort to sting Prokofiev for his non-conformism, accused him of aping Mayakovsky (N. Shebuyev in *Zritel*, December 2, 1916).

In November 1913 Prokofiev met Debussy, who had come to Russia at the invitation of Koussevitzky. In honor of Debussy's arrival in St. Petersburg the magazine *Apollon* arranged a concert on November 28, at which Prokofiev played his *Legend*, Op. 12, and one of the études of his Op. 2. Debussy displayed interest in his work. Prokofiev in his turn attended the concert given by the celebrated leader of musical impressionism, but found Debussy's music "not sufficiently meaty." It was only much later, when he lived in Paris, that Prokofiev began to appreciate the new French music to the full.

The year 1913–14 was Prokofiev's last year at the Conservatory. He conducted at public concerts frequently during this period. Pending the final examinations Prokofiev concentrated on the piano. At the same time he continued to give recitals of his latest compositions in both Moscow and St. Petersburg. His prestige as a composer was notably increasing. On February 7, 1914 the Evenings of Modern Music allotted him the entire second half of their program for the performance of his Second Sonata, *Ballad* for the cello, and a number of piano pieces, Op. 12. His Moscow opponents (Sabaneyev and others) again poured vials of abuse on the composer's head. The Second Sonata was their pet anathema. During that same winter Prokofiev was at last included in the program of a large symphony concert (Koussevitzky's symphony matinée in Moscow, February 16, 1914).

The composer's fight for the first prize when graduating from the Conservatory is an interesting episode in his *Autobiography*. "While I did not especially mind the poor rating I received for composition," he recalls, "this time ambition got the better of me and I resolved to win a first for the piano."

The sportsman in him was aroused by the excitement of the contest, the spirit that was so vividly depicted a year later in his *Gambler*. Not that there was anything of the gambler's fatalism in his make-up: his "game" was founded on cool calculation. Instead of the customary fugue from *Das wohltemperiertes Klavier* he chose one of the lesser-known fugues from *Die Kunst der Fuge*; instead of the classic concerto he included his own D-flat major Concerto. But it was not so easy to circumvent the old established Conservatory regulations. The examining board demanded that each examiner be provided with a copy of the "terrible" concerto one week before the examinations. This hurdle, however, was also overcome. At the composer's request Jurgenson printed the piano score in time for the examination so that each of the twenty examiners received his copy in good time. "When I mounted the platform the first thing I saw was my concerto spread out on twenty laps. What a sight for a composer who had just succeeded in getting some of his work published!"

The First Concerto, brilliantly played by the composer, staggered the Conservatory professors. The jury split into two sharply opposed camps: Essipova's group and a number of young professors (Kalantarova, Drozdov, Vengerova, Lemba, and Medem) were in favor, the powerful academic group headed by Glazunov (Lyapunov, Lavrov, and Dubasov) was against. The most vehement protest and expression of indignation were voiced by Dubasov. Nevertheless, the Conservatory was forced to recognize the talent of its unruly graduate. By a majority of votes the Rubinstein first prize for the piano was awarded to Prokofiev.[9] Glazunov, the director of the Conservatory, who had just voted against what he called the "harmful tendencies" reflected in Prokofiev's work, was obliged personally to announce the results of the contest. On May 11, at the graduation exercises, the First Concerto was

---

[9] Seven pianists contested for the prize, Prokofiev's closest rival being N. Golubovskaya (now professor at the Leningrad Conservatory), a pupil of Lyapunov.

played again with great success by the orchestra under Tcherepnin's direction. The entire press of St. Petersburg reported the event, carrying photographs of the prize-winner and even interviews with him. As far as the musical press as a whole was concerned, Prokofiev had arrived. Even his enemies were now compelled to recognize that an outstanding musician had entered the arena.

4 : *Sturm und Drang*

> Then I told him that I was a heretic and a barbarian . . . and that I did not care a fig for all these archbishops, cardinals, monseigneurs, etc.
>
> DOSTÓYEVSKY: *The Gambler*

BY 1914 Prokofiev was firmly established in the world of music. This erstwhile *enfant terrible*, this prankish, mischievous lad, had won universal recognition. His name was mentioned more and more often in the press of the capital. He was received in the art salons of St. Petersburg, and theatrical circles began to display an interest in his work.

The composer, who had made such a brilliant showing as a concert virtuoso, was now passionately interested in the musical theater, a sphere that had fascinated him since early childhood. Even during their Conservatory years Prokofiev and Miaskovsky had toyed with the idea of using Dostoyevsky's novels for librettos. Prokofiev's imagination had been captured by the dramatic, gripping plot of *The Gambler*, and Miaskovsky had planned an opera based on *The Idiot*.

But 1914 brought new ideas and subjects to the composer. A tremendous role in the subsequent development of Prokofiev as an artist was played by his friendship with Diaghilev, the master mind of the rising generation of painters and musicians. On the eve of the war Diaghilev's ballet seasons abroad were among the most fashionable and sensational artistic attractions in Europe. The daring and novelty of his media and his brilliance of form were indisputable. The latest sensation, following Stravinsky's *Firebird* and *Petrouchka*, had been *Le Sacre du printemps*, the barbaric brutality of which was absolutely without precedent. With all its technical brilliance this music, nevertheless, pointed the way to many anarchic extremes in postwar European music. Yet this was the last word in modernism and could not but interest the young Prokofiev, with his avid thirst for everything new.

In June 1914 Prokofiev made a special trip to London for the opening of the Diaghilev season. The trip was in the nature of a reward from his mother for his successful graduation from the Conservatory. The young composer heard Stravinsky's *Firebird* and *Petrouchka* and Ravel's *Daphnis et Chloë* for the first time. He heard Chaliapin and Richard Strauss as well. Prokofiev, however, did not unreservedly embrace the new music in all cases. "Their verve, inventiveness, and 'trickiness' interested me immensely, but I found them lacking in subject matter."

Walter Nuvel, who accompanied Prokofiev, introduced him to Diaghilev, who condescended to listen to the Second Piano Concerto. There was talk of Prokofiev's participating in the Diaghilev programs. The composer mentioned his plan to write an opera after Dostoyevsky's *Gambler*, but Diaghilev rejected the idea at once on the grounds that opera was out of date and was being completely ousted by ballet and pantomime.[1] The negotiations ended with Prokofiev receiving an order for a new ballet "on Russian fairy-tale or prehistoric themes." Diaghilev advised Nuvel and Karatygin to introduce

---

[1] In his denunciation of opera Diaghilev is known to have gone to the most absurd extremes. He gave a new interpretation to Rimsky-Korsakov's *Golden Cockerel*, making a ballet of it by shifting the singers to the orchestra and leaving the dancers in full possession of the stage. On hearing Prokofiev's Second Concerto Diaghilev also proposed producing it in the form of a ballet, but the idea never materialized.

the composer to some of the young poets, including Sergei Gorodetsky.

Diaghilev's word was law. On returning to his native land, Prokofiev laid aside his plans for *The Gambler* and com menced work on a Scythian ballet entitled *Ala and Lolli*. While Gorodetsky was finding suitable images for a Scythian plot, Prokofiev occupied himself by revising the orchestration of his *Sinfonietta*, Op. 5, which he intended for inclusion in the program of Siloti's concerts.[2]

This Scythian, prehistoric "barbarian" subject matter was actually foreign to Prokofiev's nature and inner conviction. He had essentially no sympathy for the "Scythianism" adopted by the Russian bourgeois poets, who were bored with languid yearnings and parlor mysticism and were seeking solace in the instinctive animal wisdom of primitive man. Nor had he any wish, like the symbolists, to glorify the "future Hun," the plebeian barbarian who was to shatter and destroy all bour- geois civilization. For Stravinsky, *Le Sacre du printemps* was in the nature of an ideological declaration, a glorification of the primordial elemental forces of nature, a revival of savage, pagan instincts as an antidote against the morbid atmosphere of decadence. Prokofiev, on the other hand, regarded such subject matter far more simply and soberly, without any "philosophical soul-searching" whatever. For him the ballet *Ala and Lolli* was merely a convenient opportunity to give full rein to his daring harmonic idiom — which had been seeking an outlet in the *Sarcasms* and in the Second Concerto — to "try his hand at something big," something monumental and sweeping.

After a long tussle with the ponderous and static material of Scythian mythology, Prokofiev and Gorodetsky together de- vised a plot. It was briefly as follows: The Scythians are wor- shipping their favorite gods, Veles, the sun god, and Ala, a wooden idol, when one night a cunning stranger, Chuzhbog,

---

[2] The *Sinfonietta* was first performed at Siloti's concerts on October 24, 1915.

aided and abetted by the dark forces of evil, tries to steal Ala. His spell, however, works only in the darkness; under the pale light of the moon he is powerless. To Ala's rescue comes Lolli, the warrior. Chuzhbog would slay him, but in a timely intervention the sun god smites Chuzhbog with his blinding rays.

By the autumn of 1914 the piano score of *Ala and Lolli* was ready in the rough. To compensate for the dramatic shortcomings of the plot, Prokofiev directed the whole of his composer's genius to inventing the crisp, acrid chords, the savage, archaic melodies and crude rhythms most suited to the nature of the subject. *Le Sacre du printemps*, which Prokofiev had heard in concert performance but "had not understood," may have subconsciously influenced him in this work.

In the meantime the war had broken out and the consequent high cost of living inevitably affected the material well-being of the Prokofiev family. The composer was obliged to apply more and more frequently to his publisher for advances.

In his correspondence with Jurgenson, Prokofiev insisted on his rights. "You want to pay me little more than the few rubles you will receive in your shops for the sale of one or two piano scores so that in a few years' time *my* ballet will be *yours* for all time" (letter dated May 1, 1915).

His first encounter with life's hardships brought the young artist closer to earth, opening his eyes to the reality around him.

While working on *Ala and Lolli* the composer laid aside the ballet a number of times to bring some of his own ideas to life. This was something of a relaxation from the strain of his quest for new forms. It resulted at the end of 1914 in that splendid specimen of Prokofiev's vocal lyrical music, *The Ugly Duckling*, after the Andersen fairy-tale. While in his work on the ballet the predominant features were decorative design, the wild exoticism of ritual scenes, and violently colorful sound effects, in *The Ugly Duckling* we find the warm human note confidently asserting itself against a cleverly conceived fairy-tale background. In the lyrics of *The Ugly Duckling* the deep inner content was tangibly felt; in Prokofiev's interpretation the fairy-tale was a sincere, if allegorical, story of true man contrasted with the ugly world of narrow-minded philistinism and hidebound routine. This was how the music struck Maxim Gorky, who attended several of Prokofiev's recitals. "Why, he has written that story about himself," exclaimed Gorky after hearing *The Ugly Duckling*.[3]

After an extremely successful performance of his Second Concerto played at the RMO (Russian Musical Society) on January 24, 1915, Prokofiev left for Italy on February 6 at the invitation of Diaghilev. After looking over the outline for *Ala and Lolli* Diaghilev rejected the ballet on the grounds that the plot was stilted and the music dull "*à la* Tcherepnin." By way of compensation the all-powerful entrepreneur arranged for Prokofiev to appear at a symphony concert in the Augusteo in Rome. The concert, held on March 7, 1915 — Prokofiev's first appearance on a foreign concert platform — was widely advertised and had good publicity. While few of the Italian papers were able to grasp all the complexities of the Second Piano Concerto, all paid tribute to the brilliant performance of the composer.

At Diaghilev's home Prokofiev met Stravinsky and such leading Italian futurists as Marinetti and Balla, who had been invited to discuss the current ballet production based on Neapolitan carnivals. A complete reconciliation was effected with Stravinsky, and the two composers at their host's request played a four-hand arrangement of *Petrouchka* for his Italian guests.[4] The long and rather unstable friendship between Prokofiev and Stravinsky, interrupted time and again by various disagreements in principle, dated from this time. The futurists did not particularly impress Prokofiev. Their urbanist ideas

[3] The music was first performed on January 17, 1915 at a concert of the Evenings of Modern Music. A. Zherebtsova-Andreyeva was the singer.

[4] For details of this meeting between Prokofiev and Stravinsky see the latter's *About My Life*: "At last I had an opportunity to enter into closer contact with this fine musician whose value has been recognized by the whole modern musical world" (p. 123).

were foreign to him, as can be seen from the matter-of-fact tone of his article entitled "The Musical Instruments of the Futurists," published in the magazine *Muzyka* (April 8, 1915) on his return to his native land.

His second meeting with Diaghilev played what might be termed a historic role in Prokofiev's career as a composer. When he rejected *Ala and Lolli*, Diaghilev asked Prokofiev to write a new ballet on Russian folk-tale themes. The music of the Second Concerto (the subordinate theme of the finale)

4. Second Piano Concerto, subordinate theme of finale.

showed that Prokofiev was no stranger to Russian national melody. Diaghilev felt this. "Write music that will be truly *Russian*," he told the composer. "They've forgotten how to write Russian music in that rotten St. Petersburg of yours." Looking through Afanasyev's collection of Russian folk tales,[5] they selected two amusing stories about a jester, and together worked out a ballet libretto. The stories, collected in the Perm Government, were about a jolly village wag of the type of Pushkin's Balda who outwits the village priest, the priest's wife, the rich merchant, and seven jesters. The libretto of the future ballet was given a rather long-winded title: *The Tale of the Buffoon Who Outwitted Seven Buffoons*. It is characteristic that the priest and his wife, the principal comic characters

---

[5] *Collection of Fairy-tales* by A. N. *Afanasyev* (State Literary Publishing House, 1940), Vol. III, p. 206.

in the story, were deleted by Diaghilev, who was not interested in anticlerical satire.

Of course, the Russian style embraced by Diaghilev had nothing in common with the progressive national aspirations that had distinguished the work of the Five or the *Peredvizhniki*. In the present case it was merely used as an excuse for original, ingenious stylization, for æstheticizing the primitive simplicity of the old-fashioned village folk-tale. Such, for example, were the deliberately simplified "Russian" paintings by the artists of the "Ass's Tail" group (Goncharova and Larionov) who copied the crude style of village prints and signboards. Stravinsky's *Renard* and *Histoire du soldat*, composed two or three years later, were done in the same manner. Although *The Buffoon* [6] essentially belongs in this category as well, notes of a live, warm lyricism and a keen folk humor break through the otherwise stylized music of the ballet.

The Buffoon and the quest for a national style involved in this work absorbed Prokofiev completely. He composed the first draft of all six scenes during the summer of 1915. The work went easily and pleasantly. The whimsicality of the tale lent itself to pungent musical caricature, and, what was most important, while working on the ballet the composer discovered the world of Russian song melody which he freely reproduced without quotations or ethnographical research.

His second return from abroad and his contract with Diaghilev boosted Prokofiev's prestige considerably in the business circles of Russian music. Concert organizations that had ignored him now began to shower him with invitations. In 1915 his name figured on the symphony programs of Siloti, Koussevitzky, the court orchestra, and the summer symphony seasons in Sestroretsk and Pavlovsk. The additude of the public was likewise markedly changed. "Only three years ago," wrote Karatygin, "most of our music-lovers saw in Prokofiev's compositions merely the excesses of a mischievous anarchism that threatened to upset the whole of Russian music. Now

---

[6] Usually known in the United States as *Chout*. — Editor.

they won't let him leave the stage before he has played innumerable encores" (*Rech*, No. 186, 1915).

By the end of the summer the piano score of *The Buffoon* was ready. Prokofiev sent it to Diaghilev by post, being unable to go to Italy himself owing to the war in the Balkans. In the meantime he had been working on the orchestration of the rejected music of *Ala and Lolli*, which he had decided to rewrite as a symphonic suite. This was his first large-scale and fully mature orchestral work, as until then he had written small and essentially juvenile symphonic pieces and accompaniments to concertos. The four movements of the *Scythian Suite* combined most of the material of the ballet (first movement, "Worship of Ala and Veles"; second movement, "Chuzhbog and the Dance of the Evil Spirits"; third movement, "Night"; fourth movement, "Lolli's March and the Sun Procession"). The composer wrote for a huge orchestra with eight French horns, five trumpets, additional woodwinds, piano, and a complicated selection of nine percussion instruments not counting the kettle-drum. Prokofiev's scope and originality made themselves most strongly felt in the two last movements of the suite, particularly in the grand and powerful finale depicting the powerful elemental beauty of the rising sun.

That same year, in the intervals between the more important commissioned works, the composer found time to give outlet to his own purely lyrical musical inclinations. Early in 1915 he conceived the idea for a violin concertino, but after composing a delightfully serene and lovely melody (the future leitmotiv of the D major Violin Concerto) he laid the work aside to await better times. The same year saw the advent of a number of colorful and charming piano pieces, something in the nature of pages from a diary, a record of the emotions of the composer, passing impressions of the outer world. These pieces were later entitled *Fugitive Visions*. (Nos. 5, 6, 10, 16, and 17 were composed in 1915).

It was in the summer of 1915 too that Prokofiev composed

his cycle of songs, Op. 23, which included such notable items as the *Wizard* (words by Agnivtsev) and *Under the Roof* (words by Valentine Goryansky). In the autumn he turned his attention to *The Gambler*. Recalling this period, Prokofiev says that "the Russian outweighed the foreign in the scales of my personal interests."

And if we compare these Russian interests with the problems in stylization set him by Diaghilev during his stay in Italy, we find that the composer's personal creative ideas had far greater depth and meaning. True, these ideas were not yet properly grasped and digested. Nevertheless he was intuitively groping toward the bigger human themes in art and serious problems of a social nature that Diaghilev and the modernists studiously eschewed.

The last of the *Sarcasms* already contained not only clever harmony and rhythms but also a compact philosophy akin to the "laughter through tears" theme of Gogol's *Cloak* and *Dead Souls*: "Sometimes we laugh maliciously at someone or something, but when we look closer, we see how pitiful and wretched is the object of our laughter, and then we grow ashamed and the laughter rings in our ears, but now the laugh is on us. . . ." This program was not declared. Nevertheless, its existence showed that besides laughing and scoffing (as, for instance, in the caricature *Scherzo* for four bassoons) the composer had a searching mind and a desire to perceive and feel life in his own way.

It was no accident, either, that the verses of Valentine Goryansky, who contributed to the radical satiric magazine *Novy Satirikon*, should appeal to Prokofiev. In this period the *Novy Satirikon* published the verses of Mayakovsky, his bitingly sarcastic "hymns" (*Hymn to Dinner, Hymn to the Judge*, etc.). Some of the poets of the *Novy Satirikon*, as V. Shklovsky put it, "resembled Mayakovsky, but the resemblance was not apparent until much later." Goryansky's urban, extremely prosaic and mundane lyricism expressed his sympathies for the world of city slums and the common folk crushed by the soullessness and brutal exploitation of the "machine age."

The song *Under the Roof*, written to Goryansky's text, gives a curious insight into the essence of the young Prokofiev's lyricism — his genuine love for life and nature in spite of the oppressive atmosphere of the capitalist city.

> . . . It was a week ago that someone told me
> I was blind and knew not life's joys,
> That I was all sunk in working and sweating,
> That my children were sin's ugly toys. . . .
> But that's not so, now! Really not so!
> My children have all the graces!
> But I'm poor, and that's why they starve and are famished,
> What gives them such pinched little faces.
> I see the wide world through my one tiny window,
> My soul is not blinded to light.
> Oh, I see the sun climbing higher and higher,
> Through banks of clouds and the night.

And at the end the calm and serene conclusion:

> Who said that I live not knowing nature
> Affronted me, spoke in vain.
> No! I have felt fair nature's glad smile!
> Never mind that we are beggars in town. . . .
> My children are not ugly and full of guile —
> Only wan and weak, and pressed down.

Prokofiev took this particular song very seriously, giving it a great deal of thought and "taking great pains to convey in the music every shade of feeling contained in the text." And only a certain mechanical quality in the accompaniment, a preponderance of automatic *ostinato* figures, somewhat detracted from the impression of the song as a whole.

A unique phenomenon among the Russian vocal lyrics of that period was the *Wizard*, a bold challenge to rose-colored, philistine complacency, a specimen of bitter musical caricature, a sphere unexplored in Russian vocal music since the days of Mussorgsky's *Classic* and *He-Goat*.

43

These songs were direct stepping-stones to *The Gambler,*
which Prokofiev began to compose in the autumn of 1915,
notwithstanding Diaghilev's vehement disapproval. And this
stubborn striving to continue his own work on the opera in the
face of the "anti-operatic" tendencies of the leading modernist circles was evidence of the progressiveness of Prokofiev, of
his disagreement in principle with the empty formalism of the
Diaghilev school.

The Gambler had been conceived as a realistic, lifelike performance. The composer wrote the libretto himself, striving to
retain the Dostoyevsky dialogues intact (with the fourth act
only was he assisted by his intimate friend B. N. Demchinsky).
Lively and dynamic action and flexibility of the recitatives,
which were based on the actual intonation of ordinary speech
— such were the aims Prokofiev strove to achieve in his opera
in obvious continuation of the operatic traditions of Mussorgsky, particularly in *Marriage.*

As distinct from the stylization and decorative problems of
Ala and Lolli and *The Buffoon, The Gambler* was a problem in
character-portrayal and social protest. The characters in *The
Gambler* — the stupid, fatuous General, the shameless hussy
Mademoiselle Blanche, the Marquis, the crowd of half-crazed
gamblers poisoned by their passion for gain — are wretched and
disgusting in their cynical frankness. The gambling den, with
its merciless hold on the destiny of people, ruining some and
enriching others, presented as a terrible symbol of fate, an embodiment of the soulless force of the bourgeois "hard cash"
principle, is a theme quite often chosen by Russian writers and
composers (Lermontov's *Masquerade, The Queen of Spades*
by Pushkin and Tchaikovsky). What obviously attracted Prokofiev was the opportunity to create characters in striking contrast to this repulsive world — Alexei with his sardonic humor
and provocative behavior, Babulenka (Granny), straightforward and outspoken, and Pauline, impulsive, passionate, and
nervously exalted. The composer has laid particular emphasis
on all those scenes in which Alexei shocks and scandalizes the

society around him. It is no accident that Prokofiev begins his opera with the monologue of "the virtuous father," in which Alexei exposes the cheeseparing avarice of the bourgeois family with its blind worship of all-powerful gold.[7]

In the music of *The Gambler* one is struck by a number of finely wrought details revealing the keen eye of the composer, his remarkable gift for clever, laconic character portrayal: the foolish remarks of the General, the false, hypocritical coquetry of Mademoiselle Blanche, the broad Russian melodies of

5. *The Gambler*, Act II, theme of Babulenka.

Babulenka, and the feverish dynamic effect of the scene in the gambling house.

Nevertheless, in his desire to turn his back completely on the

[7] Here is the text of this monologue: "The virtuous father, the obedient family, a stork on the roof, flowers in front of the house. All work like oxen and save money: money, money, money is the motto. The daughter is an old maid. She was given no dowry. The youngest son was sold into servitude and the money added to the capital. At last sufficient wealth had been accumulated to enable the oldest son of forty to marry. The father blesses him, weeps, moralizes, hands over his capital, and dies. And so on until six generations later there is the solid respectable firm of Hoppe & Co." Prokofiev reworked the text himself, leaving it brief and pithy.

old operatic aria the composer went to the other extreme, with the result that the unnatural, caricaturesque quality of the recitative, the fragmentary nature and deliberate dissonance of the orchestral accompaniment, are clearly overdone. From the standpoint of pure form, this opera anticipated many of the modernistic operas of the thirties. The subject matter of *The Gambler*, however, bore witness to some interesting processes at work in the mind of the young composer in 1915–16. The challenging, provocative tone of the opera, its malicious grotesqueness at that time, undoubtedly bore an affinity to the scourging satire of the young Mayakovsky.

The bulk of *The Gambler* was written in five and a half months, from October 1915 to March 1916. The "Left" extremes indulged in by the young composer in his search for harsh and unaccustomed harmony puzzled even his well-wishers. "Do you really understand what you are pounding out of that piano of yours?" was the remark made to him once by his irritated mother, who until then had patiently endured all the excesses of her talented son. "We didn't speak to each other for two days after that," Prokofiev recalls.

Work on *The Gambler* was stimulated by Prokofiev's introduction to Albert Coates, who had promised to produce the opera on the stage of the Maryinsky Theater. At that time Telyakovsky, the manager of the imperial theatres, not wishing to lag behind Diaghilev, permitted the introduction of many modernistic novelties in the Maryinsky. "Left" producers were invited and numerous interesting novelties staged, or at least rehearsed (for example, Strauss's *Elektra*). This policy was actively supported by Albert Coates, who was gradually taking over the reins of management from the aged Napravnik.

It is surprising that, notwithstanding the militant principles expressed in his music, particularly in such novel compositions as the *Scythian Suite*, *The Gambler*, and the *Sarcasms*, Prokofiev was not given to propounding his views in the kind of public declarations made by his contemporaries in other fields of art. While most of the "Left" poets and painters of his generation were constantly indulging in loud declarations of their opinions, delivering "slaps in the face of public taste," and mercilessly flaying their opponents, he preferred to act exclusively through the medium of art itself. Only from his letters and his few attempts at criticism is it possible to form an idea of his æsthetic views at that period. They were, briefly, a passionate defense of anything new and a violent distaste for all that was stereotyped and passively imitative.

"When I drew the attention of a certain pianist to the new sonata," he wrote in a review of a new piano sonata by Miaskovsky, "he said. 'What? No, thank you. I had better learn to play all of Beethoven's sonatas before tackling something new.' A weighty argument, of course, but how utterly hopeless!" (*Muzyka*, No. 210, February 14, 1915). At the end of the same article the reviewer bitterly condemned those who "fear the mob taste and are too lazy to tackle new things." Elsewhere he sharply criticized a young "Frenchified" composer for allowing himself to lose his national identity for the sake of aping the French impressionists. A letter to Jurgenson (May 1, 1915), criticizing the Moscow publisher for his niggardly methods, is annihilating in its frankness:

"You have published scarcely a single genuine composer since Tchaikovsky," wrote Prokofiev. "All the best names are invariably to be found somewhere else, while hundreds of scribblers whose names figure neither on programs nor even in the musical calendar are firmly established on your shelves. True, you can pay them in small change, but, after all, you head a first-class publishing firm and not an asylum for failures."

While working on *The Gambler* Prokofiev had experienced the satisfaction of the sensational success of his *Scythian Suite*, performed for the first time at a Siloti concert held on January 16, 1916. Once again Prokofiev's music evoked a storm of mingled enthusiasm and indignation.

"The first movement of the suite," reported one reviewer, "was received in puzzled silence, the second and third movements were applauded, the finale caused a heated skirmish between two camps, the one applauding wildly, the other violently hissing" (Dzbanovsky in the *Vecherneye Vremya*, January 17, 1916). The daring music put Glazunov to flight; he could not endure the dazzling power of the sunrise finale. The yellow press pounced on this fact with malicious glee. "One cannot but sympathize with A. K. Glazunov," said the *Petrogradskaya Gazeta*, "who, notwithstanding his notorious good nature, got up during the performance of Prokofiev's 'music' and demonstratively left the hall. . . . In appraising the new composition . . . the director of the Conservatory did not mince words" (*Petrogradskaya Gazeta*, January 17, 1916, review by N. Bernstein entitled: "A Siloti Concert, or the Incident in the Maryinsky Theater").

"Hair-raising musical rowdyism," "a new way of smudging musical score sheets," "the super-music of the future," "horse-racing," and "cacophony" were some of the stinging comments of the music critics. Even the progressive *Muzykalny Sovremennik*, organ of the St. Petersburg modernist circles, which had taken the place of the defunct Evenings of Modern Music, devoted an extremely ambiguous article, full of reservations and contradictions, in its issue No. 15 for 1916 to Prokofiev's suite.

Differences of opinion with regard to the music of Prokofiev and Stravinsky led shortly afterward to a split in the editorial board of the *Muzykalny Sovremennik*. The more radical Igor Glebov and P. Suvchinsky, unable to agree with Rimsky-Korsakov, Y. Weisberg, and other leading lights of the magazine, resigned.

It was, incidentally, in connection with the *Scythian Suite* that Sabaneyev disgraced himself. On December 13, 1916 the Moscow magazine *Nevosti Sezona* appeared with one of his customary condemnatory articles reviewing an alleged *première* performance in Moscow of the *Scythian Suite*. The article, which was the usual passionate tirade against Prokofiev's "barbarous" music, ended with the remark that "the composer himself conducted with barbaric zeal" (*Novosti Sezona*, No. 3335;

December 13, 1916). A few days later the newspaper *Rech* carried a coldly formal letter from Prokofiev to the effect that the *Scythian Suite* had not been performed in Moscow at all and that the only copy of the score could not have been in the possession of any of the critics. This was fitting revenge on Sabaneyev for his persistent nagging of Prokofiev.

The public controversy in the musical press regarding Prokofiev's work merely fanned public interest in the *Scythian Suite*. In the early part of the following season (October 29, 1916) it was performed again at one of Siloti's special concerts, and henceforth became a popular feature on concert programs both in Russia and abroad.

V. Karatygin in the *Rech* and Igor Glebov in *Muzyka* paid glowing tribute to the new composition. "The freshness of harmonic effects, originality of theme, and elemental force that permeate the *Scythian Suite* make it undoubtedly one of the most significant and valuable examples of Russian musical 'modernism,' " wrote Karatygin. "Not since the death of Borodin have we heard a voice singing so appealingly of the rich bounty of life," claimed Glebov. "Prokofiev is one of ourselves, a contemporary. It would be a sad mistake to relegate him to the unknown future, to label him with the vulgarized title of 'futurist.' "

Unlike the modernists, particularly Nurok and Nuvel, who laid emphasis on Prokofiev's experiments in harmony and modernistic coloring, Glebov, and Karatygin as well, drew attention to the intrinsic lyricism latent in many of his works. The sober strength and exalted humanity of Prokofiev's lyricism made themselves most strongly felt in five songs written to verses by Anna Akhmatova in five days during November 1916.

On April 7, 1916 a private audition of *The Gambler* was arranged at the home of Telyakovsky. Among those present were Siloti, Coates, and Tartakov, chief producer. In order to avoid unpleasantness, Coates managed things so that Glazunov, Cui, and other conservative-minded members of the jury were absent. Telyakovsky did not approve of the opera, but succumbed to the arguments of the young conductors and signed the contract. The opera was included in the repertory for 1916–17. Prokofiev devoted the entire summer of 1916 to the orchestration of *The Gambler*. He worked hard on the score, doing as much as eighteen pages a day.

By autumn the press announced that *The Gambler* had been included in the repertory of the Maryinsky and that rehearsals had begun. The leading roles were to be sung by the cream of the Maryinsky opera company — I. Yershov and I. Alchevsky (Alexei), Bosse (the General), Zbruyeva (Babulenka).

The hostile press attacked Prokofiev's latest composition in advance. "One can merely pity the poor subscribers who will be forced willy-nilly to listen to a futuristic opera," bemoaned the critic of the *Petrogradskaya Gazeta* (April 15, 1916). It was sensationally reported that Dostoyevsky's widow had claimed royalties for the operatic version of *The Gambler*, but this incipient scandal was nipped in the bud. It was rumored likewise that the signers of the Maryinsky cast were driven to despair by the insuperable difficulties of this "Left" opera. This as a matter of fact was indeed one of the main reasons why the opera was taken out of the repertory immediately after the February Revolution, before it was ever produced on the Russian opera stage.

During the war Prokofiev re-entered the St. Petersburg Conservatory to study the organ. This marked a revival of the classical tendencies in him dating back to his student days in Tcherepnin's class. At the end of 1916 he conceived the idea of a symphony in the classical manner, "as Haydn might have written it had he lived in our day." He decided to compose for the first time without the piano — on the basis of the inner ear. "The orchestral color in a piece of music like this must be purer."

The themes for the new symphony were conceived "between whiles," occasionally on his way home from the Conservatory. The first was the Gavotte (the third movement of the symphony), later to become one of the most popular of Prokofiev's miniatures. Then came the material for the *Allegro* and the slow movement. The symphony was completed in the summer of 1917. This subtle and original stylization of the musical idiom and orchestration of an eighteenth-century symphony was called the *Classical Symphony*. Without resorting to the method of museum research, the composer created a piece of music that was delightfully fresh and clever, full of an exquisite charm and touched with a faint, barely perceptible irony.

Russian local color, reminiscent of one of the themes of Rimsky-Korsakov's *Snow Maiden*, breaks through rather startlingly in the concluding A major finale, giving the effect of the eighteenth century seen through the prism of Russian national melody. The *Classical Symphony* was dedicated to Boris Asafyev (Igor Glebov), with whom Prokofiev had formed a close friendship since the death of M. Schmithof and Miaskovsky's departure for the front. At this period Prokofiev toyed with the idea of writing a miniature Russian symphony in a similar vein and dedicating it to Diaghilev. But the idea never materialized.

Coming after the extremes of *The Gambler* and the *Scythian Suite*, most of the works composed in 1916–17 — the Akhmatova songs, the Violin Concerto, the *Classical Symphony*, the *Fugitive Visions*, and the sonatas for the piano — indicated a definite turn toward quiet lyricism and a marked "softening of mood." For Prokofiev this unexpected turn toward lyricism, to gentle, dreamy moods, signified the broadening of his artistic diapason, the maturity of his versatile talent.

Came 1917, the historic year of the October Revolution. The young composer, wholly absorbed in his music, was hardly aware of the revolutionary storm-cloud that was gathering. The utter disregard for politics characteristic of the modernist and Conservatory circles in which he had moved all these years had not helped to awaken his social consciousness. His life flowed on as before. He continued to appear at symphony con-

certs and piano recitals: on November 27, 1916 he gave a recital at one of Siloti's chamber concerts; on January 14, 1917
he played his First Concerto with the RMO symphony orchestra; [8] on February 2 he gave a piano recital in Saratov, and on
February 5 appeared at an Evening of Modern Music in Moscow (first performance of the Akhmatova songs, Op. 27). This
last concert was attended by Medtner and Rachmaninoff, who
were rather unfavorably disposed toward Prokofiev's music.
It was on this occasion that Medtner uttered the phrase that
was immediately snatched up by the critics: "If that is music,
then I am no musician." On February 12, 1917 Prokofiev appeared at a literary and musical evening held in Petrograd at
an exhibition of paintings arranged by N. E. Dobychina. Besides Prokofiev, who played a number of his compositions, the
program included readings by Maxim Gorky of excerpts from
My Childhood, and violin selections by Jascha Heifetz (his
last appearance before departing for America). Gorky showed
great interest in Prokofiev. He laughed heartily over the Bassoon *Scherzo* and listened carefully to *The Ugly Duckling* and
the *Sarcasms*. "Pampered art," remarked the great writer, "but
good, very good." Prokofiev's contact with Maxim Gorky
lasted for many years.

The February days saw Prokofiev on the streets of Petrograd watching events with an eager interest and "hiding behind house corners when the shooting became too hot." He
welcomed the Revolution, but failed to comprehend its full
meaning. He saw it as some grand but incomprehensible upheaval, the expression of a mighty but chaotic primordial
force.[9] For example, the February battles inspired *Fugitive*

---

[8] The program included Stravinsky's *Petrouchka* and Miaskovsky's Second
Symphony. An interesting *feuilleton* by Alexander Amfiteatrov about this concert was published in *Russkaya Volya*, January 18, 1917.

[9] This reaction to the Revolution was typical of many other Russian artists
and intellectuals, who sincerely strove to comprehend what was happening.
Suffice it to recall Blok's *The Twelve* or Miaskovsky's Sixth Symphony. Echoes
of these moods are to be found in Prokofiev's *Cantata for the Twentieth Anniversary of the October Revolution* (Op. 74), where the revolutionary events
are likewise treated in the form of grand cosmic upheavals.

Vision No. 19 — *presto agitatissimo* — restless chaotic music that, according to the composer, depicts "the agitation of the crowd rather than the inner essence of revolution." Later, in

6. *Fugitive Vision No.* 19.

response to the revolutionary upheavals, came the cantata *Seven, They Are Seven* after the poem by Balmont. Both these works afforded clear evidence of the composer's failure to grasp the true significance of the events. The cantata *Seven, They Are Seven* for solo tenor, chorus, and orchestra was written toward the end of the summer of 1917 to the text of Balmont's version of a "Chaldean invocation" engraved in cuneiform characters on the walls of an ancient Akkadian temple. "The revolutionary events that stirred Russia," Prokofiev recalls, "subconsciously affected me and demanded expression. I did not know how to do it and hence turned to ancient themes that have been preserved through the ages."

The music of the cantata to a certain extent continued the "barbaric" tendencies of the *Scythian Suite,* but with this difference: that whereas a healthy, radiant spirit predominated in the suite, terrible destructive forces stormed and raged in the cantata, gloomy portents of fearsome cosmic upheavals and calamities. The weird and frightful Chaldean monsters that ruled the world seemed to symbolize some dread, unconquerable force that had plunged mankind into the chasm of war and hunger:

Charity they know not,
Shame they have none,
Prayers they heed not, to entreaties they are deaf.
Earth and heaven shrink before them,
They clamp down whole countries as behind prison gates,
They grind nations, as nations grind grain.
They are seven! Seven! Seven!

But what had the composer to oppose to this diabolical force that held the world in thrall? Naught but savage heathen invocation, the witch-doctor's mumblings, the mystic malediction: "*Telal, telal,* curse, curse, curse!" The cantata ends on this despairing note to the furious *glissando* shrieking of the horns and trombones, the thunder of kettle-drums and tom-toms. Such music could only leave the annihilating and morbid impression of some incredible nightmare.[10] Thus, while striving intuitively to give musical expression to his presentiment of the titanic social upheavals that were about to shake the world, the composer became entangled in the ugly web of symbolic mysticism.

Nevertheless, certain of his contemporaries believed that Prokofiev, with his healthy, earthy art and his joyous assertion of life, was the musical spokesman of the revolutionary storm that was about to break. This was the subject of a symptomatic article by Igor Glebov entitled "The Path to Joy," published in July 1917 in the newspaper *Novaya Zhizn.*[11] Viewing the conception of Revolution as an abstract idea of universal joy and freedom of creative expression, Glebov found all these qualities in Prokofiev's music. "Joy as the consciousness of one's creative powers, as faith in a better future, as a true motive force, blossomed out in Prokofiev's music in the final movement of his suite *Ala and Lolli.* . . ." In this suite, according to Glebov, "one feels the first intimation in Russian

---

[10] *Seven, They Are Seven* was first performed as late as May 1924 in Koussevitzky's concerts in Paris. In 1933 the cantata was revised by the composer and its piano score published.

[11] No. 73, July 13 (26), 1917. According to Glebov himself, this article had been ordered by Maxim Gorky and A. N. Tikhonov, who wished to publish a study on the subject of the Russian Revolution as reflected in music.

music that the path to the sun has been found, the path to that radiant joy and unclouded happiness man experiences at the discovery of the limitless fund of his creative energy. . . . Contemporary Russian music has anticipated the coming of this turning-point, and of the advance that has taken place in the country today in the direction of the assertion of the priority of will and the striving for free creative being." [12]

Even his antagonists — not without venom, of course — noted in Prokofiev's work the reflection of the new mass and democratic art principles. Sabaneyev had written on this subject a few years before, accusing the composer of pandering to the tastes of the "uninitiated" and of indulging the "mob psychology" (*Golos Moskvy*, February 18, 1914). One bourgeois æsthete took advantage of the new terminology of the time openly to accuse Prokofiev's music of "Bolshevik accessibility" (*Novy Den*, April 19, 1918, article by Kolomyitsev).

Paradoxically enough, however, while being *objectively* bound by his art to the revolutionary changes that were taking place throughout Russian culture, and being regarded by some of his contemporaries as one of the "stormy petrels" of the Revolution, Prokofiev still remained inwardly almost indifferent to it.

He spent the summer of 1917 in the country near Petrograd, studying the philosophy of Kant and Schopenhauer and working with more than his usual zeal.[13] This was an extremely productive year: in the spring he composed his remarkable Third Sonata, Op. 28, rewritten "from old folios" preserved from the Conservatory days (1907). At the same time he gathered material for a violin concerto, a new pianoforte concerto, and a string quartet conceived on the basis of strictly diatonic

[12] "Roads to the Future," another brilliant critical analysis of Prokofiev's music by Glebov, was printed somewhat later in the magazine *Melos* for 1918. In this article Glebov again speaks of Prokofiev's ties with the revolutionary epoch: "In him alone we have the sole genuine representative of the age, one in whom life is perceived as creative endeavor, and creative endeavor as life."

[13] In Schopenhauer's philosophy, as Prokofiev himself tells us, it was the maxim of practical behavior rather than the passive and despondent elements that attracted his attention.

melody ("on the white keys"). In his summer retreat the composer finished the orchestration of his Violin Concerto, completed the *Classical Symphony*, and sketched the outlines of *Seven, They Are Seven*.

The Violin Concerto, Op. 19, and the Third Sonata in one movement were perhaps the best things written by Prokofiev in the period prior to his stay abroad, the "pre-foreign period," as it has been called. One is struck by the unity of conception, the swiftness of development, and the vivid feeling of the Third Sonata, which combines a serene and gentle lyricism (subordinate theme) with fiery bursts of passion.

The broad gamut of human emotions is reflected also in the poetic Violin Concerto with its dreamy melodiousness, the wicked, satanic skepticism of the Scherzo, and the joyous embracing of nature in the finale.

In the autumn Prokofiev went to Essentuki in the Caucasus, and thence to Kislovodsk, where his mother was taking the waters. Here he completed the *Classical Symphony* and *Seven, They Are Seven*. Here too the Fourth Sonata, Op. 29, compounded of old fragments written in 1908 (the *Allegro* and part of the finale, plus the wise, meditative *Andante* borrowed from the youthful E minor Symphony), came into being.

At that time the country was in the throes of revolution; only faint echoes of the October events reached Kislovodsk. "The news was most exciting," Prokofiev recalls, "but so contradictory that it was absolutely impossible to make head or tail of it." Before long the North Caucasus was cut off from the center of the country by the Kaledin uprising on the Don. Prokofiev was stranded in Kislovodsk. "Well-wishers" whispered in his ear that there would not be much room for music in Russia now and advised him to go to America. "Immersed as I was in art, I did not have a clear idea of the scope and significance of the October Revolution and hence the idea about America took root in my mind."

Not until the spring of 1918, when the Kaledin front collapsed, did Prokofiev succeed in leaving Mineralniye Vody armed with a pass issued him by the Kislovodsk Soviet of Workers' Deputies. In Moscow he got in contact with Koussevitzky's publishing house and sold them his outstanding compositions of the last few years (*Scythian Suite, The Buffoon,* and *The Gambler*).

In April 1918 Prokofiev became associated with a group of futurist poets that included Vladimir Mayakovsky, Vassili Kamensky, and David Burlyuk. He had already heard Mayakovsky at a literary evening a year before and had been much impressed by his verse. A friendship founded on mutual artistic sympathies now sprang up between Prokofiev and Mayakovsky. Prokofiev played some of his pieces in the futurist "Poets' Café" in Nastasyinsky Pereulok and had long talks with Mayakovsky. On one such occasion the poet drew a pencil portrait of Prokofiev playing his *Diabolic Suggestions,* with the inscription: "Sergei Sergeyevich playing on the tenderest nerves of Vladimir Vladimirovich." [14] It was in this period that Mayakovsky presented Prokofiev with his poem "War and the Universe," with the amusing inscription: "To the World President for Music from the World President for Poetry. To Prokofiev from Mayakovsky."

Prokofiev met Mayakovsky subsequently both in Moscow and abroad. Mentioning his antipathy to Stravinsky's music in one of his articles from abroad written in 1922, Mayakovsky observed: "I much prefer the Prokofiev of the pre-foreign period, the Prokofiev of the crude, dashing marches" (V. Mayakovsky: *Collected Works,* Vol. VII, p. 258). This is perhaps the only positive allusion to music to be found in all of Mayakovsky's writings.

Soon afterward Prokofiev returned to Petrograd after an absence of nine months. In April 1918 he was able to arrange three consecutive concerts of his own music. In two piano recitals held in the hall of the Tenishev School on April 15 and April 17, the Third and Fourth Sonatas and the *Fugitive Visions* were played for the first time. On April 21, the *première*

[14] See V. Kamensky's book *Life with Mayakovsky* (Moscow, 1940), p. 200.

of the *Classical Symphony,* conducted by Prokofiev himself, was given by the former court orchestra.

The concerts of this "Prokofiev Week," as the press called it, were a huge success. That held in the Tenishev School was attended by numerous scientists, artists, and writers, who were most enthusiastic (*Noviye Vedomosti,* April 16, 1918; reviewer A. Koptyayev). The tranquillity and clarity of the new compositions, particularly the *Classical Symphony,* reconciled Prokofiev with his bitterest opponents. "No more grimacing, no more outrageous discords," the *Vecherneye Slovo* commented with satisfaction. "The whole music is chaste and pure, clear, simple, and reminiscent of the youthful inspiration of Haydn and Mozart" (Dzbanovsky on the *Classical Symphony* in the *Vecherneye Slovo,* April 22, 1918).

The *première* of the *Classical Symphony* was attended by A. V. Lunacharsky, People's Commisar of Education, who was much impressed by Prokofiev's talent. When, a few days later, Gorky and Benois introduced Prokofiev to Lunacharsky, Prokofiev mentioned his desire to go to America. "You are a revolutionary in music," replied the People's Commissar, "we are revolutionaries in life. We ought to work together. But if you wish to go I shall place no obstacles in your way."

Prokofiev was sent to the United States on a trip on which he was to combine "matters pertaining to art" with care of his personal health. He left Petrograd on May 7, 1918, bound for Vladivostok. His baggage consisted mainly of sheafs of music, including the scores of the *Scythian Suite,* the First Concerto, the *Classical Symphony,* and several piano pieces. Moreover, he took with him a number of ideas for a new piano concerto and the scenario of his future opera *The Love for Three Oranges,* the name given to a magazine published during the war by a group of theatrical modernists who upheld the conventionalized parody theater of Carlo Gozzi. A scenario based on *The Love for Three Oranges* by Gozzi, published in one of the issues of this magazine, had been recommended to Prokofiev as a subject for an opera.

5 : Style[1]

THE SPRING of 1918, as we have seen, marked the dividing line between the early period in Prokofiev's career and the subsequent period of his travels abroad. The early period, represented by thirty *opera* for the piano, symphony orchestra, and theater, constitutes a truly *classic* period, one of the last brilliant pages of the Russian pre-Revolutionary musical classics. It was in these years (1908–18) that the musical style of the composer became clearly defined. The musical interests of the young Prokofiev were focused on two main spheres.

The first was the *theater*, the art of concrete images and situations, the striving to reproduce in theatrical forms objects and phenomena taken either from life or from books. To this category belong the early operatic experiments and the subsequent work on ballets and operas, as well as the largest and best part of his symphonic music — likewise generated to a lesser or greater degree by the theater — and even many of his piano compositions, which constituted something in the nature of sketches for future theatrical scenes (the numerous marches, gavottes, and scherzos, or, on the other hand, *Phantom, Despair*, and *Diabolic Suggestions*).

Secondly, the *piano*, which from Prokofiev's childhood had been his favorite medium. The piano, treated not on the intimate, contemplative "drawing-room" plane (the pianoforte style of the impressionists and Scriabin had always been alien to Prokofiev), but as a means of delivering thunderous ora-

---

[1] In this chapter I have endeavored to outline my observations of the musical style of the *young* Prokofiev. However, since even in these years the composer's style was quite mature, the evaluation given here applies to a considerable extent also to the outstanding compositions of his subsequent period, particularly of the last few years. From this standpoint I have touched upon some works of the more recent period in the present chapter.

tions from the concert platform, for holding mass "concert meetings" as it were.

The peculiar stylistic features that make it possible to recognize Prokofiev's music from the first few bars, just as we recognize the music of Liszt, Grieg, Borodin, or Scriabin, asserted themselves at an early date. "The combination of the simple and the intricate, the complexity of the whole with the schematization and simplification of the particular," such is the general definition of Prokofiev's style given by V. Karatygin.[2]

The simplest and most classical features in Prokofiev's music are its forms, rhythm, and pianoforte texture. The complex and unusual are to be found in the harmonic idiom, the polyphonic methods, and sometimes the melody. Deliberately simplifying the piece, stripping it down to the bare, clear-cut rhythmic framework, Prokofiev combines this with an unusual vividness of harmony and melody. At times his music is almost schematic in form, but it is invariably enlivened with fresh and original modulation.

Perhaps the most powerful of the expressive media of the young musician are his peculiar rhythms. He turns from the delicate ultra-refined, wavy rhythms of Debussy and Scriabin to clear and concrete outlines. His predilection for common time (marches and gavottes), 6/8 time,[3] and the basic rhythms is common knowledge. Prokofiev's gravitation toward old and established chiseled dance patterns or the ceaseless tattoo of *perpetuum mobile* is clearly a return to the stable canons of seventeenth- and eighteenth-century classical music. But his rhythms as well as other elements of his style are at times a

---

2 Article entitled "Prokofiev's Music," published in No. 1 of *Iskusstvo* (1917). Other valuable observations pertaining to the musical style of Prokofiev are to be found in a number of reviews by Karatygin (see his *Collected Works*, pp. 194–204), in the works of Igor Glebov (*Melos*, No. 2, 1918, and *Russkaya Muzyka*), in the article by Y. Ekgel (*Russkiye Vedomosti*, February 10, 1917), and, more lately, in the writings of V. Zuckermann (article on the Soviet opera in *Sovietskaya Muzyka*, No. 12, 1940) and in the lectures delivered by B. L. Yavorsky.

3 We find triplets in the First, Second, and Third Sonatas, in the First and Second Concertos, in the Violin Concerto and many pianoforte pieces.

combination of the most far-fetched extremes: over-simplified designs of crude and archaic form (*Ala and Lolli*), childish primitive playfulness (*The Buffoon*), and sharply accentuated, tense rhythmic effects abounding in convulsive, spasmodic tirades and sudden bursts of movement (see *Sarcasms* Nos. 1 and 5, or the subordinate theme of the First Piano Concerto).

Prokofiev's *harmonic idiom* is characterized by a simple clarity in his basic chords combined with extreme daring in his use of incidental and transition chords. As a matter of fact, he rarely emerges from the realistic sphere of the stable major-minor harmonic relationships. On the contrary, after the modal extravaganza of impressionism, he demonstratively brings his hearers back to the more earthy and "plebeian" tonalities, to the accustomed C major (one of the keys that occur most frequently in Prokofiev's music),[4] to G major, D major, and the commonest minor keys (A minor, D minor, and G minor); yet with Prokofiev the familiar C major is apt to perform such unexpected tricks, such sudden transitions to distant tonalities, such fresh chord combinations, as to make it appear an entirely new key with unsuspected possibilities (see, for example, the main theme of *Zdravitsa*). The composer is very fond of stringing together long chains of parallel or diverging chords, each of which is more or less ordinary and common, but which are combined in such a way as to produce sound effects that are both new and original (for example, the finale of the March from the *Three Oranges*).

All these deliberate dissonances, including the weird effects produced by chance combinations of non-harmonic sounds, are employed by Prokofiev chiefly for descriptive purposes. He is not afraid of unusual chord combinations, however polytonal the effect may sometimes be, for these are merely incidental features of polytonality and are nearly always compen-

[4] The Third Concerto, the Fifth and Eighth Sonatas, the finale of the Fourth, the Prelude, Op. 12, *The Ugly Duckling*, much of *The Buffoon*, and, most recently, the *Russian Overture*, *Zdravitsa*, *Peter and the Wolf*, and a great deal of *Semyon Kotko* are written in C major.

sated for by a clear and sober tonal conclusion.[5] Sustained *ostinato* figures, which lend themselves to the most pungent combinations of developing melody with a constantly repeated bass, are a favorite method of the composer. An important element in Prokofiev's harmonic style is the linear principle: many angular chords emerge as a result of the crossing of two or more horizontal lines, and sometimes even of two different chord progressions. This trick of superimposing parallel and apparently independent melodic figures is most strikingly represented in the *Scythian Suite;* Karatygin has compared this method with Greek heterophony.[6] And side by side with crudely decorative, blatant harmonic blotches like the favorite C—F-sharp chord or the simultaneous combination of the D-major and A-major triads at the opening of the gambling scene in *The Gambler,* we find pure diatonic melody and harmony, alternating modes emanating from the Russian folk-song and used with amazing flexibility — the clear unblemished world of white keys, almost totally devoid of chromatic effects, that is so typical of Prokofiev.

Prokofiev's music is famous for its rich abundance of melody. And here, too, the composer strives primarily to bring musical style back to the clear-cut melody of the classics, a reaction from the pernicious "absorption of melody by harmony" of which the impressionists and Scriabin in the latter period were guilty. In the foreground of most of Prokofiev's longer instrumental works we find clearly defined, lapidary melodic lines, built up, like the classics, on the essential major or minor triads (the principal themes of the Second, Third,

---

[5] Characteristic in this conection is the bi-tonal *Sarcasm* No. 3; ostensibly written in a simultaneous combination of B-flat minor (bass) with F-sharp minor (melody), it is actually a complicated B-flat minor.

[6] It would be most illuminating to compare some of the harmonic and orchestral methods of the young Prokofiev with the emphatically earthy, constructivist methods of the Russian painters, the followers of Cézanne and Matisse, the "Jack of Diamonds" group. V. G. Karatygin cleverly pointed to this analogy in his reviews. Prokofiev himself tells us that as early as 1913 he took an interest in the paintings of P. Konchalovsky, attracted to them by the deliberately lapidary quality of their line and color.

and Sixth Sonatas, the First and Second Concertos, the First and Second Violin Concertos, the String Quartet, and *Peter and the Wolf*), or else on the simplest scale movement. A characteristic example of the diatonic movement is the theme of Juliet from *Romeo and Juliet* and of the chromatic movement of the Scherzo of the First Violin Concerto.

It is true that, while outwardly classical in form, these themes almost invariably tend to sprout the startling, unexpected effects that are so unmistakably Prokofiev. In melody — in rhythm and harmonic idiom, for that matter — the composer frequently indulges in curious juxtapositions of the simplest and most firmly established classical effects with the most unusual and startling angularities. Who does not know those deliberately broken themes with the incredibly wide skips in melody? Distortion and shifting of melodic lines are used for ridicule, for caricature, or for powerful emotional emphasis. The particularly uncanny, jarring interval of the ninth, for example, is employed in many themes associated with grief and despair (death theme in *Romeo and Juliet*, funeral theme in *Semyon Kotko*, subordinate theme in the First Concerto, etc.).

At times this fantastic distortion of chromatic melodic design seems artificial, and in such cases the striving for originality clearly takes the upper hand over the natural and logical. It is symptomatic that while such melodies were relatively rare in the Prokofiev of the period prior to his foreign tour (the theme of *Sarcasm* No. 4, and here and there in *The Gambler*), they occur much more frequently between *opera* 40 and 60. A true master of long instrumental melodies of the vocal type (first movement of the Violin Concerto, *Andante* of the Fourth Sonata, introduction to the first movement and the theme for the variations in the Third Concerto), he nevertheless frequently cultivates petty melodic nuclei, leitmotiv melodies, the embryos of thematic development; his rejection of broad and sweeping melodic forms is particularly irritating in his opera music, where keen and pointed declamatory detail

nearly always predominates over the vocal cantilena. It is gratifying, however, to observe that in recent years Prokofiev has
been showing marked tendencies toward clarity and melodiousness employing unmistakable cantilena forms in choral and
solo singing.

The classical quality of Prokofiev's music is perhaps most
strongly felt in his choice of *form*: the most universal classical
forms — the sonata, the one-movement symphonic poem in
the Liszt manner, rondo, variations, three-part forms, etc. —
are to be found in his instrumental music. Preserving the basic
attributes of classical forms, he frequently violates one or another essential element. Such, for example, are the methods
almost invariably employed by Prokofiev for modifying the recapitulation. The latter may be conceived as a continuation of
the development (Third Sonata) or the themes may be combined in contrapuntal manner (*Andante* of the Fourth Sonata, finale of the Violin Concerto); in other cases the recapitulation is entirely deprived of a subordinate theme, or is
reduced to the minimum, taking the form of a sort of repeat
and coda rolled in one. With Prokofiev some violation of the
principles of the sonata form is almost invariably the rule.

Sometimes he follows the example of the romanticists, now
narrowing down the classical sonata to a one-movement form
(First Concerto), now employing the leitmotiv development
of theme (echoes of themes from the first movement in the
finales of the Second and Sixth Sonatas). When, however, the
sonata form is consistently preserved, he uses unusual tonal
relationships to offset the classical form: instead of the generally accepted tonic and dominant keys, Prokofiev prefers an
augmented fourth or second up or down the scale. Novelty of
form in Prokofiev's music is frequently determined by new
and original treatment of some part of the form from the standpoint of expression and ideas; for example, the development
of his sonatas and concertos sometimes gives rise to a curious
distortion, a shifting of image either toward the grotesque or
toward an exaggerated condensation of expression, instead of

the customary dramatization of the main images or their reproduction in a new color. The range of emotions revealed in
the diverse parts of the variations (the second movement of
the Third Concerto) becomes extremely broad.

Except in instrumental concertos and sonatas, Prokofiev
rarely uses the grand sonata or symphonic forms. The sphere
of purely philosophical symphonic music has but little attraction for him.[7] In the sphere of orchestral music, the program
suite, which has concrete theatrical associations, is his predominating form. There are great freedom and absence of
constraint in his large vocal forms; here the text is the principal factor, with rare attempts to impart a formal polish by
means of instrumental refrains (*The Wizard* and *The Ugly
Duckling*).

Characteristically, it is in the earliest of Prokofiev's instrumental compositions (First, Third, and Fourth Sonatas) that
unity and completeness of thematic development are most
strongly defined. Even in such pieces as the First Concerto and
the Second Sonata, however, one can discern a tendency to
string together separate small contrasting episodes — sound
pictures. This cinematographic development makes itself most
strongly felt in the instrumental works having theatrical associations (for example, the suite from *The Buffoon* or the
"Battle on the Ice" from *Alexander Nevsky*). The regrettable
mosaic quality of the form in works of this kind, its excessive
dependence upon the program, are in some measure compensated for by the brilliance of the musical description and the
dynamic cascade of sounds. The integrity and symphonic
breadth of form perceived as a developing entity and not as a
mechanical juxtaposition of contrasting fragments appear
again in some of the later compositions (Second Violin Concerto, Sixth Sonata).

---

[7] Two of his five symphonic compositions (the four symphonies and one
Sinfonietta) are stylized (the *Classical Symphony* and to a lesser degree the
Sinfonietta), while two others are associated in some way with theatrical images
(Third and Fourth Symphonies).

A few words should be said about the technical methods of Prokofiev's music, about the principal features of his orchestral and piano style.

The most daring and original of Prokofiev's early scores are the *Scythian Suite* and *The Buffoon*. In them he most vehemently rejects the academic manner of the composers of the St. Petersburg school, with its accurately poised orchestral groups and smooth voice-leading. Prokofiev's music, on the contrary, is distinguished by its unusual hypertrophy of orchestral tone color — strident, crudely material, and almost invariably subordinated to some descriptive purpose. The rich intricacies of these scores, their innumerable pedal effects, the abundant use of *sostenuto*, insistently recurring phrases, and all manner of sound effects lend them a similarity to some of the orchestral traditions of Wagner and particularly of Strauss. Prokofiev's scores are as colorful as his harmonic texture. His orchestration abounds in harsh daubs of tone color, unexpected, pungent combinations of instruments to bring out some bizarre dramatic effect. "What difference does it make how the composer produces the effect of horror, whether by two beats of the drum and three notes on the clarinet or by a prolonged melody on the violins? If the result is horror, then he has achieved his purpose," one American critic wrote about Prokofiev's orchestration.

In contrast to the ethereal water-color imagery of the impressionist orchestra, Prokofiev often deliberately resorts to the use of crude, earthy orchestration. The sharp timbres of the brasses (the unforgettable high pitch of the brasses in the finale of the *Scythian Suite*), the complex system of the percussion instruments, the dry, brittle sting of the piano, peculiarly descriptive uses of the strings (*con legno, sul ponticello, pizzicato*) — these are some of the effects most commonly employed in his orchestra.

Sharp contrasts are as inherent in Prokofiev's orchestration as in the other elements of his musical style. Side by side with the vertiginous complexities of *Ala and Lolli* we have the translucent score of the *Classical Symphony*, built almost exclusively on pure solo timbres. Prokofiev's tendency toward pure timbres and greater economy of orchestral coloring has become more marked in his latest works, *Alexander Nevsky*, with its amazing wealth and abundance of tone color, being an exception.

While on the subject of Prokofiev's orchestral style, I might mention one curious trait of the composer's personality: his persistent striving for rationalization and efficiency in the practical technique of music-writing. While still in the Conservatory (1914), he revised the generally accepted system of score-writing by discarding the complicated practice of transposition, and by writing all the instruments in his scores in the tonic key — that is, just as they sound on the piano. The work of transposing the corresponding parts (French horn, clarinet, English horn, etc.) is left to the copyist. The only clef remaining apart from the treble and bass is the alto (for viola, trombone, and English horn); the tenor clef is dispensed with altogether (the treble and bass clefs serving for the bassoons and cellos as well). All of Prokofiev's scores are written according to this simplified system. They are extremely easy to read, and it is to be regretted that other composers, from a reluctance either to violate traditions or to trust the transposition to the copyist, have failed to follow his example.

Another interesting labor-saving device introduced by Prokofiev in the sphere of orchestration dates from the period of his foreign tour. Commencing with *Le Pas d'acier* (1925), he began to outline the whole plan of each future work, down to the minutest details, in the piano score. Having allocated all the sounds to the various instruments, marked all the details, and written on a separate staff all the additional voices or complex *divisi*, he considers the orchestration complete. All that remains is to transfer all the orchestral voices marked in pencil on the piano score, a purely technical job that can be entrusted to any intelligent assistant. In this way the composer saves a tremendous amount of time and labor. Most of his scores written in the course of the past fifteen years, with the exception of *Alexander Nevsky,* were done by this method.

In the sphere of the piano as well, Prokofiev's early work marked a violent reaction from the ultra-refinement of impressionism. From the cloying sweetness and spirituality of Scriabin and Debussy he returned demonstratively to the piano of the classical epoch, strongly accentuating its hammer-like quality. Prokofiev's construction — two voices or three voices, with a parallel movement in octaves — is pre-eminently simple and unadorned. The technique of skips and hand-crossings in his pieces is strongly reminiscent of Domenico Scarlatti; the technique of scale runs springs from the piano style of Haydn and the early works of Beethoven. Common features of Prokofiev's piano works are the toccata effects consisting of alternating chords in the right and left hands (a method used by Liszt and Balakirev), of emphasized *non legato,* and so on. Offsetting these dominant features we find a few echoes of impressionistic style in blurred, mellow passages and vibrant chords of rich sonority, and at times — especially in the slow movements of his sonatas and concertos — a striving toward complexity of structure and complex polyphonic development (the central episode of the First Concerto, the third movement of the Second Sonata, much of the Second Concerto).

The declamatory style peculiar to Prokofiev's vocal music as well as his musical dramaturgy are likewise of considerable interest. The student of Prokofiev's style might be recommended to trace the continuation and development of some of his trends in Soviet music, especially in the music of Dmitri Shostakovich. But this is a subject for special research.

The scope of the living phenomena reproduced by Prokofiev — as clearly defined as they are multiform — reveals several distinct parallel trends in his musical style.

For example, there is Prokofiev the classic, the Prokofiev of imposing sonatas, who knows the secret of impeccable form, who is capable of developing his theme in the grand classical manner with the convincing power of a Beethoven. This is the Prokofiev of the first piano concertos, of the Violin Concerto, the Third and Fourth Sonatas. At times his neo-classicism acquires the character of subtle stylization, a deliberate revival of the old through the medium of the new (the *Classical Symphony*, partly the *Sinfonietta*, Op. 5, much in Op. 12, later in the music of *Lieutenant Kije* and *Romeo and Juliet*). With his tongue in his cheek, the composer revives the dance patterns of the eighteenth century — gavotte, *rigaudon*, and minuet — the graceful, courteous world of absurd ceremonies and conventions. In this predilection for the forms of the old, pre-romantic music his work bears a certain affinity (while at the same time retaining its essential difference) to the neo-classicism of Reger, Brahms, and Taneyev.[8]

To this same "classical line" belong the toccata effects, the impelling dynamic runs that are to be found chiefly in his music for the piano; for example, the deliberately simplified passages in the form of five-finger exercises (First and Third Piano Concertos), patterns of mechanical motion, *perpetuum mobile* (Scherzo of the Second Concerto, Scherzo in A minor, Op. 12, Toccata, Op. 11). Incidentally, these violently dynamic, high-pressure figures not only bring us back to classical piano technique, but at times acquire a modern and somewhat machine-like form. Thus, the line runs from the rigid, locomotive rhythms of the Toccata, Op. 11, to the harsh images expressive of modern city life in *Le Pas d'acier* and the Toccata of the Fifth Concerto. "This line," the composer himself has observed, "is perhaps the least significant."

Secondly, an important role in the work of Prokofiev is played by the expressionist guignol — theatrically tragic im-

---

[8] In this respect he has undoubtedly anticipated many of the neo-classical tendencies of Shostakovich, particularly his scherzo and minuet images (scherzos of the Fifth Symphony and the Piano Quintet, finale of the Sixth Symphony).

ages of horrific fantasy or nervous, spasmodic emotions. These images are almost invariably associated with the quest for new harmonies, new timbre and polyphonic media. Sometimes the new harmonic devices engendered by the composer's rich imagination, the fantastic, brittle melodic effects, the bizarre and barbaric harmonies, sought an outlet in blood-curdling or primitive, archaic subjects. And while in some cases these guignol forms remained within the sphere of instrumental music (*Phantom, Despair, Diabolic Suggestions,* the subordinate theme of the First Concerto, the cadenza in the first movement and the Intermezzo of the Second Concerto, the development of the Third Sonata, and much of the *Sarcasms*), in other cases they were embodied in the descriptive sphere of the theater or in sound pictures: in the cruel visions of *Magdalene* and *The Flaming Angel,* in the symbolically decorative satanism of *The Love for Three Oranges,* in the savage atavistic archaicism of the *Scythian Suite* and *Seven, They are Seven.*

To this same line belong the most mocking of Prokofiev's grotesques, in which laughter becomes malicious and diabolical (*Sarcasms, The Wizard,* the Scherzo from the First Violin Concerto, and much of *The Gambler*).

The third significant line in Prokofiev's music is that of pure lyricism, now pensive (as in *Reminiscence,* the unpublished miniature *Reproach,* the subordinate theme in the Third Sonata, *Fugitive Visions* Nos. 1, 7, 16, 20, the slow movement of the First Concerto and the Second and Fourth Sonatas, songs, Op. 9, *Dreams,* main theme of the First Violin Concerto), now associated with the patriarchal world of old fireside legends, "grandmothers' tales" (*Story,* Op. 3, *Legend,* Op. 12, subordinate themes in the first movements of the Violin Concerto and the Third Concerto, in the finale of the Second Concerto, *Tales of the Old Grandmother,* chief refrain of *The Buffoon*). The composer's lyricism is most originally blended with the influences of Western romantic art (Schumann) and with the Russian traditions emanating primarily from Mussorgsky (slow passages of the *Pictures at an Exposition*, songs of the type of *Sunless*, etc.), or directly from the Russian folk-song.

There are lyrical pages in almost all of the larger compositions of the young Prokofiev, even in the most daring and barbaric (for example, the beginning of the third movement in the *Scythian Suite*, the central part of the first and third *Sarcasms*, or the lyrical passages from *The Gambler*). This lyricism is nearly always expressed by the typically Prokofiev diatonic line — "the white keys" (the most typical examples are the introduction to the Third Concerto, the Akhmatova songs, the subordinate theme in the Third Sonata). It is rather surprising that the majority of his early contemporaries failed to give the young Prokofiev any credit for lyrical talent, perceiving merely the crude impulses and cruel mockery in his music. "Tender lyricism is foreign to Prokofiev's nature," wrote A. Koptyayev, "and when he attempts any allusion to it I discern the hideous grin of malice" (*Birzheviye Vedomosti*, July 23, 1915).

And, finally, the fourth of the basic lines that run through the work of Sergei Prokofiev is humor, humor in all its gradations, from the good-natured smile to withering mockery. Prokofiev's humor is part of a long tradition that began with the experiments of Dargomizhsky and Mussorgsky and was later so brilliantly developed in his own works and those of Shostakovich. This tradition is one of the most characteristic features of Russian music. It is a clear sign of a striving to broaden the sphere of musical expression to the utmost, to embrace the whole gamut of human emotions and feelings. Prokofiev's humor is expressed diversely, now in the form of boisterous and gay whimsies (the *Badinage*, Op. 3, *Scherzo* for four bassoons, Scherzo from the Second Sonata, much from *The Buffoon*, and *The Love for Three Oranges*), now coming as a result of ridicule or caricature, or as a negation of some lyrical theme (development of the First Violin Concerto, much in the Second Sonata and the First Piano Concerto).

There is also a faint touch of mockery in the neo-classical pages of Prokofiev's music (the *Classical Symphony*); and there are bitterly ironic notes even in his love lyrics (the Akhmatova songs, *Gray Dress*, etc.).

In the best instrumental compositions of the young Prokofiev—the Second Piano Concerto, the Third and Fourth Sonatas, and the First Violin Concerto—the composer resorts to dramatic contrasts, making radiant dreams and romantic impulses clash with brutal fury or with waggish buffoonery. Adopting a method once used by the romanticists, the composer often lampoons, distorts, and derides his own lyrical ideals. In such cases the lyricism is either eliminated suddenly or effaced by a wicked grimace, an amusing impish movement (the first part of the Second Sonata, the First Piano Concerto), or is distorted in the course of the development (Violin Concerto) or variations (Third Concerto). In a number of works written toward the end of this period (*Sarcasms, The Gambler, The Buffoon, The Wizard*) it is the horrific, the malevolently caricatured reflection of reality that predominates. In these works the composer laughs bitterly at the ugliness and loathsomeness of existence. In this self-flagellation, this tendency to scoff at one's own emotions or at external phenomena, one can discern the skepticism of the young artist who has little faith in the purity and sincerity of human ideals.

At the same time, however, a wholesome perception of nature and faith in the triumph of human energy have taken the upper hand over skepticism and sarcasm in many bright pages of Prokofiev's music. This is apparent in the First Piano Concerto, in the *Classical Symphony*, in the finales of the *Scythian Suite*, the First Violin Concerto, and the Fourth Sonata, and later in his magnificent Third Piano Concerto.

In his striving to mock at all that was smooth and pretty in the old art, in his extensive use of deliberate prosaisms (rigid rhythms and stark, trenchant emotionalism), in his restless dissatisfaction and lack of faith in accepted ideals, the young Prokofiev bore a marked resemblance to the young Mayakov-

sky. But the difference between the two was that, while Mayakovsky succeeded in finding the path to real truth, to the assertion of positive ideals, subsequently turning from sneering
skepticism and desperate explosions of feeling to conscious
service in the cause of the Socialist Revolution, Prokofiev, in
his gropings toward truth, was to a considerable extent bound
by his stagnant, non-political musical environment, as well as
by certain influences emanating from the modernist and Diaghilev circles.

The temptations of the Diaghilev-modernist trend, with its
cult of form and brilliant inventiveness, its total indifference
to man, and its repudiation of the idea in art — this was the
force that diverted the young Prokofiev from the true path of
his artistic development.

While Prokofiev himself [9] from his early years intuitively
strove for an art that would carry on the traditions of the romanticists and the Russian school (Schumann, Grieg, and
Mussorgsky) toward an art founded on a profound love for
man and nature, on keen observation of human speech, intonation, and gesture, the Diaghilev trend, on the other hand,
impelled him in a different direction, toward the poetization
of Scythian, atavistic savagery, to the cult of rollicking buffoonery, stylization, and witty decorative invention, away from
the lofty purpose of art and serious positive ideals.[10]

The sphere of his own humanistic tendencies and the sphere
of the modernist influences were by no means mechanically
divided in Prokofiev's music. In his instrumental works or his
operas, which were the fruit of his own artistic quests, one
finds elements of mechanical, constructivist, cold and rational
art, limiting the vibrant human qualities in his music. Such,

---

[9] In his own artistic experiments he was always supported by the best and
most discerning of the critics — Miaskovsky, Karatygin, and Igor Glebov. The
latter two frequently drew attention to the *lyrical* aspect of his talent.

[10] We recall again Prokofiev's differences of opinion with Diaghilev and
Stravinsky on the question of the development of opera. Advancing the modernist ballet, a semi-acrobatic performance, as a substitute for opera, they rejected
opera in principle as much too realistic and democratic a genre.

for example, is the mechanical and exaggerated caricature of many scenes in *The Gambler*.

And on the other hand in the Diaghilev type of compositions, written to order, the warm pulse of life made itself felt time and again, side by side with the cult of the inanimate, the amusing quirk, or original decoration. Such, for instance, is the lyricism and humor of *The Buffoon, The Love for Three Oranges*; the perception of the elemental force of nature, the titanic energy of the sun in the *Scythian Suite*; the vivid and original refraction of Russian folk-melody in *The Buffoon*.

The search for the human and realistic elements in the art of the young Prokofiev is closely interwoven with healthy and, at first, intuitive manifestations of the Russian national style. The lyricism of the Third Sonata and the Third Concerto, the patriarchal lullaby forms in the finale of the Second Concerto, the profoundly national portrait of Babulenka in *The Gambler*, and, finally, *The Buffoon* and much of the *Fugitive Visions* and *Tales of the Old Grandmother* reveal a strong leaven of the national in the artist, his unusual feeling for the melody and harmony of the Russian song. How typical of Russian folk-music, for example, is Prokofiev's favorite harmonic idiom, with its clear, translucent, diatonic harmony and its characteristic vacillations between the major and minor!

It was precisely these humanistic tendencies in Prokofiev's music, least of all discerned by his contemporaries, that distinguished his music from the openly bourgeois trends of Diaghilev and Stravinsky and brought him finally onto the path of Soviet art. What was it, then, that predominated in his music of the pre-foreign period — the concentration of eccentric and decorative music, the world of mechanical dolls, the fantastic creatures of his imagination, or the poetry of the human soul, the art of living emotions and exalted social ideas?

It is obvious that, had this second tendency, which clearly existed in the best of Prokofiev's compositions, been predominant, had it been fully comprehended by him as a principle, had the sarcasm and force of negation been offset by strong positive ideals, he would inevitably have been one of the first to join the camp of the artists of the Revolution. But unfortunately this did not happen. The foreign period cut him off from his Soviet homeland for almost fifteen years.

Book II
Years of Wandering

6 : Inertia of the Past

> "Whither, madmen?"
> "To search for the three oranges."
> "But they are in Creonta's castle!"
> "I do not fear Creonta."
> GOZZI: *The Love for Three Oranges*

THE THIRST for new keen impressions, the desire to breathe "the fresh, invigorating air of seas and oceans," a persistent and confident striving for world renown prompted Prokofiev to launch upon the risky adventure of going abroad. These motives must indeed have amounted to an obsession, for to have left seething, revolutionary Petrograd and set off on a voyage round the world, across a country in the throes of social upheaval and civil war was a hazardous proposition.

The journey from Petrograd to Vladivostok took eighteen days, for the Trans-Siberian line was jammed with Czechoslovakian troop trains. Fighting had flared up between Red Guard detachments and Ataman Semyonov's bands. Prokofiev's train was the last to get through before the Czechoslovakian front was formed. "It was only in retrospect that I appreciated the dangers to which I had been exposed," recalled Prokofiev.

On June 1 he was in Japan, where he stayed for two months. As luck would have it, he arrived in Japan shortly after the publication of a book on modern European music by M. Otaguro, one of the chapters of which was devoted to Prokofiev.[1] The Japanese were much interested in the young Russian musician and arranged three recitals of his works, two in Tokyo's Imperial Theater and one in Yokohama. Many Tokyo newspapers reviewed the concerts. In Tokyo the bulk of the audience was Japanese, in Yokohama European.

Early in August Prokofiev left Yokohama bound for New York via Honolulu and San Francisco. His long trip through Siberia, across the Pacific Ocean and the entire American continent, his acquaintance with new, exotic countries, and his contacts with new people did not interfere with his work. In the course of his four months' travels he composed the themes for the White Quartet, conceived in Russia, and worked on the plan for the opera *The Love for Three Oranges*.

Arriving in New York in September, he discovered that the conquest of America of which he had dreamed would not be so easy as he had expected. American concert audiences at that time did not manifest much interest in musical novelties. What new music was accepted had to bear the stamp of European approval. Penniless and friendless, Prokofiev found himself up against the American music-business machine.

His first piano recital, held in New York on November 20, 1918, was fairly successful, however, and evoked a host of articles under glaring headlines. *Savage, furious, new, weird*, and *Russian* were some of the adjectives used by the reviewer in *Musical America*. "A piano titan," "His fingers are made of steel," "Russian chaos in music," "Godless Russia," "Bolshevism in art," "ultra-modern," "a carnival of cacophony," commented the American reviewers, taking advantage of the strong public interest in revolutionary Russia.

---

[1] The data for this chapter have in part been borrowed by the author from Montagu-Nathan's comprehensive article which appeared in the London *Musical Times* in October 1916 (the first monographic work on Prokofiev).

Both reviewers and newspaper reporters gave detailed descriptions of his appearance ("the blond Slavic rather than the Turco-Slavic type"), spoke of his virile rendition, his primitive forcefulness "*à la* Jack London," and his fantastic imagination "akin to Edgar Allan Poe's." Most of the critics did not take the trouble to make any serious detailed analysis of his style. One found influences of Chopin, Wagner, and Beethoven in Prokofiev's music, others maintained that "Prokofiev originates from Scriabin," another dubbed him "Mendelssohn played on the wrong notes."

"Take one Schönberg, two Ornsteins, add a little Satie, mix all these with Medtner, put in a drop of Schumann, add some Scriabin and Stravinsky, and the result will be something like Prokofiev," wrote the reviewer in *Musical America* (November 30, 1918). One prominent critic said that the finale of the Second Sonata "reminds one of a herd of mammoths charging across an Asiatic plateau . . . when the dinosaur's daughter graduated from the Conservatory of that epoch her repertory must have included Prokofiev." His music was regarded as something extremely savage and exotically Asiatic.

The first piano recital, in Aeolian Hall, barely covered expenses. But Prokofiev had attracted public attention. One firm invited him to record some of his compositions for the player piano. Two publishing firms ordered several piano pieces from him. This resulted in the Four Pieces, Op. 32, *Dance, Minuet, Gavotte,* and *Waltz,* and the excellent *Tales of the Old Grandmother,* Op. 31. Who would have thought that these enchanting lyrical pieces, so full of the flavor of old Russia, could have been written to order in the bustling American metropolis?

Dissatisfied with the publishers' offers, Prokofiev finally preferred not to sell his manuscripts.[2]

On December 10 Prokofiev appeared for the first time at a symphony concert with Modest Altshuler, a Russian conductor who had at one time invited Scriabin to America. The

---

[2] These pieces were later published by Gutheil. The first performance of *Tales of the Old Grandmother* was given on January 7, 1919 in New York.

concerto (First Piano Concerto) evoked a storm of abusive articles. "If this is music I am inclined to prefer agriculture," was the sarcastic comment of one reviewer. "The composer wreaks havoc with the keyboard. The duel between his steel fingers and the keys led to the slaughter of harmony" (*New York Times*, December 11). "He is the Cossack Chopin of future generations. A musical agitator," predicted Huneker. This was the beginning of a protracted war between Prokofiev and the New York music critics.

His longer works had a much better reception in Chicago, where they were performed by one of America's leading symphony orchestras, conducted by Frederick Stock. His Chicago debut with the First Concerto and the *Scythian Suite* was a success. The leading Chicago critics correctly appraised the historical mission of Prokofiev's music. "Russia, it appears, is giving us the long-awaited antidote to French musical impressionism, to the fragrant delicate twilight that pervades the music of pre-war Europe," said the *Chicago Daily News* (December 7, 1918). Nearly all the critics persisted with naïve assurance in speaking of the "Bolshevist" nature of the *Scythian Suite*. "The red flag of anarchy waved tempestuously over the old Orchestra Hall yesterday as Bolshevist melodies floated over the waves of a sea of sound in breath-taking cacophony," said the *Chicago Herald and Examiner* on December 7, 1918. The *New Majority* (October 25, 1919), a labor paper, enthusiastically hailed Prokofiev as a representative of revolutionary Russia.

Before long Prokofiev was approached by Cleofonte Campanini, chief conductor of the Chicago Opera Company, who proposed producing one of his operas. Prokofiev had only the piano score of *The Gambler* to offer, the orchestral score having been left behind in the library of the Maryinsky Theater. When he mentioned his plans to write a new opera, *The Love for Three Oranges*, Campanini was delighted by the idea of a light opera on a classic Italian theme. A contract was signed in January 1919, and the new opera was to be submitted for rehearsals by autumn. Work on *The Love for Three Oranges* proceeded at great speed. Notwithstanding a bout of illness (scarlet fever and diphtheria) lasting for six weeks, the composer completed the piano score of the opera by June 1919, and by October 1, according to agreement, the orchestral score was submitted.

"The mixture of fairy-tale, humor, and satire in Gozzi's play, and especially its theatrical qualities, had a strong appeal for me," Prokofiev recalls. Conceived when the composer was still in Russia, *The Love for Three Oranges* was connected with the new trends in the theater directed against the naturalism and backwardness of the pre-Revolutionary theater. These were the same tendencies that in 1922 gave rise to one of the most striking productions of the new Soviet theater, *Princess Turandot*, staged by E. Vakhtangov. Like Prokofiev, Vakhtangov chose a Gozzi theme because of the splendid material it afforded for gay and sparkling fun and ingenuous exposition of theatrical methods. In this sense there is a close affinity between *Princess Turandot* and *The Love for Three Oranges*.

In contrast to the stark realism of *The Gambler*, everything in *The Love for Three Oranges* is presented in an ironic tone with deliberately accentuated parody and make-believe. The Prince is not a real, living character, but a comedian with a gift for expressive singing and, more important still, the ability to move, dance, and gesticulate to music. We admire the actor's skill and follow the development of the plot without for a moment believing that it is all true. A light musical performance, remarkably laconic and dynamic, *The Love for Three Oranges* is at the same time a subtle parody of the old romantic opera with its false pathos and sham fantasy.

The music is much less harsh and exaggerated than that of *The Gambler*. In *The Love for Three Oranges* the composer revealed the finest aspects of his talent: natural, vivacious declamation, spicy, exuberant humor (the jolly Truffaldino and the Odd Fellows; the laughter scene, the gay music of the

March and Scherzo), brilliant harmony and tone color in the decorative descriptions and mass scenes (the magician Celio, Fata Morgana, the festivities, etc.), and, last but not least, enchanting although transient lyrical moments (love of the Prince and Ninetta).

7. *The Love for Three Oranges*, theme of Truffaldino.

The Love for Three Oranges proved to be the most popular of Prokofiev's operas. The March from this opera has been played all over the world and has moved the most indifferent and skeptical of concert-goers.

The new opera was followed shortly afterward by the *Overture on Hebrew Themes*, Op. 34, for string quartet, clarinet, and piano. This composition, too, was called forth by Prokofiev's old associations. In New York he had met a group of former fellow students from the St. Petersburg Conservatory who had formed a Jewish chamber ensemble known as the *Zimro* (I. Mestechkin, G. Bezrodny, Karl Moldavan, I. Chernyavsky, Simeon Bellison, and L. Berdichevsky). At their insistent request he wrote, in the space of two days, an excellent short overture based on genuine folk motivs suggested by the ensemble. The rhythmic forcefulness and scherzo character of the Jewish dance melody of the *freilachtanz* type cleverly off-set the slow and mournful cantabile melody.[3]

When the time came for *The Love for Three Oranges* to be produced (the settings had already been ordered from the Russian artist Boris Anisfeld), Campanini suddenly died. The production was postponed until the following season. "This put me in a most awkward position," the composer recalls. "I had been engaged on the opera for almost a year and had completely neglected my concerts." Indeed, after the brief sensation occasioned by his initial appearances, Prokofiev's name had been forgotten by the concert world. It was with difficulty that he succeeded in arranging a number of recitals. He was obliged to submit when the managers demanded that his own compositions be kept to the minimum because the American public could not understand them. And so Prokofiev's piano recitals included Mussorgsky's *Pictures at an Exposition*, Schumann's *Carnaval*, and even pieces as foreign to his nature as Rachmaninoff's preludes, Scriabin's études, and Chopin's mazurkas. Only at the end of the program did he play two or three of his own pieces, usually his early piano miniatures (Gavotte, Op. 12, *Diabolic Suggestions*). Prokofiev gave several unsuccessful recitals with this program, including those on his tour of Canada in the early part of 1920.

"Out of sheer despair" Prokofiev started another big opera in December 1919. This time it was the plot of Valery Bryusov's *The Flaming Angel* that attracted him. "As a matter of fact, my interest was not altogether timely," the author admits. *The Love for Three Oranges* like *The Gambler* was already shelved. To write a new opera with no prospects of its production meant working purely for personal satisfaction. But Prokofiev's passion for the musical theater and his keen interest in Bryusov's characters outweighed all practical considerations.

---

[3] The Overture had its *première* in New York in January 1920. Later it was orchestrated for a small symphony orchestra, but some of the specific flavor of the national ensemble was lost thereby.

The libretto and the first two acts of the opera were written in an amazingly short time. While *The Love for Three Oranges* was to a considerable extent a synthesis of the humor, parody, and decorative fantasy characteristic of Prokofiev's work (the world of the gay scherzos, festive marches, and fantastic *Diabolic Suggestions*), in *The Flaming Angel* the composer gave full rein to his gift for tragic expression, his interest in the cruel and revolting sides of life, in horrific theatrical phantasmagoria and the guignol.

Valery Bryusov's story, with its subtle imitation of the German humanistic art of the sixteenth century, the epoch of Dürer and the Counter-Reformation, its blood-curdling scenes of the Inquisition, religious mania and hysteria, and interweaving of sober historical narrative with gloomy and powerful fantasy, could not have been better suited to Prokofiev's purposes. In the music of this opera Prokofiev discarded grotesquerie and humor in order to depict dramatic emotions and oppose two contrasting worlds: that of clear and sober rationalism (Ruprecht, his friends, and Agrippa, the philosopher) and the morbid religiously erotic ecstasy of Renata.

The composer gave battle, as it were, to mysticism and medieval obscurantism, depicting these survivals of the past in all their repulsive nakedness and gloomy grandeur. The scenes of Renata's religious paroxysms, her frightful imprecations and hysterical outcries, are produced with fearsome, almost pathological expressiveness.[4] The music is based on the principle of complex symphonic development, utilizing a number of clearly delineated leitmotivs. Some of the latter were taken from the sketches of the unfinished quartet "on the white keys" (Renata's love theme and the monastery theme). These same melodies later returned to the domain of pure instrumental music when the composer used them as thematic material for his Third Symphony (1928). The pro-

---

[4] A reflection of these expressionist trends can be found later in certain scenes of *Semyon Kotko* (the scene of Lyuba's insanity) and partly in the music of *Alexander Nevsky* ("Crusaders in Pskov").

8. *The Flaming Angel*, Act I, Renata's love theme.

duction of this opera was seriously hampered subsequently by
its excess of musical and dramatic material, its pathological
effects, and a few rather serious violations of the rules of
dramaturgy. Prolonged negotiations for the production of
The Flaming Angel with a number of American and European
theaters ended in failure.

By the spring of 1920 the composer became finally convinced that America had nothing more to offer him. "I wan-
dered through the enormous park in the center of New York
and, looking up at the skyscrapers bordering it, thought with
cold fury of the marvelous American orchestras that cared
nothing for my music and of the critics who reiterated what
had been said a hundred times before . . . and who balked
so violently at anything new, of the managers who arranged
long tours for artists playing the same old hackneyed programs
fifty times over."

He thought of returning to his homeland, but Russia at that
time was blocked on all sides by White Guard fronts. Moreover, his youthful pride was as strong as ever: he could not
think of returning to Russia without having won world recognition. The grandeur of the revolutionary struggle that was
raging in his native land in those years was still uncompre-
hended by him.

In April 1920 Prokofiev went to Europe. In Paris and later

in London he met Diaghilev and Stravinsky. And again he fell under the spell of Diaghilev's personality, his energy, enterprise, limitless fund of ideas, and ability to mold the artist to his will. Diaghilev proposed to produce *The Buffoon*, (*Chout*) the piano score of which he had carefully preserved for five years. At his suggestion Prokofiev altered a few ballet numbers, added five entr'actes (so that all six scenes could proceed without a break), and rewrote the final dance. Stravinsky took a keen interest in the work and offered a number of suggestions, chiefly concerning orchestration. The final touches to *The Buffoon* were completed in Mantes, near Paris, where the composer took up his residence for the summer. The ballet was scheduled for the opening of Diaghilev's season in 1921. In this period the composer completed several piano transcriptions: the arrangement of an organ fugue by Buxtehude and a series of Schubert waltzes and *Ländler* forming a complete suite.[5] Both these pieces were intended for future American tours.

His return to America in the autumn of 1920 was another disappointment for the composer. The production of *The Love for Three Oranges* again failed to materialize, this time because the composer demanded compensation from the Chicago Opera for breach of contract. "I preferred to sacrifice the production rather than allow them to wipe their boots on me." His demands were rejected and Prokofiev had to limit himself to concert tours, including a most pleasant six weeks' tour of California. The programs of his concerts again included a large amount of classical music: Beethoven's Sonata in A major, Op. 101, Chopin's études, his own arrangement of Schubert's waltzes, pieces by Lyadov and Rimsky-Korsakov. But these concerts lacked the exciting, sensational atmosphere of his initial appearances. Prokofiev was obliged to appear on the same program with other touring artists, mainly singers.

[5] The idea of using Schubert's waltzes was Stravinsky's. Later, in 1924, Prokofiev revised this suite in a two-piano arrangement (this time with changes in harmony and counterpoint).

The American newspapers now mentioned him merely as a pianist, forgetting him as a composer: the caption of a photograph in the *Musical Courier* read: "Composer Stravinsky and Pianist Prokofiev."

During his Californian tour Prokofiev wrote five songs without words for voice and piano in a refined lyrical manner, something in the style of the Akhmatova songs. These songs, first performed in March 1921 by Nina Koshetz, were not especially successful owing to the absence of text; later (1925) the composer rewrote them for the violin on the advice of Paul Kochanski, the violinist.[6]

It was not until the spring of 1921, when the management of the Chicago Opera Company was changed, that the question of the production of the *Three Oranges* was finally settled. The new director, the progressive-minded singer Mary Garden, celebrated for her performance of the roles of Mélisande and Salome among others, finally included the opera in the repertory of the following season.

Much pleased with his victory, Prokofiev went off to Europe again to supervise the production of his *Buffoon*. His debut in Paris with the *Scythian Suite*, on April 29, 1921, before the ballet had its *première*, was given an enthusiastic reception by the press. "It is impossible to resist such a happy combination of skill and freshness," *L'Éclair* commented (May 19). Shortly afterward Diaghilev opened his season with the *première* of *The Buffoon*. The famous producer had taken great pains with this ballet. The settings and costumes by Larionov were executed in the style of exaggeratedly primitive signboard drawing and futurist show-booth manner. The composer himself conducted. The *première* attracted the attention of the whole musical world of Paris. The bulk of the press comment was extremely laudatory: "A veritable cascade of ideas, inexhaustible fund of color, rhythms, melody. . . ." For the Pa-

---

[6] This writing of a whole series of extremely emotional vocal miniatures without text is extremely symptomatic. It was a sign that Prokofiev could not find adequate textual material with which to express the rich fund of ideas he possessed.

risian gourmets, long since sated with hothouse impressionist culture, this music coming after the Stravinsky ballets was but one more specimen of barbarous Russian exoticism, so deliciously titillating to their jaded appetites.

The Buffoon is an extremely contradictory phenomenon in Prokofiev's music. In the very conception of the ballet, to say nothing of its stage reproduction, Diaghilev's influence was clearly evident in the tendency to " work for export" — that is, to display for the benefit of the Parisian bourgeois everything fantastic and eccentric that could be found in Russian art and life. The grotesque in *The Buffoon* is exaggerated to the limit, and is essentially an end in itself. It has neither the social satire of *The Gambler* nor the bitter philosophical skepticism of *Sarcasms*. Hence its humor is deceptive, the underlying spirit of the music being infinitely pessimistic. The careful emphasis laid on the crude and cynical scenes, the accentuated mechanical rhythms, and the predominance of sharply exaggerated, mercilessly caricatured masks would have had the most depressing effect on the modern Soviet audience.[7]

Nevertheless, the composer's amazing gift for musical narrative, his ability to give the most accurate and laconic expression to his ideas, reached a high-water mark in *The Buffoon*. The orchestration, spare, stinging, sharply graphic, with abundant use of the piano and percussion instruments (no doubt the influence of Stravinsky's *Noces* made itself felt here), with subtle and ingenious employment of diverse string effects, is extremely striking. There is a host of brilliant new harmonic and tone-color effects in the music: the cries of Molodukha when beaten, the amusing pranks of the Buffoon, the confusion and horror of Stryapka, the cook, the mock funeral of the seven wives of the buffoons. It is difficult to enumerate all the details and nuances revealing the author's keen powers of

---

[7] The ballet is a long succession of brutal jests, violence, and murder: in the first scene the Buffoon beats his partner with a whip, in the second scene the seven buffoons kill their seven wives, in the third the buffoons beat up Molodukha, in the fourth they attempt to thrash the go-betweens. The fifth demonstrates the brutal treatment of Kozlukha, etc., etc.

observation, his ability to depict human gestures, movements, and emotions with the swift, sharp lines of the cartoonist. But what is most appealing about *The Buffoon* is the Russian lyrical quality, which now and then sounds sincere and almost serious, despite the mocking irony implicit in the staging by Diaghilev and Larionov (the theme of the Merchant's love, Molodukha's theme, the main theme of the Buffoon himself,

9. *The Buffoon (Chout)*, Scene I, central theme.

which runs through the whole ballet in a manner similar to the famous Promenades in Mussorgsky's *Pictures at an Exposition*). It is interesting to note that the "Left" critics who demanded exotic show-booth clowning from the Diaghilev ballet were not altogether satisfied with *The Buffoon*, some of whose elements struck them as being too realistic. "The production is not quite consistent, the grotesque and doll movements are not sustained throughout: two figures — the young Buffoon and the Merchant — strike a jarring note because of their realism" (review by N. Zborovsky in *Posledniye Novosti*, May 1921).

The Buffoon proved to be the last grimace of the Prokofiev grotesque, the wickedest and most malicious of them all.[8] It is not surprising that soon after *The Buffoon* Prokofiev himself, as if sensing the danger to his future development, began to depart more and more from the grotesque as an end in itself, endeavoring to grope his way toward a more serious and intelligent art. Thus began the long quest that was crowned with success only upon the composer's return to his native land.

If *The Buffoon* was given a warm reception in Paris, where Diaghilev's excesses were taken as a matter of course, its London *première* caused quite a scandal. Nearly all the English papers attacked the authors of *The Buffoon* with frank abuse. It was in almost every respect a repetition of the reception accorded the *Scythian Suite* in Petrograd five years before. One of the critics called *The Buffoon* a ballet absurdity; another, stupid and puerile music; whereas a third, on the other hand, considered it a "revelation of musical genius" (*Daily Graphic*, June 16, 1921). One of the reviewers in all seriousness advised ballet-goers to "stuff their ears in order not to hear the music." Most rabid of all was Ernest Newman in the *Sunday Times*. "Few composers," he wrote, "would venture to write long scores so poor in ideas or so primitive in technique as Prokofiev in *The Buffoon*."

Diaghilev in a fury replied to the English critics in a long and strongly worded letter to the editor of the *Daily Telegraph* (July 16, 1921). "Man has invented air navigation and telephones, and yet people still use these telephones to exchange the same imbecile remarks about any new idea, any new phenomenon," he wrote. "When I was sixteen, I heard someone say that Wagner had not composed a single melody; at twenty I was assured that the music of Rimsky-Korsakov was nothing but mathematics, at twenty-five that Cézanne and Gauguin were merely buffoons. And Debussy! And Strauss! And Rous-

---

[8] A rather clever explanation of Prokofiev's "buffoonery" was once given by Lunacharsky. "His rich personality, confined within the environment of a mechanized world, feels lost. This explains why buffoonery plays so large a role in his music. The buffoon after all is the plaything of society" (*Zhizn Iskusstva*, No. 88, 1926).

seau! And Matisse! For fifteen years people have been sneering at them without suspecting how stupid they looked as they did so. It is not difficult to imagine how stupid and banal all the abuse the learned critics are leveling at Stravinsky, Picasso, Prokofiev, and Larionov sounds. . . ."

The London hullabaloo over *The Buffoon* was evidence of the fact that Prokofiev's music had preserved its challenging, iconoclastic force under European conditions, exciting — as it had done before in St. Petersburg — the fury and malice of those critics who clung to the old traditions.[9]

After the *première* of *The Buffoon*, Prokofiev moved in the summer of 1921 to the coast of Brittany and applied himself with enthusiasm to his work on the Third Piano Concerto, begun in Russia. Most of the themes for this concerto had been accumulated over a long period of time: the lovely E-minor theme of the variations (second movement) dates back to 1913, the first two themes in the first movement and two variations to 1916–17; the first and second themes of the finale are taken from the White Quartet, conceived in 1918 [10] Even the difficult passage of parallel triads in the recapitulation of the first movement had been preserved from the youthful sketches of 1911, when, besides a D-flat major Concertino, Prokofiev had projected a large concerto full of virtuoso passages.

Adding a few themes that were still missing (the subordinate theme of the first movement and the third theme of the finale) and combining all into a harmonious three-movement design, Prokofiev created one of his finest works, the result of many years of experimentation in the field of piano music.

---

[9] Subsequent performances of *The Buffoon* abroad — for instance, in Cologne in 1928 — likewise provoked hostile comment. "This Soviet music declares war on all the laws, ignores all the rules, overthrows all methods . . . plunges us into a morass of dissonances, into a vertigo of harsh, disconnected, savage shrieking sounds. It is like a lunatic asylum!" (*La Gazette de Liége*).

[10] The quartet was originally conceived in two parts. Fearing lest sustained diatonic style should prove monotonous, Prokofiev in 1921 dispersed the thematic material of the quartet, including part in *The Flaming Angel* and part in the Third Piano Concerto.

Prokofiev's favorite world of juxtapositions and contrasts is presented with classic coherence in the Third Concerto, with its soulful Russian lyrical touches (introductory theme to the first movement), its virile dynamic forcefulness (main themes of the first movement and finale), and its elegant dance quality (theme of the variations). The multiformity of Prokofiev's music made itself most strongly felt in the remarkable variations (second movement), where the theme is now "mechanized," subjected to spiteful caricature distortions reminiscent of *The Buffoon,* now floating away into the realm of pure fantasy, now again changing to the powerful springy movement of the piano runs. The finale of the concerto, like that of the First Piano Concerto, is a hymn to the triumph of human will and energy. Here is a composition that deserves a place alongside the concertos of Liszt, Tchaikovsky, and Rachmaninoff on our concert programs.

Simultaneously Prokofiev composed five songs, Op. 36, to the pretentious and morbidly mystical poetry of Balmont. These songs (particularly the last of them, *Pillars*), depressingly gloomy and despondent in mood, possess features of over-refined chromatic style and elements of exoticism in the spirit of Gauguin's vivid canvases not at all in keeping with Prokofiev.[11]

At last the long-awaited *première* of *The Love for Three Oranges* was due. In October 1921 Prokofiev made his third trip to America, to participate in the preparations for the *première.* He supervised the direction of the performance and gave instructions to the solo singers and the chorus, ignoring the presence of the stage director. The role of Fata Morgana was played by Nina Koshetz.[12] The *première* of *The Love for*

---

[11] When Prokofiev wrote music to the poetry of the symbolists he almost invariably began to speak in a "foreign language," as it were, searching for all manner of palate-tickling harmonies and refined contemplation: for example, the "symbolist" songs *In My Garden* and *Trust Me* in Op. 23. There is an eery mystical flavor, not without a shade of sarcasm, in the *Gray Dress,* song to words by Z. Hippius (Op. 23, 1915).

[12] The Prince was sung by José Mojica. — *Editor.*

Three Oranges, on December 30, 1921, was warmly received by the Chicago public. The press too was extremely favorable. In New York, on the other hand, where the Chicago company presented the opera in February 1922, the reception was definitely hostile. The critics again foamed at the mouth. "The cost of the production is 130,000 dollars, which is 43,000 dollars for each orange," was the facetious comment of one of the reviewers, "but the opera fell so flat that its repetition would spell financial ruin."

A similar fate awaited the first American performance of the Third Piano Concerto: Chicago, where it was played on December 16 and 17 under the baton of Frederick Stock, gave it a warm reception, while New York (December 26 and 27, under the direction of Coates) condemned it.

Prokofiev's hopes that Mary Garden would produce *The Flaming Angel* at the Chicago Opera fell through when she unexpectedly resigned her post. "The American season, which had begun so promisingly, fizzled out completely for me. . . . I was left with a thousand dollars in my pocket and an ache in my head, to say nothing of a fervent desire to get away to some place where I could work in peace."

Prokofiev left America and in March 1922 settled in Ettal, a small, picturesque hamlet in Bavaria, two miles from Oberammergau. After four years of incessant wandering and tense struggle, the composer felt an urgent need of a change of environment in order to review his work over a period of many years. He stayed in Ettal for a year and a half, making occasional trips to various European centers for concerts and *premières.*[13] *The Flaming Angel,* begun in America, finally took definite shape in Ettal. Oberammergau was famed for its medi-

---

[13] In April 1922 the *première* of his Third Concerto was held in Paris (Koussevitzky) and in London (Coates). In June *The Buffoon* was revived in Paris. In January 1923 the *Scythian Suite* caused a sensation in Brussels, where the two hostile camps into which the audience divided almost came to blows. In the spring of 1923 Prokofiev made concert tours to Barcelona, Paris, Antwerp, Brussels, and London. Germany had not yet recovered from the effects of the war and took little interest in new Russian music: the performance of the *Hebrew Overture* and fragments from the *Three Oranges* passed unnoticed.

eval Passion Play and it occurred to the composer that the witches' Sabbaths described in Bryusov's story must have taken place somewhere in the vicinity. Here too he wrote the Fifth Piano Sonata (1923), prepared the piano scores of *The Buffoon* and *The Love for Three Oranges* for publication, made a symphonic suite out of *The Buffoon*, and rewrote the Second Piano Concerto, the score of which had been lost in Petrograd.

In the course of 1922 and 1923 the Gutheil and Koussevitzky firm published nearly all of Prokofiev's works written in that period. Koussevitzky, with his extensive opportunities as publisher and concert manager, was, with Diaghilev, the main force that kept Prokofiev abroad by tempting him with the prospects of world renown.

In the summer of 1922 after the revival of *The Buffoon* Prokofiev met Stravinsky again. The latter sharply criticized the *Three Oranges*, refusing to listen to more than one act. The result was a conflict between the two composers. In his turn Prokofiev told Stravinsky of his antipathy to the latter's recent work. The two collaborators in the Diaghilev ballet were thus estranged for several years. Diaghilev, disappointed in *The Love for Three Oranges*, also lost interest in Prokofiev's work.

On the other hand, Prokofiev had resumed contact with the Soviet Union. In May 1923 the Moscow magazine *K Novym Beregam* published a report by Prokofiev on his work abroad. His Soviet friends Miaskovsky and Asafyev, with whom he corresponded, kept him well informed about the musical activities that had been revived in Moscow and Petrograd with the termination of civil war. Beginning with 1923, a growing interest in Prokofiev's music arose in the U.S.S.R. A series of Musical Exhibitions arranged by the International Book Society in Moscow and several Evenings of New Music held somewhat later in Leningrad were largely responsible for this. About this time the Music Department of the State Publishing House began to put out some of Prokofiev's compositions, the first to appear being the score of *Seven, They Are Seven*, in 1922.

The leading article in the 1924 New Year's issue of the Leningrad magazine *Zhizn Iskusstva* mentioned Prokofiev as an eminent Russian composer who had been stranded abroad. "However wide we have thrown open the 'window into Europe,' nothing will compensate us for the protracted absence from Russia of some of her finest musicians. In the coming year we shall await news of the repatriation of our 'foreign' composers."

But the Soviet journal's appeal never reached Prokofiev. "I had not at that time fully grasped the significance of what was happening in the U.S.S.R.," Prokofiev explained later. "I did not realize that the events there demanded the collaboration of all citizens — not only men of politics, as I had thought, but men of art as well. Moreover, I was tied down by the routine of the life I was leading: publishing compositions, correcting proofs, attending concerts, endeavoring to prove my point in arguments with other composers representing different musical trends. Family affairs too played no small part: the long illness of my mother, ending in her death, my marriage, and the birth of my son."

The brief pause in Prokofiev's activities during his sojourn in Bavaria was something in the nature of a summing up of his creative endeavors over the past period. The Fifth Sonata, Op. 38, the only new thing he wrote here, excluding his work on *The Flaming Angel*, was on the borderline between the former Prokofiev style relating to the Petrograd period and the new "foreign" Prokofiev. While in the C-major first movement the classical clarity of idea, the characteristic emphasis on fresh harmonic juxtapositions and unity of development (in the spirit of the Third and Fourth Sonatas) still predominate, we find in the main theme of the finale an intricate chromatic style, an unnatural complexity of melody, with invention clearly taking the upper hand over genuine feeling. Similar themes are thenceforward quite common in Prokofiev's music.

His departure for Paris from Ettal in October 1923 marked

94

a new period in Prokofiev's work, perhaps the least significant of all.

What can we say about the five years (1918 to 1923) that mark the first stage of Prokofiev's "foreign period"? From the the standpoint of his career as a composer, the first five years spent abroad marked the culmination of all he had achieved until then: the enormous running start he had taken in the years 1916 and 1917, the powerful creative impulse, had continued to operate under foreign conditions, giving rise to such significant works as the Third Concerto, *The Love for Three Oranges*, the *Hebrew Overture*, the piano pieces, Op. 31 and 32, songs, Op. 35 and 36, and, last but not least, *The Flaming Angel*. It is noteworthy that the best of these compositions, which are inseparably bound up with Russian art trends of the pre-Revolutionary times, had been conceived before the composer left Russia (the *Three Oranges*, the themes for the Third Concerto and *The Flaming Angel*). Op. 31 and 32 are directly associated with the style of the *Fugitive Visions* and other piano pieces of the "pre-foreign" period. *The Flaming Angel* was likewise an expression of the composer's former interests, the expressionistic guignol tastes that had made themselves felt in *Magdalene* and such of the earlier piano pieces as *Phantom* and *Despair*.

During these years Prokofiev had completed, revised, and prepared for production or publication a number of compositions that had likewise originated in Russia (*The Buffoon*, Violin Concerto, Second Concerto for piano, etc.).

His numerous appearances as a conductor, and especially as a pianist, consolidated abroad the renown he had won by his attainments while in Russia. The excesses begun in St. Petersburg and Moscow were continued in approximately the same forms in the concert halls of New York, London, and Chicago. The powerful oratorical nature of Prokofiev's piano style astounded, shocked, and frightened the academic audiences of the West. Regardless of his personal intentions and convictions, Prokofiev the composer and pianist was in the eyes of the Western public a bearer of the new Russian culture, the artistic expression of the revolutionary processes that were at work in Russia.

But the inertia of the past could not last forever. Having broken away from the national and social sources that had nourished him for so long even at such a distance from his homeland, Prokofiev had found no new potent creative stimuli for himself in the West. From 1924 on, his absence from his native land began to exercise an increasingly negative influence on his work.

7 : The Crisis

> How could I have failed to emerge for a quarter of a year from the thrall of demons and devils — I who am so accustomed to the clear and distinct world of ships' rigging and military maneuvers?
> VALERY BRYUSOV: *The Flaming Angel*, Chapter vi, p. 137

PARIS, where Prokofiev took up his residence in October 1923, became his chief headquarters for the next ten years. He had already made a name for himself in Parisian music circles with the *Scythian Suite*, *The Buffoon*, and the Third Concerto. His removal to the French capital coincided with the *première* of his Violin Concerto, played on October 18 by Darrieux under the direction of Koussevitzky. The serene lyrical quality of the concerto had but little attraction for the Paris public, with its insatiable desire for new thrills. The more celebrated violinists, including Hubermann, refused to play it. Incidentally, this remarkable piece of music was first played by an ordinary concert-master.[1] The Paris critics gave

[1] During the summer of 1924 the concerto was performed at a musical festival of new productions in Prague by Joseph Szigeti, thanks to whom it subsequently won world recognition.

the concerto a rather cold reception. For the first time Prokofiev found himself criticized from the Left for writing music that was too lucid and not sufficiently intricate in pattern. Among those who disapproved of the concerto were the composers Nadia Boulanger, Georges Auric, and the White émigré Scriabinite critic Boris de Schloezer. Auric found traces of artificiality and what he called Mendelssohnism in the concerto.

The living and human quality in Prokofiev, that quality which was stubbornly breaking through all his modernistic formalist Leftism, could not find favor with the sophisticated public of the French capital. Hence, from the very beginning of his stay in Paris, Prokofiev felt strong hostile pressure from the Left formalistic art circles. Somewhat later this attitude to Prokofiev's art was expressed with brutal frankness by Stravinsky in a conversation. Praising Prokofiev for his talents, the Paris *maître* admitted that there was "something he did not like" about Prokofiev's music: "A certain instability of his culture, some indefinable quality in his musical gift, *precisely that quality, incidentally, which is now making him such a success in Russia*" (*Zhizn Iskusstva*, June 14, 1927, Leningrad, "A Conversation with Stravinsky").

The art world of Paris in the twenties fundamentally differed but little from that noisy, blatant market-place, with its essential indifference to genuine art, so vividly described by Romain Rolland in *Jean-Christophe*. The names alone had changed: the cult of Debussy was replaced by the cult of Stravinsky. A new sextet of composers was being strenuously pushed to the fore (Milhaud, Honegger, Poulenc, Auric, etc.), proclaiming the principles of constructivism and polytonality, the cult of urbanist, machine-like art. France in those years was jealously striving to promote her own national youth, a group of arrogant young musicians totally indifferent to tradition.

Essentially, however, musical life remained the same as that described in Rolland's *La Foire sur la place*: "Composers searched assiduously for new chord combinations in order to express — does it matter what? New expression. Just as the organ, it is said, creates the need, so also will expression finally generate thought; the important thing is that it be new. Novelty at any price! They lived in morbid dread of anything that had been 'said before.' Even the most talented of them were paralyzed by this dread."

This tendency toward pseudo-innovation made itself most strongly felt in the art of postwar France, where Left artists of all shades and descriptions vied desperately with one another in upsetting every known æsthetic canon. Impressionist art, in which the artist's subjectivity had nevertheless sprung from some perception of reality, was replaced by a whole series of new and more Left trends in which subjectivity in art was carried to the extreme.[2] Reality ceased to exist for the artist; indeed, nothing mattered except subjective impulse, the untrammeled license of the artist himself. Turning his back on living nature, the artist gave expression exclusively to his own ideas, concocting things and splitting them up into their component parts, distorting them in any way he pleased. Imagining himself a superman, capable at will of solving and explaining the riddle of the universe, the artist depicted an object not as he saw it in life but as he knew or sensed it. The result was that his work not only lost all reality, but carried no message. Its value was measured solely by the ingenuity and originality of the artist, whose perception of life was governed by laws known to him alone.

Such were the canons of the new art that flourished in western Europe during the period of the First World War.[3] This

[2] To this category belonged such varied trends as cubism and constructivism, with their cult of pure form and business-like lack of feeling, or, on the other hand, German expressionism, with its mystical symbolism and morbid high-pitched emotions.

[3] I do not intend to touch here upon the question of the great internal contradictions in this art, its rebellious tendencies reflecting the protest of the artistic intelligentsia against the antiquated standards of academic art. It is no accident that many artists brought up on expressionism or constructivism subsequently took the road of revolutionary social art (the German painters George Grosz and others, and Hans Eisler and Honegger in music).

was the atmosphere in which Prokofiev's music developed during his years in Paris. Finding no support for the best and healthiest tendencies in him manifested in the past, the composer was gradually drawn into the vortex of the Paris art world, enticed by ultra-radical advisers from the Left.

In the spring of 1924 Koussevitzky again presented Prokofiev to the Paris public. On May 8 the composer appeared with a new version of his Second Concerto and on May 29 the cantata *Seven, They Are Seven* was performed for the first time. Both compositions, particularly the savagely mystical Chaldean invocation, suited the tastes of the Paris musical world. This time, however, Prokofiev was accused of using old compositions to win new success. Determined to show the Parisians that he could write music no less modernistic than the fashionable *Six*, he conceived a plan for a new symphonic work "made of iron and steel." The Second Symphony in D minor, Op. 40, which took him all of 1924 to compose, is one of the least successful of Prokofiev's works. Employing the sharp cubistic methods of the *Scythian Suite* (simultaneous movement of continually recurring figures at various levels of the orchestra), and using a huge orchestra, the composer created an edifice of sound that was extremely complicated and overloaded, whose barbaric savage noises were this time not justified by the subject. Most of the themes, especially the principal theme of the first movement, are strikingly artificial, angular, zigzagged, and almost geometrical as to melody. Borrowing the outline of the symphony from one of Beethoven's later works (two-part structure of the sonata Op. 111 — a long *Allegro* followed by a theme with variations), the composer was unable to find adequate ideas and emotions to inspire it. The development of its

10. Second Symphony, 1st movement, main theme.

idea was sacrificed to noise effects and contrapuntal intricacies, and the variations seemed artificial and lacking in that rich multiformity in genre which was so enchanting in the variations of the Third Concerto. On the whole, the symphony is a queer cross between chaotic primitive barbarism and the ultra-modern urbanist machine style of the period.

While working on the symphony Prokofiev wrote the music for a short ballet, *Trapeze*, for the Romanoff, a roving ballet company. As the plot (which dealt with circus life) did not particularly interest him, the composer regarded the work in the light of a purely technical problem in instrumentation: namely, to write a piece of chamber music for an unusual combination of instruments: oboe, clarinet, violin, viola, and doublebass. The piece was subsequently published as a quintet, Op. 39, and performed as an independent chamber work.[4] The chromatic style of the quintet, its excessive refinement of expression, the complex constructivist technique of its simultaneously developed melodies, and the studied artificiality of its ideas place it in the same class as the Second Symphony.

Following a number of recitals in the 1924–5 season,[5] Prokofiev submitted his new composition to the judgment of Paris. When, however, on June 6, 1925, his Second Symphony was performed at a Koussevitzky concert, even the sophisticated Parisians were puzzled by it. The critics were unanimous in expressing their disapproval of the piece and their disappointment in Prokofiev's gifts. "It occurred to me that I might perhaps be destined to become a second-rate composer," Prokofiev confesses. And, indeed, fickle Paris was as capable of exalting a fashionable name to the skies as of trampling it in the gutter. "The vogue did not last long and the idol invariably awoke one fine morning to find himself on the rubbish-heap" (*Jean-Christophe*). This was the sad fate that threatened

---

[4] Later the composer added several more items to the six original numbers (those included subsequently in *Divertissement*, Op. 43).

[5] December 5, recital of four sonatas in Paris; January 24, first pianoforte recital in Berlin; March 14, first European performance of *The Love for Three Oranges* (Cologne).

Sergei Prokofiev. Poverty, disillusionment, the lot of the deposed idol stared him in the face. His Soviet friends watched this disastrous decline of the Prokofiev vogue in Europe with deep regret. "Paris is adamant: Stravinsky, Stravinsky, and Stravinsky! No wonder Prokofiev's star is setting on that horizon," commented *Zhizn Iskusstva* a year later, "and . . . art circles are speaking of him as if he were dead. Prokofiev does not exude the odor of putrefaction so dear to the nostrils of the Paris bourgeois . . ." (*Zhizn Iskusstva*, No. 21, 1926, article by N. Malkov).

At this critical moment Diaghilev, his former patron, remembered him again. Shortly after the performance of the Second Symphony, Diaghilev made Prokofiev a new and quite unexpected offer. This time the famous *maître* asked for a ballet depicting life in Soviet Russia. "I could not believe my ears," Prokofiev recalls. "It was as if a fresh breeze had blown through my window." Georgi Yakulov, Soviet theatrical constructivist artist, was invited to write the libretto. It was decided to present a number of scenes from the period of the Civil War and the new industrial upsurge in the U.S.S.R. The first part of the ballet was to show the break-up of the old order: meetings, speeches by commissars, trains full of food speculators, a former duchess bartering her gowns for food, a Revolutionary sailor, and homeless waifs. The second part was to present a picture of Socialist construction, the building of new plants and factories, yesterday's sailor turned worker, and so on. Prokofiev launched into this work with enthusiasm. He welcomed it, firstly, as an opportunity to write music with a truly Russian flavor and, secondly, to proclaim his repudiation of the chromatic intricacies of the quintet and the Second Symphony and his return to a strict, purely diatonic style. By the autumn of 1925 the piano score of the new ballet was ready. Diaghilev accepted it for production, naming it *Le Pas d'acier*. Prokofiev's symptomatic turn to Soviet subjects was noted with interest by the press of Moscow and Leningrad. The production of the new ballet in Paris, however, was hampered by diverse political considerations. Diaghilev, chary of startling his Paris clients with such an unexpected subject, was in no hurry to produce it.

While working on the orchestration of *Le Pas d'acier* Prokofiev made a long concert tour through the United States in the winter of 1925–6, this time received as a recognized master. The American tour was followed in the spring of 1926 by a number of concerts in Italy. In Naples Prokofiev met and was most cordially received by Maxim Gorky, who carried the composer off with him to his villa in Sorrento for a long, heart-to-heart talk lasting far into the night.

The year 1926 saw Prokofiev's name once again in the limelight, both in western Europe and in the U.S.S.R., as a result of a few performances of *The Love for Three Oranges*.[6] Much was done to popularize Prokofiev's music in this period by the Moscow Persimfans orchestra, the first symphony ensemble without a conductor. Composed of leading Moscow musicians, Persimfans gave concerts every Monday in the Moscow Conservatory in the period between 1922 and 1932.

Bruno Walter also became interested in Prokofiev at this time, and offered to produce his *Flaming Angel* at one of the Berlin theaters. In the summer of 1926 Prokofiev orchestrated and revised *The Flaming Angel* and worked on his B-flat major American Overture. The latter, ordered by a New York music firm for the opening of a new concert hall, was intended for a seventeen-piece orchestra.[7] In the center are two pianos, doubled by two harps and a celesta; five woodwinds take the lead, supported by two trumpets and a trombone, with two cellos, a doublebass, and a few percussion instruments for accompaniment. The music of this overture was distinguished

---

[6] On February 18 the opera had its *première* in the former Maryinsky Theater in Leningrad (conductor, Dranishnikov; producer, S. Radlov). On October 9 it was produced in Berlin (conductor, Leo Blech). In Paris the opera was not a success; and a symphonic suite adapted from the *Three Oranges*, first played on November 29, 1925, was coldly received by Paris circles. This suite, written in 1924, consisted of six numbers: "Odd Fellows," "Scene in Hades," March, Scherzo, "The Prince and the Princess," and "Flight."

[7] Later, in 1928, the overture was revised for a large orchestra.

by clarity of form, simple harmonies in a gay, festive dance manner, offset by pleasant lyrical episodes, now contemplative, now stirringly poetic. Were it not for several deliberate eccentricities in some of the episodes (for example, the absolutely unwarranted intrusion of the percussion instruments in the main theme with the obvious intent of marring the over-commonplace flow of the music), one might have thought that the composer had completely abandoned the stylistic excesses of his Paris period.

Beginning with 1925, Prokofiev's connections with Soviet music circles began to grow, through correspondence with the Persimfans and with the management of the Maryinsky Theater. After having been dropped so abruptly by the Parisians, the composer felt that the interest of the Soviet public in his music was much more solid and sincere.[8] To the West Prokofiev had always been a stranger from a distant land, evoking little more than a passing curiosity (the Americans usually referred to him as "that young Russian"). To Soviet musical circles, on the other hand, he was "our Prokofiev," one of the outstanding representatives of the new Russian music. In one of his numerous articles on music written in the spring of 1926, Lunacharsky said of Prokofiev's work: "The freshness and rich imagination characteristic of Prokofiev bear testimony to his unusual talent. . . . His pure lyricism is tremendously significant. . . . In order that his talents may blossom to the full, Prokofiev must return to us."

In the course of his travels in America and Europe in 1926 Prokofiev decided to visit the U.S.S.R. In January 1927, after an absence of nearly nine years, he returned to his native land. One of the first steps he took upon reaching his homeland was to take Soviet citizenship.

---

[8] In addition to the Leningrad production of *The Love for Three Oranges*, much interest was aroused by Feinberg's performance of the Third Concerto (Moscow, March 22, 1925, under the direction of K. Saradzhev), the Violin Concerto by Joseph Szigeti (1924-5), the first performance of the *Scythian Suite* in Moscow (Persimfans) and a number of performances of the March and Scherzo from the *Three Oranges* (Oscar Fried).

His three months in the U.S.S.R. proved to be a grand triumph, the like of which the composer had never before experienced. He was extremely happy to meet many of his old friends and fellow musicians — Miaskovsky, Asafyev, Saradzhev, and others. In Moscow Prokofiev gave eight concerts with tremendous success. Here is a description of one recital given on January 26: "It was not a concert, it was an event. The few dissenting voices were drowned out by the flood of unanimous recognition and approval. There was a sort of peculiar magic in the performance and, indeed, the composer himself played with an élan that was quite natural, considering that he was playing for an audience that could not but be particularly near and dear to him" (*Sovremennaya Muzyka*, No. 20, 1927, article by K. Kuznetsov). More cordial still was the reception accorded Prokofiev in Leningrad. "Between concerts I roamed the streets and embankments recalling with tenderness the city in which I had spent so many years."

Prokofiev acquainted himself with the works of the young Leningrad composers, and was especially attracted by the talents of twenty-year-old Shostakovich and Gabriel Popov.[9] He was much pleased by the brilliant production of *The Love for Three Oranges*. Lunacharsky, who was with him at the opera, compared it to a "glass of champagne."

After Leningrad the composer visited Kharkov, Kiev, and Odessa, giving two pianoforte recitals in each city before returning to Moscow, where he gave another three concerts.[10]

His visit to the Soviet Union was brief this time. Although much impressed by the new culture that was being created in his Soviet homeland, and deeply flattered by the warm and friendly reception he had been given, the composer was not

---

[9] In subsequent years Prokofiev exerted no small effort to popularize abroad the work of Soviet composers — Miaskovsky, Shostakovich, Shebhalin, Khachaturyan, and others. On one of his American tours he played some of Miaskovsky's *Whimsies*.

[10] At one of these concerts his quintet with woodwinds (Op. 39) was performed for the first time. During this visit to the U.S.S.R. the Overture for a seventeen-piece orchestra (Op. 42) had its *première* in Europe.

yet ready to sever his ties with the West. The Diaghilev *première* of *Le Pas d'acier* was due and there were hopes of having *The Flaming Angel* produced in Germany. Notwithstanding his Soviet passport, Prokofiev continued to be a Parisian for another six years.

At last, in June 1927, *Le Pas d'acier* had its sensational *première* in Paris. On July 4 Diaghilev even risked presenting the ballet in London. The London *première* was attended by the whole English fashionable world, including the Prince of Wales. The majority of the critics gave the ballet an enthusiastic reception.

"For one familiar with the Russian ballet . . . the presentation of Prokofiev's Bolshevist ballet was something of a shock. . . . But . . . if the 'Red' composer writes better music than Stravinsky, then let us hear it by all means," said the *Daily Telegraph* (July 5). "He travels through the civilized world but refuses to belong to it" (*Daily Mail*, July 11). "As an apostle of Bolshevism he has no peer. Writers and orators have been telling us about all this for years, but Prokofiev's ballet expresses the spirit of modern Russia better than all their efforts taken together" (*Empire News*). "With the exception of the *Noces* this is the most powerful Diaghilev production of the postwar period" (the *Musical Times*, August 1927). Some critics were frankly puzzled: was this another product of the inexhaustible imagination of the famous Russian producer, or was it merely Bolshevik propaganda? "A queer production from start to finish, can it possibly be intended to replace *A Life for the Tsar?*" one Paris paper wondered. "You think the public was scandalized? Not in the least. Snobs, casting their eyes upward, breathed: '*charmant,*' '*épatant,*' '*rigolo,*' and called for the authors seven times at the end of the performance." No less sensational was the success in England. "Like the Parisians before them, the Londoners looked and listened, thrilled by the spectacle, and at every pause the hall rocked with applause" (*Boston Evening Transcript*, July 23). In reactionary White émigré circles, haunted by the specter of Communist propaganda, *Le Pas d'acier* evoked a storm of wrath and indignation.

For Prokofiev this ballet was a sincere attempt to draw a true picture of revolutionary Russia. However, Diaghilev made use of the idea to produce for the Paris snobs another extravagant spectacle, a dash of Bolshevist exoticism to tickle the palates of the élite. It showed a comical sailor tattooed from head to foot, with an ear-ring in one ear and a single felt boot, jolly cigarette and candy venders, the shabby aristocrat selling her possessions on the market, and steam hammers raising an ear-splitting din. As for the music of the ballet, the composer, who had never actually known Soviet reality, had to limit himself to depicting externals in a starkly graphic manner. He was primarily concerned with the naturalistic reproduction of factory noises and the rattle and din of the machinery. Here the purposeless urbanism of the Second Symphony sought for a justification. The Russian melodies he invented to portray the sailor, the commissar, and the working woman seemed jagged and uneven, and were almost invariably mutilated by deliberately discordant counterpoint. The whole idea of revolutionary reconstruction in Russia was reduced by the authors of *Le Pas d'acier* to a noisy though picturesque hurly-burly, motley crowds and the grinding roar of engines, all of which in no way differed fundamentally from the mechanical types of Western urbanistic art. Presented in this way, the Soviet types were actually discredited, notwithstanding the composer's good intentions. Few and far between in the score of *Le Pas d'acier* were the fresh, unblemished Russian themes that showed that the composer had not yet forgotten his native language (for example, the A-minor theme in the "Train of Speculators" episode.

Several other *premières* of Prokofiev's works occurred simultaneously with *Le Pas d'acier*: on May 7 the ballet *Die Erlösten*, to the music of *Ala and Lolli*, was presented in Berlin; [11]

---

[11] Max Tempis, ballet-master at the Berlin Opera, supplied the music of the *Scythian Suite* with a mystical plot full of angels, cherubs, demons, etc. Prokofiev considered the production a failure.

11. *Le Pas d'acier*, The Train of Speculators.

on May 19 *The Love for Three Oranges* was produced at the Moscow Grand Opera (not quite so successfully as in Leningrad); on October 11 a ballet to the music of *Ala and Lolli* was performed in Buenos Aires; and in the beginning of January 1928 *The Buffoon* was given at the Kiev Opera House.

Opera still continued to loom large among Prokofiev's interests. In the summer of 1927 he completed the orchestration of *The Flaming Angel*. However, although the Berlin Opera had accepted it and the piano score with the text in German was printed, the opera was never produced. Then, discovering the manuscript of *The Gambler* in the library of the former Maryinsky Theater exactly as he had left it, Prokofiev resumed work on this opera. Much of the original version, written eleven years before, struck him as unnecessarily complex and overloaded with musical horrors. He simplified a number of episodes, discarding everything that encumbered the vocal parts. In this way the second version of *The Gambler*, produced on April 29, 1929 at the Royal Theater of Brussels, came into being.[12] Somewhat later, in 1930–1, *The Gambler* was used as a basis for a symphonic suite entitled *Portraits*, Op. 49, which included all the principal musical characteristics of the opera (first movement, Alexei; second movement, Babulenka; third

[12] The opera was carefully produced, but was not understood by wide sections of the audience. A pianoforte arrangement of the opera was published in 1930 by Gutheil and Koussevitzky.

movement, Pauline; forth movement, the General; fifth movement, Gambling Den).

After two virtually barren years (apart from the small American Overture and the revision of *The Gambler* he wrote nothing in 1926 and 1927) a certain creative revival occurred in Prokofiev's work. 1928 saw the advent of the two most significant fruits of the Paris period: namely, the Third Symphony, Op. 44, and the ballet *L'Enfant prodigue*, Op. 46.

The Third Symphony represents an independent non-program composition incorporating the chief musical images of *The Flaming Angel*.[13] It is the most dramatic and emotional of Prokofiev's four symphonies. After his graceful imitations of court music (*Classical Symphony*) and the dizzy intricacies of his iron and steel music (Second Symphony), the composer wrote a powerful and stirring narrative of human passion and suffering. The two basic themes of the first movement are those depicting Renata's mental anguish in *The Flaming Angel*: her despair (chromatic *ostinato* figures in the introduction) and her love for Madiel (a broad, lilting melody on the "white keys"). In contrast to these is the calm, confident subordinate theme of Rupprecht the Knight. The suffering and pain depicted in this music is by no means a humble submission to the forces of destiny; it is presented as a powerful expression of emotion, couched in harsh, biting, unequivocal phrases. The forces opposing man are presented not as abstract symbols, but as a palpable world of revolting, frightful apparitions. Hence the stark discordant harmonies, the polytonal touches, and so forth. In sharp contrast to the first movement is the detached, ethereal music of the *Andante*, with its archaic diatonism (from the beginning of Act V in *The Flaming Angel*: Renata in the monastery). The wild tempestuous movement of the Scherzo, as the composer himself admits, was suggested by the finale

---

[13] The composer vehemently protests against attempts to regard the symphony as a program work based on the themes of *The Flaming Angel*, on the ground that the principal themes of the piece were written as purely instrumental motivs before he began working on the opera (see his "Notes" in *Sovietskaya Muzyka*, No. 3, 1933).

of Chopin's B-flat minor Sonata, here intensified tenfold by the furious, chaotic torrent of orchestral color. The finale brings us back to the world of tragic visions and monstrous invocations, partly repeating the material of the first movement. "I feel that in this symphony I have succeeded in deepening my musical language," Prokofiev wrote several years later. "I should not want the Soviet listener to judge me solely by the March from *Three Oranges* and the Gavotte from the *Classical Symphony*." It was evidently to confirm the seriousness and depth of his symphonic quests, as well as in tribute to a friendship of many years' standing, that Prokofiev dedicated this symphony to Miaskovsky, one of the most confirmed symphonists of our time.[14]

But if the Third Symphony was something of an "echo of the past," being made up chiefly of materials relating to 1918 and 1919, *L'Enfant prodigue* represented a new departure in Prokofiev's music.

It was Diaghilev's last order to Prokofiev for his ballet troupe. Having given the Parisians a taste of "Bolshevist exoticism" with *Le Pas d'acier*, the indefatigable producer proposed a new subject to Prokofiev, this time from the Gospel according to St. Luke. The Diaghilev ballet, it will be seen, had an absolutely unlimited range of themes to choose from: yesterday scenes from the Bolshevik Revolution in Russia, today the Biblical parable of the prodigal son. And inasmuch as the fifteenth chapter of Luke is not exactly suitable for a ballet libretto in its original form, Diaghilev and his colleagues added some of the necessary details. The Prodigal Son, leaving his father's home, meets his friends, who make him drunk and rob him, after which he returns, beaten and humiliated, to his father. For the love intrigue they introduced a liaison

---

[14] The Third Symphony was first played in Paris on May 17, 1929. In the United States it was frequently performed by Leopold Stokowski. It has been given several times in the U.S.S.R. (Dranishnikov, Hauck, and the composer himself), meeting with the approval of the critics (see the article by A. Alschwang in *Sovietskoye Iskusstvo*, November 1935). There is a four-hand arrangement of the symphony by Miaskovsky (in manuscript).

between the leading character and a certain Beautiful Maiden. The scene with the elder brother, which drives home the moral of the fable, they discarded altogether, adding instead the Prodigal's sisters, moving characters, and his wicked friends. The story ended, as in the Bible, with the repentance of the Prodigal Son and complete absolution for his sins. Diaghilev's choice of a Biblical theme was rather symptomatic. Disillusioned by the excesses of cubism and the emptiness of contemporary art, many French artists as far back as the first half of the twenties had turned to ancient or Biblical themes, thus giving rise to a certain type of neo-classicism. After his subjectless cubistic designs Picasso went back to Ingres; Stravinsky after *Mavra* and *L'Histoire du soldat* wrote *Œdipus Rex* and later the *Symphonie de psaumes*, blazing the trail to a sort of deliberate neo-Bachism. Tired of its own childishness and anti-æsthetic nihilism, art attempted to become rational, subtle, and intelligent. It sought to save itself in eternal themes, in the imitation of a classical style that had died out long since, from the complete ideological and artistic degeneration to which superficial experimentation was inevitably leading. But the dead Latin revived by Stravinsky in his *Œdipus Rex* was even more of a sealed book to the living human listener than the blatant primitiveness of his make-believe world. Absence of ideas and principle, the worship of form for its own sake, continued to serve as the banner of French bourgeois art, notwithstanding the employment of more serious themes of universal human interest.

It is difficult to imagine that Diaghilev's *L'Enfant prodigue*, exquisitely stylized by the artist Rouault, with the gay sinner executing all manner of dizzy *battements*, could seriously broach any philosophical problems. For as keen and vital an artist as Prokofiev, who had striven always to give his own individual musical interpretation of his concrete observations of life, the parable as a theme could not have been much more than an abstraction.

Nevertheless, the philosophical aspect of the subject, notwithstanding its remote Biblical setting, had a certain positive influence on his work. Unwilling to follow the lead of Stravinsky's museum-like neo-classicism,[15] Prokofiev was obliged to grope his way alone toward a new lyrical and melodic style. The ballet was written in Paris in the autumn of 1928, and the piano score was ready in three months. Diaghilev was astonished at the composer's speed.

Bound neither by problems of style nor by decorative description (unlike *The Buffoon* and *Le Pas d'acier*, *L'Enfant prodigue* had no elements of local color), the composer strove to bring out primarily the purely emotional aspect of the work. This gave rise to some extremely fine lyrical music: the theme of the parting between the parents and the Prodigal Son, the Beautiful Maiden's theme, and the theme of the Prodigal Son in the scene of his encounter with his friends. The composer's interest in a new melodic style, intimately lyrical and contemplative, requiring neither the colorful harmony of opera nor the rich timbre of orchestral music, was evident in these themes. Complex harmonic constructions and the search for entirely new modal and harmonic combinations ceased to attract Prokofiev; he frequently conducted his themes in unison or octave, rejecting harmonic support altogether.[16] The music was clear in tone, discords occurring only as a result of thin contrapuntal superimpositions or blots. There emerged a new orchestral palette, thin, economic, pencil-drawn, with the lone and delicate timbres of flutes, oboes, clarinets. After the heavily splashed color and fiery tones of the *Scythian Suite* and the stinging orchestra of *The Buffoon*, this palette seemed rather exaggeratedly ascetic.

In the Beautiful Maiden a new Prokofiev character was evolved, that of the young Botticelli ethereal maiden endowed

---

[15] "For my own part I am not satisfied with his latest works, with all their Bachisms and false notes," Prokofiev said in an interview (*Rabochi Teatr*, February 22, 1927).

[16] Prokofiev had also had recourse to these methods previously in certain lyrical passages; for example, *Fugitive Vision* No. 11, and even more often in tense, dynamic themes (first and third parts of the Third Concerto).

with a sad, exquisite grace. Her emotions are far more restrained and virginal than the passionate exaltation of Pauline in *The Gambler* or Renata in *The Flaming Angel*. She is undoubtedly the prototype of Juliet and perhaps also of Cinderella. In *L'Enfant prodigue* the composer relegated sound description to a secondary plane (the pure character scenes of the Prodigal Son's encounter with his comrades, the carousal and the robbery), abandoned sheer decorative landscape music altogether, and reduced to a minimum the elements of pure dancing (the only real dance number is the "Men's Dance" No. 4, perhaps the weakest item in the whole ballet).

At the same time the music of *L'Enfant prodigue* brought out the negative aspects of Prokofiev's new style: his deliberate rejection of logic, the incoherence of his different thematic formations, his arbitrariness, the incomprehensible harshness of some of his polyphonic passages, and his studied combination of musical episodes, which are repeated without any attempt at development.

The poetical qualities of *L'Enfant prodigue*, the sincere lyricism expressed in its pale, autumnal, yet delicate and human images, were brought out subsequently with far greater force in the music of *Romeo and Juliet* (which, incidentally, also brought out its negative qualities, particularly a certain mechanical combining of thematic scenes).

In the summer of 1928, spent in a little village near Paris, Prokofiev composed two small piano pieces that he called *Things in Themselves* (Op. 45). This was his first reversion to his favorite sphere of piano music since the Fifth Sonata, written five years before. The new piano technique evolved in Paris, however, was far removed from that active, healthy, virile piano style which had distinguished his earlier works. The *Things in Themselves* was followed by a series of piano miniatures similar in genre and style: two sonatinas, Op. 54, in E minor (1931) and G major (1932), three pieces, Op. 59 — *Promenade* (1934), *Landscape* (1933), and *Pastoral Sonatina* (1934) — and, finally, three pieces called *Thoughts* (1933–

4). It was difficult to recognize the old Prokofiev in these pieces. The rhythmic elasticity and clarity of idea had disappeared. Fervor of feeling and youthful vigor had given place to a cold, rational outlook. The old impulsiveness and use of rich tone color had given way to dull, bare outlines. The composer had even renounced his former predilection for the dance, song, and theatrical action.

This was both new and strange. A musician whose art appeared to spring wholly from the stage and concrete theatrical depiction suddenly plunged into a realm of intellectual construction and rational speculation utterly foreign to his nature. The reasons for this sudden metamorphosis were not difficult to guess. In the first place, new French bourgeois art, with its emphasis on rationalism and its new puristic tendencies, could not but have affected him. Most important, however, was the fact that Prokofiev had lost his ties with the living sources of his art. Having neither the practical possibilities nor the favorable external stimuli for the creation of music reflecting one or another aspect of reality, the composer was forced to draw upon his own personal abstract reflection. The result was extremely paradoxical: Prokofiev, who in his youth had rebelled against ivory-tower aloofness and the contemplative introspection of modernist piano music, himself finally revived the typical parlor style, intended for a narrow circle of select connoisseurs.

True, the new Prokofiev piano pieces as well as the lyrical passages of L'Enfant prodigue did show evidences of a determined attempt to write profound and earnest music. But that which the composer had conceived as an expression of a philosophic principle, as music of the mind (Things in Themselves, Thoughts), might have been taken for the mere mechanical reflection of his thought-processes.

The few years remaining before his final return to the U.S.S.R. saw the aggravation of the crisis in Prokofiev's work. He had more and more frequent recourse to his former compo-

sitions, revising them or incorporating them into new works.
In 1929 he completed a new version of his youthful *Sinfonietta*, Op. 5, somewhat encumbered by new harmonic
details, revealing a growing preference for smaller forms
(added second and fourth movements), and renumbered
as Op. 48.

Out of the material for the ballet music written in 1925 for
the Romanoff troupe, with the addition of two new numbers,
emerged a four-part *Divertissement* for orchestra, Op. 43 (the
first movement, "Moderato," and the third, "Dance," were
written in 1925; the second movement, "Nocturne," and the
fourth, "Epilogue," in 1929).

From the music of *L'Enfant prodigue* came three new
works: the Symphonic Suite, Op. 46–A, the Fourth Symphony,
Op. 47 (1930), and a number of pianoforte transcriptions, Op.
52 (six pieces written in 1931 include three fragments from
L'Enfant prodigue, a transcription of one of Prokofiev's songs,
Op. 35, the *Andante* from the String Quartet, Op. 50, and
the Scherzo from the *Sinfonietta*).

On May 21, 1929 the *première* of *L'Enfant prodigue* was
performed in Paris. It was given on the same program with
Stravinsky's *Rénard*. Both composers conducted their own
music.

The ballet was a success. Particularly impressive was the
final episode, in which the repentant Prodigal Son crawled on
his knees toward his father across the whole stage. Shortly
afterward Diaghilev presented the ballet in Berlin and London. Press comment was favorable everywhere. This was Diaghilev's last ballet, for in the summer of 1929 he died in
Venice. One of the most important threads binding Prokofiev
to the West had snapped. "The brilliant master of ceremonies
of Russian art," as Alexandre Benois, the artist, had called
him, ended his days as an émigré, having long since ceased to
represent the progressive art of his day.

In 1929 the Paris press commented on a few of Prokofiev's
new symphonic compositions: the Third Symphony (May

1929), the *Sinfonietta* and *Divertissement* (performed in December 1929 at a Koussevitzky concert).

In the autumn of 1929 Prokofiev made his second trip to Moscow, to discuss the production of *Le Pas d'acier* at the Grand Opera. He was unable to give any recitals on this trip owing to some trouble with his hands (his only appearance was to conduct a radio concert of his own music). His reception this time was considerably cooler than in 1927.

The year 1930 was marked by a grand tour of the United States, where Prokofiev gave twenty-four concerts with leading American orchestras. On this tour he received a number of orders: the Fourth Symphony was written for the Boston Symphony Orchestra, and the Quartet, Op. 50, for the Library of Congress in Washington. Hopes of producing *The Flaming Angel* in one of the American theaters were revived, but again nothing came of them.

The relatively unproductive year 1929 was followed by three significant compositions in 1930: the Fourth Symphony,[17] the string quartet, and the ballet *Sur le Borysthène*.

The most interesting of them was the Quartet in B minor, Op. 50,[18] which was somewhat unusual in form (three movements: an *Allegro* in sonata form, a Scherzo, and a slow lyrical finale). The music, like that of *L'Enfant prodigue*, is here predominantly deep, calm, and contemplative — for example, the subordinate theme in the first movement, the introduction to the Scherzo and, finally, the main part of the quartet, a soothing, sorrowful *Andante* with some passages almost frankly reminiscent of Mussorgsky.

---

[17] Written for the fiftieth anniversary of the Boston Symphony Orchestra, it was played for the first time in Boston on November 14, 1930. It is the gentlest and most intimate of all Prokofiev's symphonies. The first and fourth movements were new versions of *L'Enfant prodigue* themes; the rest was almost completely borrowed from the music of the ballet (second movement, return of the Prodigal Son; third movement, description of the Beautiful Maiden).

[18] The Library of Congress in Washington has been in the habit of ordering new works from renowned modern composers to add to its manuscript department. The quartet was first performed in Washington on April 25, 1931, at a special festival.

12. Quartet, Opus 50, *Andante*.

More typical of Prokofiev were the classical main theme of the first movement (anticipating the main theme of the Second Violin Concerto) and the sparkling semi-dance theme of the Scherzo. The music is marred only by a few rather unusual and apparently unjustified polyphonic effects.

The history of the advent of the ballet *Sur le Borysthène,* Op. 51, is striking evidence that Prokofiev's talent had reached a crisis in its development. The ballet had been ordered by the management of the Paris Opéra in the summer of 1930. There was no definite subject, and, indeed, it was not easy to find a subject for an opera theater with no dominating artistic principles. It was decided to solve the problem simply: the composer wrote the music on the basis of a purely abstract plan providing for a succession of "intensifications," "lyrical moments," and "upsurges." When and where the action was to take place, what characters were to be depicted — all these questions were to be shelved for the time being. All that existed was the general framework of the piece, worked out in conjuction with the ballet-master: a "lyrical moment" here, a variation in fast tempo there, a pensive mood here, a passionate outburst of emotion there. When this abstract skeleton was filled with music, a more or less suitable story was to be woven around it. Could an artist as discerning and observant as Prokofiev possibly have departed farther from reality than this?

The plot turned out to be extremely simple. A soldier falls in love with a peasant girl; this is demonstrated by tender love scenes and sentimental *pas de deux*. But the father wants the girl to marry someone else. The betrothal takes place and the rejected soldier turns up at the feast and fights the bridegroom. The fight is the dramatic culmination of the ballet. The soldier is seized and tied to a tree. In the end he is released by his sweetheart to the accompaniment of soft music.

The fact that the action takes place *sur le Borysthène* (on the Dnieper) was decided upon at the last minute, evidently as a concession to the Russian artists Larionov and Goncharova, who were responsible for the settings. The very mention of the Dnieper was carefully disguised by the use of its ancient Greek name Borysthène.[19] And although Larionov did try to depict the beauty of the Ukrainian landscape in spring with the apple trees in bloom, there was essentially nothing Ukrainian about the performance.

In the music of this ballet Prokofiev repeated the experiment of *L'Enfant prodigue* with its extremely abstract action beyond time and space. There was of course no question of introducing any Ukrainian color into the music. The lyrical images were much less human and warm than in *L'Enfant prodigue*, and the character episodes not nearly so poignant and dramatic. The fact that Prokofiev as composer and dramatist had no real subject to work on could not but have affected the music.

Sur le Borysthène was the last major work for the theater written by Prokofiev abroad. By this time the composer saw clearly that in western Europe of his day there was no room for development in musical drama. No one was interested in his operas. *The Flaming Angel* could find no producer, and to write new operas was useless when no one would produce them. In any case there were no subjects, no leading ideas left for operas. "It often seems that one subject is just as useless as another."

Soon after the *première* of *Sur le Borysthène* and a new

---

[19] The ballet *Sur le Borysthène* (dedicated to the memory of Diaghilev) was presented by Serge Lifar on one program with two other short ballet novelties at the Paris Opéra on December 16, 1932. It was not a success, and was soon taken out of the repertory.

chamber piece — a sonata for two violins — Prokofiev left for his sixth concert tour of the United States. He played his Third and Fifth Piano Concertos with Frederick Stock, Bruno Walter, and other distinguished conductors. Some of his more complex works of the latter period puzzled the American public. After the performance of the *Portraits*, Prokofiev recalls, one American concert-goer, sitting in the box adjoining his, said loudly: "I'd like to meet that guy [the composer]. I'd tell him a thing or two!" "I hastily took my leave," Prokofiev says.

The last of Prokofiev's foreign compositions were purely instrumental: the Fourth and Fifth Piano Concertos, the Sonata for two violins, Op. 56,[20] *Symphonic Song*, Op. 57, and a Concerto for the cello, Op. 58.

The Fourth Piano Concerto (for the left hand) was written to order for the repertory of the one-armed pianist Paul Wittgenstein (1931).[21] The Fifth Concerto (1932), on the other hand, showed evidence of new experiments in the sphere of piano technique, resumed after a lapse of eleven years. The machine-like Toccata, in the athletic style of the earlier Prokofiev, presents his bold jumps, hand-crossing, and Scarlatti technique in highly exaggerated form. The tendency to wide skips *à la* Scarlatti is carried to monstrous extremes; sheer feats of piano acrobatics completely dominate the principal movements of the concerto (first and third movements, *toccata*; fifth movement, finale). In the precipitate Toccata this dynamic quality degenerates into mere lifeless mechanical movement, with the result that the orchestra itself seems to be trans-

---

[20] The Sonata for two violins was composed in Paris in 1932 for the Triton, a society for popularizing modern chamber music, which was supported by a group of composers including Milhaud, Honegger, Poulenc, and Prokofiev himself. The sonata was first performed at the inauguration of the society on December 16, 1932, the same day as the *première* of *Sur le Borysthène*.

[21] The Austrian pianist Wittgenstein was extremely popular at that time in European musical circles; concertos for the left hand were written for him by Richard Strauss, Maurice Ravel, and other composers. Prokofiev's extremely complex concerto displeased the pianist to such an extent that he refused to play it, and it was never performed. It consists of four movements, the first and fourth of which abound in virtuoso passages; the second movement is an *Andante*, and third an *Allegro* in sonata form.

formed into a huge mechanism with fly-wheels, pistons, and transmission belts.

The brittle, urbanistic style of this work is relieved by only a few oases of gentle lyricism — for example, in the subordinate theme of the first movement in the spirit of the lyrical themes of *L'Enfant prodigue*, in the gavotte-like theme of the second movement, later swamped by the floridity of the development in the form of variations, in the lilting "lullaby" theme of the fourth movement, and at the beginning of the finale.[22]

The foreign period in the work of Prokofiev ended rather aptly with the *Symphonic Song*, Cello Concerto, and Three Pieces, Op. 59. The first two of these compositions made no impression whatsoever on the Soviet audiences.

How, then, can the so-called foreign period in Prokofiev's musical career be summed up in a nutshell. Although the foreign period covers the years between 1918 and 1927, it made itself felt in his writings between 1924 and 1934, when the bourgeois Paris influences were still strong in him. This latter period was incidentally the least productive of his career.

Even a superficial chronological review of this period evinces certain ominous signs. Instead of the thirty-four opus numbers produced between 1909 and 1919, the decade 1924–34 saw only twenty opus numbers, among them many duplications, revisions, and rearrangements of old compositions. To this period belong a number of works made to order or written for chance occasions, and instrumental pieces devised from the material for all manner of music for the stage.

Prokofiev did not write a single opera or vocal work in these ten years. His favorite sphere, music born of living human intonation, was neglected. His piano style acquired a rather domestic, introspective flavor, and even became somewhat pallid and anemic. The virtuoso compositions (Fifth Piano Concerto) had lost their former realism and theatrical vividness

[22] The first performance of the Fifth Concerto was given on October 31, 1932 in Berlin.

and were reduced to a cold and sober neo-Scarlatti trend. While striving to avoid the influence of the bourgeois vogue, and sometimes even making a stand against it, Prokofiev was nevertheless tied down by the Paris artistic environment. This explains his vacillations between the constructivist excesses of the Second Symphony and the quintet, the machine-like naturalism of *Le Pas d'acier* and the purist rationality of *L'Enfant prodigue* and the later piano pieces.

At the same time certain compositions of the Paris period gave evidence of new and vital style features: namely, the dramatic tensity of the Third Symphony, the original lyrical images in *L'Enfant prodigue*, the search for Russian melody in the quartet, *Le Pas d'acier*, and some of the piano pieces (*Pensées*, Op. 62). This yearning for Russian melody was expressed both in Prokofiev's unconscious emulation of Mussorgsky and in his interest in folk-songs; Prokofiev first attempted to adapt Russian folklore to music in the two songs *White Snowflakes* and *Guelder-Rose*, published in Paris in 1931.

Many years before, Karatygin and Igor Glebov had predicted the growth of a lyrical trend in Prokofiev's music, which had not appeared too frequently in his earlier compositions. "It seems to me," wrote Glebov, "that Prokofiev, stormy and temperamental in his conception of external phenomena, is utterly transformed as soon as he ventures into the sphere of intimate feeling. I feel that he has not yet fully revealed himself in this sphere, that he has great potentialities there" (*Sovremennaya Muzyka*, No. 19, 1927, article "Eight Years").

And Glebov was right. For a long time Prokofiev had been persistently seeking an outlet for his pent-up, repressed lyricism. But the pointless art of bourgeois Paris had not been conducive to the realization of these tendencies. Hence the abstract and deliberate reticence of his lyricism in *Things in Themselves* and *Thoughts*. Most of his work belonging to the end of the twenties and the early thirties was actually no more than experimentation in a new lyrical style that took final shape after his return to the Soviet Union. The search for a new melodic style that began with the lyrical episodes in the Overture, Op. 42, and continued in the lyricism of *L'Enfant prodigue* and the Quartet, Op. 50, brought Prokofiev at last to the melodic wealth of the Second Violin Concerto, *Romeo and Juliet,* and other compositions of the Soviet period.

It remains to be added that the years spent abroad had initiated Prokofiev into all the secrets of the technique of modern composition. He had learned from the bottom up all there was to know about contemporary music in the West. And what he had learned had convinced him that the professional mastery of the Western composers was pointless, without a future, and utterly devoid of content. The year 1933–4 marked a sharp dividing line in Prokofiev's work. The crisis of the Paris period had ended with the *Symphonic Song* and the Cello Concerto, and the composer now launched upon a new path under new, Soviet conditions.

Book III
Soviet Artist

8 : New Views

> For four years I fought, and now I am
> home again.
>
> *(Semyon Kotko)*

IT gives me great joy to be home again in the Soviet land," Prokofiev said to Moscow newspapermen in November 1932 (*Sovietskoye Iskusstvo*, November 27, 1932). "Two things struck me about the U.S.S.R.," he wrote at that time, "the unparalleled creative activity among the Soviet composers . . . and the colossal growth of general interest in music clearly evidenced by the huge new contingents of the public that now fill the concert halls" (*Vechernaya Moskva*, December 8, 1932).

Moscow in 1932–3 was, as it is today, one of the liveliest art centers of Europe.

Prokofiev was swiftly drawn into the orbit of new artistic interests. He undertook to write music for the cinema and theater, planned to teach practical composition in the Moscow Conservatory, sought assiduously for new opera librettos, hoping under Soviet conditions to be able at last to see his ideas in the field of musical drama take shape. In numerous statements to the press he emphasized the sharp contrast between bourgeois opera, utterly devoid of purport, and the wealth of themes and subjects suggested by Soviet life. "The ordinary subject matter of the West now repels me," he said. "It strikes me as rather useless and is tinged with an indifference that might be called formalism. . . . One subject is as pointless as another — that is the inevitable impression one gets from the recent products of Western music. . . . When you come to the U.S.S.R. from abroad, you are instantly aware of an essential difference: here music for the theater is really necessary and there is no doubt as to the subject matter: the subject must be heroic and constructive (creative), for these are the traits that best characterize the present epoch. I have a great desire to write an opera on Soviet themes. . . . In my spare time between concerts I have been reading a large number of librettos with the greatest interest" (*Sovietskaya Muzyka*, No. 3, 1933, "Notes" by S. Prokofiev).

Prokofiev spent 1933 and 1934 taking stock of his surroundings, gradually finding his own place in the Soviet scheme of things. During this time his world outlook became more clearly defined and purposeful. His credo during the period of his wanderings abroad had been innovation in general, the quest for new sounds and harmonies, the creation of an original music unlike anything known theretofore. He admitted as much in one of his American interviews: "The cardinal virtue (or, if you like, vice) of my life has always been the search for originality, for my own musical language. I hate imitation, I hate hackneyed methods. I do not want to wear anyone else's mask. I want always to be myself."

But in this distaste for routine, this constant striving for something new, it was difficult to find any positive conviction that would determine the meaning and the purpose of his work. Such inordinate passion for novelty at all costs had been sharply ridiculed by Lenin in one of his conversations with Clara Zetkin: "Why should we turn away from the truly beautiful, why reject it as a point of departure for further development merely because it is old? Why is it necessary to worship the new as one might worship a god to whom we must submit merely because 'it is new'?" (Clara Zetkin: "Reminiscences and Meetings," *Moskovsky Rabochy*, 1925).

It was not until he returned to the Soviet Union that Prokofiev began to strive consciously toward a goal worthy of a great artist: namely, to create for the people, for the broad masses of music-lovers who understand and appreciate real creative art.

"In the Soviet Union music exists for the millions who formerly had to live without it or who rarely came in contact with it. It is to these new millions that the modern Soviet composer must cater," wrote Prokofiev in an article published in *Izvestia* on November 16, 1934. True, in his theoretical utterances one could at times detect echoes of his former modernistic views on art, of a tendency to divide music into two categories: a higher category for the "connoisseurs" and a lower category for everyone else. As a matter of fact, this idea had been current at one time in musical criticism and had given rise to a corresponding classification of compositions. In his article Prokofiev speaks on the one hand of "great music," capable of "posing problems even to leading musicians," and on the other of "lightly serious" or "seriously light" music, comprehensible to all. Appraising his own works of this period he places his *Symphonic Song, Sur le Borysthène*, and Third and Fourth Symphonies in the first category, and *Lieutenant Kije, Egyptian Nights*, and his popular songs in the second.

This theoretical misconception took practical shape in his music, giving rise to a deliberately simplified style in some of his popular songs, which were clearly intended, according to his own classification, for the "second group" (especially most of the songs of Op. 79). On the other hand, in the case of his best works (*Romeo and Juliet* and *Alexander Nevsky* suites, etc.) he refuted his own æsthetic standards by producing music that appealed equally to connoisseurs and to the general public.

Three years later Prokofiev gave a much deeper and more

correct analysis of the tasks facing the Soviet composer in an article published in *Pravda*. Real innovation in art, he pointed out, could not be based on any attempt to meet the "low" tastes of the average audience half-way, but, on the contrary, must take its stand on the constant development of the Soviet public. "Music in our country has truly come to belong to the wide masses. Their artistic taste, the demands they place upon art, are growing with incredible speed. And, bearing this in mind, the composer must make the corresponding 'amendments' to every new work he produces. It is something like shooting at moving targets. Only by aiming ahead at tomorrow will he avoid lagging behind today's requirements. That is why I feel that every attempt at simplification on the part of a composer is a mistake" (*Pravda*, December 31, 1937).

"What is real, what is good?" Prokofiev asks in another article. "Not vulgar tunes that are pleasing at first but soon become incredibly boring, but music with its roots in the classics and in folk-songs" (the magazine *Pioneer*, No. 7, 1939).

In accordance with his new aims and principles, his choice of subject matter changed. Under Soviet conditions there is no need for the artist to obscure his ideas with the hazy ambiguity of "things in themselves," comprehensible only to himself and a select circle of the initiated. Under Soviet conditions it would be similarly unnatural for an artist to indulge in sheer grotesque, distortion, or caricature of reality. "What subject do I seek?" the composer asked himself. "Not a caricature of shortcomings ridiculing the negative features of our life. At the present moment this does not attract me. What interests me is a subject asserting a positive principle. The heroics of construction. The new man. The struggle to overcome obstacles. These are the moods and emotions with which I should like to fill large musical canvases" (*Vechernaya Moskva*, December 6, 1932). Prokofiev's new declarations were not mere words. Once he had planted his feet firmly on the ground and felt himself a participant in the great community of Soviet intellectuals building a new culture, the composer began to work with redoubled energy. His music beginning with 1934–5 is amazing for its intensity and for the significance of its creative ideas.

On the face of it this period in his career was uneventful. Long journeys and concert tours were few and far between. The composer was utterly immersed in his composing. Even his favorite medium, the piano, was unfortunately neglected.[1]

Composition possessed him to the exclusion of everything else. When G. G. Neuhaus, on behalf of many admirers of Prokofiev's pianoforte performance, advised him to arrange a recital, he replied: "I can't do it. It would cost me half a sonata."

The sole diversions from his creative work were his social activity in the Moscow Union of Composers, of which he was a member of the board and chairman of the Consulting Committee, or an occasional game of chess, a favorite pastime from childhood.

9 : Composition

LET us make a brief survey of the highlights of Prokofiev's work in recent years.

The first of his Soviet works, written in 1933, was the music for the film *Lieutenant Kije* after the story by Y. Tynyanov (Leningrad *Belgoskino* Studios, director A. Feinzimmer). This was in the nature of a trial of the pen under the new Soviet conditions. For the first time after wandering so long in a maze of subjectless music the composer was at last able to tackle a concrete problem: to provide the musical settings of old St. Petersburg under the reign of Paul, with its parades, its

---

[1] Incidentally, his later solo performances, particularly his performance of the First Piano Concerto in February 1941, again astounded his hearers by the inexhaustible power and energy of his gifts as a pianist.

military ceremonies after the Prussian pattern, and its dashing
Hussars. The anecdote about the lieutenant who existed on
paper only because of a mistake made by the secretary, offered
rich possibilities for grotesque effects. But Prokofiev resisted
the temptation and gave instead an almost realistic reproduction of the epoch, complete with the Russian snows, the dull
parade-ground ceremonies, the sentimental ditty with a faint
flavor of parody to it, and the tinkling sleighbells. His St.
Petersburg was closer to the stylized, gently ironic engravings
of Dobuzhinsky than to the cynical caricatures in Stravinsky's
Mavra or Shostakovich's *The Nose*. A year later, in 1934, Prokofiev revised the orchestration and made a symphonic suite
(Op. 60) out of this music.

The music for *Egyptian Nights*, staged by A. Tairov in the
Moscow Kamerny Theater (1933), was written almost simultaneously with *Lieutenant Kije*. Carried away by the image of
Cleopatra, Tairov attempted to combine three texts written
in three distinct styles: *Antony and Cleopatra* by Shakespeare,
Egyptian Nights by Pushkin, and *Cæsar and Cleopatra* by
Bernard Shaw. The result was artificial and cumbersome. Yet
for Prokofiev this, his first encounter with Shakespeare's great
passions and strong, cruel heroes, was most fruitful indeed.
The music for *Egyptian Nights* provides settings masterfully
executed in rich, somber tones — tense, thrilling night alarms,
echoes of fierce battles, the austere grandeur and majesty of
the ancient world. Against the subtly conveyed historical background the contours of powerful human characters take shape
in the themes of Antony and Cleopatra. The best episode in
the symphonic suite made in 1934 from the music of *Egyptian
Nights* is, in the composer's own estimation, No. 6, "Eclipse
of Cleopatra"; No. 3, "Alarm," written for percussion instruments alone (bass and side drum plus kettle-drums), is also
particularly interesting.

Prokofiev spent part of 1933 abroad, where he wrote his
Symphonic Song, several piano pieces, sketches for a cello concerto, and a symphonic suite from the ballet *Sur le Borysthène*.

All this was in the nature of a summing-up of the Paris period of his work. The three-movement *Symphonic Song* was conceived by the composer as a complex lyrical and philosophical work representing three successive states: obscurity, struggle, and achievement. But the exposition proved to be so confusing that even Koussevitzky, who had invariably upheld all of Prokofiev's most Left compositions, was at a loss.

The *première* of the *Symphonic Song* in Moscow, on April 14, 1934, failed to arouse the interest of the public. *Sovietskaya Muzyka* (No. 6, 1934) criticized it severely. The *Symphonic Song*, said this magazine, "has no cantabile quality; it is not a song at all in our sense of the word. We regard it as a symphonic monologue for the few, as the sad tale of the eclipse of the fading culture of individualism." The gist of the article was that any continuation of the tendencies evinced in the *Symphonic Song* would be quite unsuitable under Soviet conditions.

Prokofiev spent a large part of 1934 in the U.S.S.R., putting the finishing touches to suites adapted from the music of *Lieutenant Kije* and *Egyptian Nights*, trying his hand at mass songs, and interchanging ideas with Soviet musicians. He spent the summer in Polenovo, where the artist P. Konchalovsky painted his portrait. At the end of the year he conceived the idea for a new major work; together with the producer S. Radlov he outlined the plan for a ballet on the theme of *Romeo and Juliet*.

In the meantime Prokofiev's standing was high in the West. In 1934 the Academy of Music in Rome elected him to honorary membership. A group of French musicians asked him to write a new major violin piece for the famous violinist Robert Soetens, giving Soetens exclusive rights in the piece throughout the first year. First conceived as a sonata for violin and orchestra, this work finally assumed the dimensions of a grandiose composition — the Second Violin Concerto (Op. 63). It was composed in the first half of 1935, in the intervals between numerous concert appearances. One part was written in Paris, another in Voronezh, a third in Baku, and so on. The score was completed in Baku on August 16, 1935. That same summer Prokofiev concentrated on his new ballet, *Romeo and Juliet*, which, apart from a few additional sections, was ready early in September 1935.

In Polenovo, where he spent the summer of 1935, the composer wrote a number of simple pieces for childern, with typical program titles (*Morning, The Walk, Fairy-tale, Repentance, Grasshoppers' Parade, Rain and Rainbow*). As he himself admits, his former predilection for the sonatina had reawakened in him. The last of these pieces, *The Moon Goes over the Meadows*, executed in the style of a Russian folk-song, was inspired by the scenery at Polenovo. To the imposing list of compositions produced in 1935 were added a few popular songs to texts by Soviet poets — *Partisan, My Country is Growing, Anyutka*, and others. *Anyutka* won second prize at a contest of mass songs arranged by *Pravda* (no first prize was awarded). Prokofiev's first six mass songs, collected as Op. 66, marked the beginning of a long series of compositions on Soviet themes. Thus by the end of the third year of his work in the Soviet Union there were already definite signs of a considerable change in Prokofiev's output in the direction of serious themes replete with ideas and a new simplicity and clarity of style.

Early in October 1935 the composer gave a public performance of the music of *Romeo and Juliet* at Moscow. Commenting on the concert, *Izvestia* spoke with undisguised approval of Prokofiev's new "realistic language" (*Izvestia*, October 6, 1935). A controversy at once arose in connection with the dubious attempt to tack a happy ending on to the Shakespearean plot; in the original version, Juliet was to be resurrected, and the ballet was to have ended with a joyous dance of the lovers. Most of the critics, however, opposed making any such modernization of Shakespeare for the sake of the old ballet traditions, and the original plot was finally restored.

During the winter of 1935–6 Prokofiev accompanied Robert Soetens on a long concert tour that included Spain, Portugal, Morocco, Algeria, and Tunis. The new violin concerto had its *première* in Madrid on December 1, 1935.[1] In their joint appearance Prokofiev and Soetens played chamber pieces by Beethoven and Debussy. A year later the Second Violin Concerto was played in Moscow by Fischmann, and in 1937 became part of the repertory of the famous American violinist Jascha Heifetz.

In April a new symphonic composition came into being — *Peter and the Wolf,* a symphonic fairy-tale for children. Prokofiev himself wrote the story of the brave Pioneer Peter, who cleverly outwitted the wicked Wolf. The music and the spoken text are given simultaneously in the form of a musical monologue. This was an entirely new departure for Prokofiev, his first attempt to write an orchestral piece for children, giving in attractive form an object lesson in instrumentation. "Every character in this story," wrote the author in his introduction to *Peter and the Wolf,* "is represented by a corresponding instrument in the orchestra: the flute is the Bird, the oboe the

13. *Peter and the Wolf,* theme of Peter the Pioneer.

---

[1] In a concert conducted by Enrique Fernández Arbós. — *Editor.*

Duck, the clarinet played *staccato* in the low register is the Cat, the bassoon is Grandpa, three French horns are the Wolf, the string quartet is Peter, and the kettle-drums and bass drum are the hunters' rifle-shots. Before the performance it is advisable to show these instruments to the children and to play the leitmotivs on each instruments. In this way the children will be able without the slightest effort to recognize the diverse orchestral instruments in the course of the performance."

Thus, twenty-two years after *The Ugly Duckling*, Prokofiev once again created a gallery of clever and amusing animal portraits as vividly depicted as though painted from nature by an animal artist. The carefree twittering of the Bird, the languorous purring of the Cat, the blood-curdling howls of the Wolf, the quacking of the Duck as it waddles lazily along, are all presented with the gentle tolerant humor of a story-teller who understands the musical tastes and requirements of children.

The piece has since been performed many times in Moscow and in the larger cities of the United States for adult audiences as well as for children. The American public was particularly enthusiastic. In Chicago, *Peter and the Wolf* was presented on the stage as a ballet (by Adolph Bolm). The text of the story was published in a special de luxe edition. The critics compared Prokofiev's gift for depiction with that of Walt Disney.[2]

Prokofiev's interest in themes for children induced him to write three more small songs to words by Soviet poets: *Chatterbox* (Barto), *Sweet Melody* (Sakonskaya), and *Little Pigs* (Mikhalkov). These songs were collected as Op. 68.

The Soviet art world in 1936 was preparing for two important jubilees: the twentieth anniversary of the October Revolution and the centenary of the death of Pushkin. Both these occasions were reflected in Prokofiev's music. At the end of 1935 he conceived the idea of writing a large piece for orches-

---

[2] The piano score of *Peter and the Wolf*, Op. 67, was published by the State Music Publishing House in 1937; the orchestral score appeared in 1940. The piece was first performed by the Moscow Philharmonic in May 1936.

tra and chorus to depict the history of the October Revolution. In the course of 1936 and the early part of 1937 this idea gradually took shape. The composer's plan was an ambitious one. He proposed to write music for chorus and orchestra to the actual words of Marx, Lenin, and Stalin. "Lenin wrote in such graphic and convincing language that I did not want to resort to any versified exposition of his ideas," declared the composer. "I wanted to go right to the source and use the actual words of the leader" (*Vechernaya Moskva*, June 22, 1936).

The cantata written for the twentieth anniversary of the October Revolution, and completed in 1937, consists of ten parts:

Part One: orchestral introduction (the epigraph to this is the phrase from the *Communist Manifesto*: "A specter is haunting Europe — the specter of Communism");

Part Two: *Philosophers* (chorus to the text taken from Marx's theses on Ludwig Feuerbach: "The philosophers have interpreted the world in various ways; the point, however, is to change it");

Part Three: orchestral interlude;

Part Four: "We are marching in a compact group along a precipitous and difficult path" (chorus to Lenin's words from *What is to be Done?*);

Part Five: orchestral interlude;

Part Six: *Revolution* (chorus to texts from articles and speeches by Lenin, October 1917);

Part Seven: *Victory*, orchestra and chorus (to texts from Lenin);

Part Eight: *Stalin's Pledge* (chorus to text taken from Stalin's speech at the bier of Lenin);

Part Nine: *Symphony*, for symphony orchestra and accordion orchestra (theme, Socialist construction);

Part Ten: *The Stalin Constitution* (chorus to text taken from Stalin's speech at the Eighth Extraordinary Congress of Soviets).

The cantata was intended for a huge number of performers,

no less than five hundred people: two choruses, professional and amateur, and four orchestras, symphony, brass, percussion, and accordion.

The grandeur and novelty of the artistic problem posed by the composer are indisputable. Moreover, the salutary effect on the composer of this, his first attempt at a subject of such vast political significance, cannot be overestimated. Nevertheless, the cantata, Op. 74, will remain interesting merely as an experiment in the development of Prokofiev's art. Brilliant as the utterances of the great leaders of the Revolution undoubtedly were, they were never intended to be sung in the form of choral recitative, and when transferred to the métier of choral singing, they not only encumber the melodic idiom itself, but lose much of their oratorical power. The most impressive parts of the cantata were, naturally enough, the symphonic interludes in which the idea of Revolution is not merely introduced into the music through the text, but translated into the specific language of musical images. And even here the most convincing are not those episodes in which the composer chose to depict the external tumult of upheaval, but the few images giving the inner feeling of joy in the victory of the Revolution: the radiant and confident calm of Part Seven. However, the cantata has never been performed, and to pass any final judgment on its musical qualities now would be premature.

Pushkin themes were tackled by Prokofiev in a similarly bold and sweeping manner. For thirty years, since his youthful experiment with the *Feast during the Plague*, he had not attempted to set Pushkin's poetry to music. In modernist circles — especially in the West — Pushkin themes would have been regarded as an intolerable anachronism, and if Stravinsky did use Pushkin for his *Mavra*, he tried his best to make a comic caricature out of it. With his Pushkin songs (1936) Prokofiev returned to vocal lyrics, a sphere he had neglected for fifteen years. Of the three songs, Op. 73, to Pushkin texts (*Pine Trees, Roseate Dawn, In Your Chamber*), the first, written in serene narrative tones, is the best. The text of this

song has an autobiographical value for the composer, who
sees in it a calm statement of his joy at returning to his homeland:

> Ten years have passed since then — and much
> Has changed in life for me,
> I, too, obedient to life's laws,
> Have altered — but here again
> The past enfolds me in its arms
> And lo, it seems but yesterday
> I roamed these woods. . . .

The verse ends with praise of the "young glade" that had
sprung up in the poet's absence, and a joyous welcome to the
"new, young, unknown tribe."

In the second half of 1936 Prokofiev worked simultaneously
on three major Pushkin themes: his music to the poem *Yevgeny Onyegin* (libretto by S. D. Krzhyzhanovsky for the
Kamerny Theater), for the film *The Queen of Spades* (Moscow Film Studios, director M. Romm), and for the play *Boris
Godunov*. Thus Prokofiev entered into competition with the
great classics Tchaikovsky and Mussorgsky.

The greatest difficulties, on the composer's own admission,
were presented by *Yevgeny Onyegin*, and sprang from the tremendous popularity of Tchaikovsky's music for the opera of
that name. "The play *Yevgeny Onyegin* in Krzhyzhanovsky's
version stressed precisely those aspects of Pushkin's poem that
had been omitted from Tchaikovsky's opera," wrote Prokofiev.
"I believe it would be extraordinarily interesting to see Lensky
arguing heatedly over a bottle of wine with Onyegin, or Tatyana visiting the latter's empty house, or Onyegin on the banks
of the Neva. . . . It is my intention," he maintained, "to
keep as close as possible to the original text" (*Vechernaya
Moskva*, June 22, 1936).

In the music of *Yevgeny Onyegin* Prokofiev concentrated on
the characterization of the principal dramatis personæ: a few
themes for Onyegin, three leitmotivs for Tatyana, developing
with the growth of her passion. The ball scene at the Larin

home (waltz, polka for two pianos, etc.) and the music depicting the serene rural atmosphere at the Larin estate were executed with Prokofiev's customary subtlety of stylization.

Prokofiev found much to interest him also in *The Queen of Spades*, the tragic high-strung character of Hermann having a particular appeal for him.

Unfortunately, not one of the three Pushkin works was ever produced. Including all three of them in the list of his compositions (*The Queen of Spades* and *Boris Godunov* under Op. 70, and *Yevgeny Onyegin* under Op. 71), Prokofiev subsequently used several themes from them for instrumental works.

To the long list of works written in 1936 must be added two symphonic suites adapted from *Romeo and Juliet* and a new large symphonic piece, *Russian Overture*, Op. 72, written for the Moscow Philharmonic (first performed on October 29). Moreover, four marches for brass band were composed in 1936 and 1937.

The two symphonic suites from *Romeo and Juliet* included the essential parts of the ballet.[3] The first suite, first played by the Moscow Philharmonic Orchestra on June 24, 1936, was unanimously hailed by Soviet critics as a sign of a fundamental change in Prokofiev's work, of a definite transition to a new realistic style. In 1937 the music of *Romeo and Juliet* was used for a cycle of piano pieces, Op. 75, written without any of Prokofiev's former frills and furbelows. Notwithstanding the almost ascetic simplicity of the exposition, very similar to a piano arrangement of an orchestral score, the pieces were quickly taken up by Soviet pianists and included in their concert repertories.

Long before the *première* of the ballet itself the music of

---

[3] The First Suite, Op. 64-A, consists of seven parts: (1) "Folk Dance," (2) "Scene," (3) "Madrigal," (4) "Minuet," (5) "Masques," (6) "Romeo and Juliet," and (7) "The Death of Tybalt." The Second Suite, Op. 64-B, also has seven items: (1) "The Montagues and Capulets," (2) "Juliet as a Child," (3) "Friar Laurence," (4) "Dance," (5) "Romeo and Juliet before Parting," (6) "Dance of the Young Antillean Girls," and (7) "Romeo at Juliet's Tomb."

Romeo and Juliet won the sympathy of the Soviet performer and concert-goer. It was similarly successful abroad.

Early in 1937 Prokofiev undertook a long concert tour through Europe and the United States. His creative work during that year included the completion of the cantata, Op. 74, the piano cycle *Romeo and Juliet,* and a series of songs for chorus and orchestra entitled *Songs of Our Days.* "In the music written in this productive year," the composer wrote at the end of 1937 in *Pravda,* "I have striven for clarity and melodious idiom, but at the same time I have by no means attempted to restrict myself to the accepted methods of harmony and melody. This is precisely what makes lucid, straightforward music so difficult to compose — the clarity must be new, not old."

In *Songs of Our Days* Prokofiev turned again to Soviet themes that he had embraced for the first time in the songs, Op. 66, using, besides the verses of Marshak, Lebedev-Kumach, and Prishelets, a number of poetic folk texts (Russian, Ukrainian, Byelo-Russian).[4] In these songs Prokofiev strove to express all the multiform phenomena of our life: the new life on the collective farms, the heroism of the Soviet border guards, the enthusiasm of the young girls who went to the Far East to take part in the new construction there, the daring of a Young Communist who saved children from a fire. The author's sincere desire to achieve a new simplicity and comprehensibility was unfortunately not always combined with a clear, vivid perception of the images he attempted to reproduce. Only when he clearly felt the drama of a situation, the passion and intensity of his poetic material, did he produce vivid and truthful images in the ballad genre. Such, for example, is the lovely song *Brother for Brother,* about the heroic border guard who took the place of his brother killed at his post.

---

[4] The *Songs of Our Days* suite consists of nine parts: Orchestral introduction (a march), "Over the Bridge," "Be Well," "Golden Ukraine," "Brother for Brother," "Girls," "The Twenty-Year-Old," "Lullaby," "From End to End."

In the early part of 1938 Prokofiev made another long tour abroad, visiting Czechoslovakia, France, Britain, and the United States. While in Los Angeles, he visited Hollywood and made a detailed study of the technical methods used for the musical backgrounds of American sound films. America welcomed Prokofiev as an old friend and gave him a most cordial reception. In the United States the composer found a serious interest in his work. He was pleasantly surprised to discover that two student societies named after him had been formed for the express purpose of studying and popularizing his music, one at Hanover, New Hampshire, the other at Wheaton, Illinois.

Following his American trip, Prokofiev collaborated with Sergei Eisenstein, the film-producer, and Eduard Tisse, the cameraman, on the historical film *Alexander Nevsky*. His association with Eisenstein, one of the outstanding representatives of Soviet art, was a source of great satisfaction to Prokofiev. He made many interesting sound experiments, using some of the methods employed in Hollywood. In turn, Eisenstein and Tisse treated the ideas of their collaborator with the greatest respect and regarded him as a co-producer of the film (Tisse wrote about this in one of his articles in the newspaper *Kino*). Indeed, *Alexander Nevsky* proved to be one of the few Soviet films in which the music not only illustrates, but leads the action.

In the same year (1938) the composer completed the score of his Cello Concerto, Op. 58, which had existed in rough draft since 1933, and composed music for a production of *Hamlet*. It was in writing the music for *Hamlet* that the exquisite gavotte, in actual fact the fourth of Prokofiev's gavottes, came into being. The Cello Concerto, performed in November 1938 during the second Festival of Soviet Music (solo by Berezovsky), made no particular impression on the public, but was the cause of a heated controversy between the newspaper *Sovietskoye Iskusstvo*, which had praised it even before its public performance, and the magazine *Sovietskaya Muzyka*. Later the composer made some changes in the score on the basis of some of the critical comments. In 1940 the concerto was performed in the United States by the well-known cellist Gregor Piatigorski.

The failure of the Cello Concerto and *Songs of Our Days* at the musical festival in 1938 was partly compensated for by the enthusiastic reception accorded at the same time to the Second Piano Concerto, interpreted by the excellent pianist M. V. Yudina.

The year 1939 was extremely productive for Prokofiev. It saw the completion of the *Alexander Nevsky* cantata, the opera *Semyon Kotko*, the cantata *Zdravitsa*, written for Stalin's sixtieth birthday (December 21, 1939), a number of popular songs for various contests, sketches for a violin sonata, Op. 80, and the project for three new piano sonatas — the Sixth, Op. 82, the Seventh, Op. 83, and the Eighth, Op. 84. In April 1939 the *Alexander Nevsky* cantata, a revised and reorchestrated version of the film music, was first performed by the Moscow Philharmonic Orchestra. Repeated in November of the same year during the third Soviet music festival, the cantata was given an enthusiastic reception by both the public and the press.

Similarly successful was the cantata *Zdravitsa*, performed by the chorus and orchestra of the All-Union Radio Committee in December 1939. The text of the cantata was a successful combination by the composer himself of seven folk-songs to Stalin by various Soviet nationalities (Russian, Ukrainian, Byelo-Russian, Mordovian, Mari, Kurd, and Kumykian). Russian folk-melody predominates in this music, which is written in an extremely clear melodic idiom, colored by Prokofiev's own individual style.

In 1939 the ballet *Romeo and Juliet* found a producer in the Soviet Union.[5] The best ballet troupe in the country, that of the Kirov Theater in Leningrad, undertook its production with

---

[5] The first production of this ballet had been staged in Brno, Czechoslovakia, in 1938.

great enthusiasm. The *première* of the ballet, on January 11, 1940, took the form of a festival of the Soviet ballet. Glowing tribute was paid to the work of the ballet-master, L. Lavrovsky, the artist P. Williams, and the exceptionally talented performance of Galina Ulanova in the role of Juliet. The performance was also a tremendous success in Moscow during the visit of Leningrad theaters to the Soviet capital in May 1940.

In February 1940 a new sonata, the Sixth, was completed, and it was played shortly afterward by the composer himself in a radio recital. Later a brilliant rendering of this sonata was given by the young Moscow pianist Svyatoslav Richter.

Throughout the 1939–40 season Prokofiev took an active part in the preparations for the production of *Semyon Kotko* in the Moscow Stanislavsky Theater.[6] The *première* of the new opera was given at the end of June 1940 (producer S. Birman, conductor M. Zhukov). Not one of Prokofiev's compositions in the latter period had given rise to so many conflicting opinions in musical circles as this opera. Some considered it one of the first full-fledged Soviet operas, others actually found traces of formalism in it. The *Semyon Kotko* controversy (see *Sovietskaya Muzyka*, Nos. 9, 10, 11, and 13, 1940) shifted in December 1940 to the platform of the All-Union Opera Conference, where the opera was severely criticized by some of the delegates. By this time Prokofiev had written another opera, *Betrothal in a Convent*, after Sheridan's *Duenna*. This lyrical comic opera, of which Prokofiev wrote the libretto himself, was completed in the summer of 1940 and was intended for the Moscow Stanislavsky Opera Theater. It was soon orchestrated and ready for production. Several dress rehearsals in June 1941 won it not a few enthusiastic admirers among Moscow's musicians. Because of the outbreak of the war, however, the Moscow public was prevented from seeing it.

---

[6] The opera was first called *I, Son of the Working People*, after the novel by Valentin Katayev about the struggle of the Ukrainian guerrillas against the German invaders in 1918.

On the eve of the war the composer was engaged on his symphonic suite from the music of *Semyon Kotko* and a new ballet, *Cinderella*, to a libretto by N. Volkov, for the Kirov Theater in Leningrad. Prokofiev collaborated with Vakhtang Chebukiani, the eminent Leningrad ballet-master and dancer, in working out the details of the ballet. "Although every nation has its Cinderella," wrote Prokofiev, "I wanted to treat it as a real Russian fairy-tale. Moreover, I see Cinderella herself not only as a fairy-tale character, but as a living human being. . . ." [7]

Add to this the voluminous *Autobiography*, written with genuine literary brilliance in the early part of 1941 at the request of *Sovietskaya Muzyka*, and this brief summary of his activities between 1933 and June 1941 will be exhausted.

June 22, 1941, when the Nazis launched their sudden and treacherous assault on the U.S.S.R., was a turning-point in the lives of all Soviet people. Prokofiev was living at the time in Kratovo, a suburb of Moscow, where he was working on *Cinderella*. In the early days of the war he could frequently be met, excited and agitated, in the halls of the Moscow Union of Composers, at the State Music Publishing House, or at the Committee on Arts. With all other Soviet artists, Prokofiev was anxious to give unstintingly of his efforts and talent to his country.

In July 1941 he wrote his *Symphonic March*, Op. 88, and the March in A flat, Op. 89, intended for a brass band. Somewhat later he wrote a number of popular songs to anti-fascist and war verses by Soviet poets. [8] But his most important task during this period was the creation of a large historical opera on the theme of Tolstoy's great novel *War and Peace*. In July 1941 Prokofiev worked out the scenario and libretto for this heroic opera depicting Russia in 1812 and the self-sacrificing

---

[7] From a letter to me dated July 18, 1942. A brief excerpt from *Cinderella* (introduction to Act I) was published as a musical supplement to the magazine *Sovietskaya Muzyka*, No. 4, 1941.

[8] *Admiral Trash* (Mayakovsky), *Song of the Brave* (Surkov), *Tankist's Pledge, Son of Kabarda, Soldier's Sweetheart, Fritz, Your Country Needs You*.

struggle of the Russians against the Napoleonic invasion. There are eleven scenes in the opera. The first six scenes are devoted almost exclusively to the emotions of Natasha Rostova and her relations with Andrei Bolkonsky and Pierre Bezukhov. The pure, tender, maiden-like lyricism is interwoven with musical pictures of the life of the old Russian nobility: the whole of Scene iii, for instance — a ball in the house of Hélène Bezukhova — is permeated with old-style Russian waltz rhythms. At the end of the sixth scene there is a sharp break in the action when the news comes that Napoleon's troops have approached the Russian border. Then the lyrical drama is transposed to the plane of broad historical narrative. The Russian people in the struggle and historical figures like Field Marshal Kutuzov and Napoleon are now in the foreground. Much space is given to monumental choruses of Russian soldiers and portrayal of individuals from among the common people, such as Platon Karatayev, the soldier, Vasilissa, the woman guerrilla, and a village elder. The dramatic culmination of the opera comes in Scene ix, where the fire of Moscow and the fury of the people at the foreign invaders are shown. The tense scene of the battle that ends with the victory of the Russians over the French is given in the music of the eleventh and final scene. The personal experiences of the heroes of Tolstoy's novel — the wounding and death of Andrei, the despair of Natasha, the arrest and release of Pierre — are woven into the opera in the form of a subordinate plot. The opera ends with the triumphant entry of Kutuzov into Moscow and the popular rejoicing at the victory.

Air raids, which began in Moscow at the end of July, compelled the Soviet Government to evacuate a number of the leading members of the world of art and science to the rear. With Miaskovsky, Shaporin, Nemirovich-Danchenko, Kachalov, and others, Prokofiev went to the Caucasus. In Nalchik, center of the Kabardino-Balkarian Autonomous Republic, situated at the foot of Mount Elbruz, a handsomely equipped sanatorium was placed at their disposal. Prokofiev resumed his creative work with his former zeal. He at once took a great interest in the unusually fresh, piquant, and little explored musical folklore of Kabardino-Balkaria. Kabardinian and Balkarian songs inspired his Second String Quartet, which was written on the basis of this local national music.

The composer defined his purpose in this connection as the "combination of one of the least-known varieties of folk-song with the most classical form of the quartet." Rejecting all the classical traditions of Russian Oriental music, Prokofiev combined the Caucasian folk-melodies with his own individual harmonic and polyphonic style. The result was a unique composition giving a sharply individual and fresh, if perhaps disputable, interpretation of the Caucasian scene. In the harsh harmonies of the first movement we feel the stern, warlike, vengeful Caucasus. The poetry of the Caucasian love-songs is subtly reproduced in the slow second movement, with its flowery, ornate violin grace-notes, so characteristic of Oriental music. The flexible syncopated rhythms of mountain dances dominate in the rhapsodic finale of the quartet. This composition soon found first-class interpreters in the Moscow Beethoven Quartet (D. Tsyganov, V. Shirinsky, V. Borisovsky, and S. Shirinsky), one of the finest Soviet chamber ensembles.

In Nalchik and later (from November 1941 on) in the Georgian capital of Tbilisi, Prokofiev worked intensively on the opera of *War and Peace*, with only occasional diversions in concerts of his works in Tbilisi, Baku, and Erivan. Simultaneously he undertook a symphonic canvas of the patriotic war. This was his symphonic suite 1941 (Op. 90). It is in three parts: "In Battle," "At Night," and "For the Brotherhood of the Peoples." The composer himself tells us: "The first part is a scene of fiery battle, heard by the auditors both from afar and on the very battlefield; in the second part there is the poetry of night, through which pours the tension of approaching battles; the third part is a triumphantly lyrical hymn of victory and of the brotherhood of all peoples." Prokofiev's firm friend and his companion on the evacuation to the Caucasus, the composer Nikolai Miaskovsky, soon made a four-hand piano arrangement of the new suite. Arousing no particular interest in musical circles because of the simplified solution of its problems, giving too superficial a description of the war theme, the music of 1941 was employed as a score for the new film *Partisans of the Ukrainian Steppes*, directed by Igor Savchenko. Prokofiev's use in this score of a Ukrainian folk-song, *Oh, You Galya*, made this one of the most popular soldiers' songs of the war.

10 : Maturity

EVEN the brief chronological survey given here will suffice to show the marked revival in Prokofiev's creative activity after his return to the U.S.S.R. An examination of the figures will show that during the seven years between 1934 and 1940 Prokofiev composed almost one and a half times more than in the entire decade 1924–33 (twenty-seven Soviet works as against twenty "foreign"). Moreover, there were almost no rehashes in the new crop of compositions. The fountain of his creative energy burst forth anew as in the best years prior to his departure from his homeland.

His passion for the stage, for music of the theatrical pictorial variety, for opera and ballet, returned. His subject matter became richer and more profound: Shakespeare, Pushkin, and other literary geniuses now attracted him as never before. He worked with interest and enthusiasm on subjects of Revolutionary history (cantata, Op. 74, *Semyon Kotko*), on motives borrowed from folk poetry and legend (*Zdravitsa, Songs of Our Days, Cinderella*) and heroic themes from the history of the Russian people (*Alexander Nevsky*).

Once again after long years of enforced silence the living human voice sounded in his music (cantatas, romances, mass songs). The composer turned again with avidity (after an interval of seventeen years!) to the piano sonata, adding three large sonatas to his list of compositions.

Once again, as in the best years of his youth, Prokofiev's music evoked passionate controversies in the musical world. Whereas the *Symphonic Song,* the "Portraits" from *The Gambler,* and the Fifth Piano Concerto had left the public cold or puzzled, *Semyon Kotko, Romeo and Juliet,* and *Alexander Nevsky* aroused a veritable storm of discussion, dispute, and argument. Only a live, talented, and audacious art can evoke such reactions from the audience. Prokofiev's gift had indeed blossomed forth anew.

The new invigorating influences flowed into his music along two main channels: firstly, through vivid subject matter, theatrical concreteness, and the ideological import of his new compositions, and, secondly, through the extensive and now quite conscious and deliberate interest in Russian national melody. A keen and far-sighted artist who had for so many years worked as though blindfolded, Prokofiev at last returned for his inspiration to nature, to the great and beautiful world inhabited by living men and women and illumined by a real sun. While *Lieutenant Kije* and *Egyptian Nights* still belonged to the category of pictorial, theatrical stylization, the Second Violin Concerto and *Romeo and Juliet* were the expression of new lyrical tendencies, the composer's return to the world of profound and serious human emotion.

After the drab, somber tones of *Thoughts,* the Violin Concerto impresses by its wealth of emotional contrasts: the warm lyricism of the main G-minor melody in the first movement (remotely related to a theme in Tchaikovsky's First Symphony), gives way to a passionate, tremulous romanticism in the subordinate theme in B-flat major (one of the finest melodic discoveries of Prokofiev). The charmingly pensive second movement, with its melancholy figurational patterns gradually

14. Second Violin Concerto, 1st movement, subordinate theme.

unfolding in the spirit of Beethoven *adagios*, changes to the gay carnival rhythms of the finale, done in the sparkling Latin festive manner.

It is not difficult to trace the connection between the Violin Concerto and the music of *Romeo and Juliet*: in the subordinate theme of the first movement of the concerto we feel the anticipation of the love scenes of *Romeo and Juliet*; in the finale, the carefree gaiety of the masked ball and nocturnal revelry.

Prokofiev's return to the traditional classical construction of the concerto after neglecting the orthodox sonata forms for so many years is symptomatic.[1] Similarly classical is the use of the violin itself as a cantilena instrument (second movement). For Prokofiev, who for years had been considered a confirmed opponent of romanticism, the concerto marked a return to the lyrical and romantic tendencies of his early youth. As if convinced of the emptiness and cold indifference of his abstract experimentation, Prokofiev the Schumannist and poet returned to the point from which he started, but now considerably richer in ideas and technique.

This restoration of lyrical and romantic tendencies made itself even more strongly felt in *Romeo and Juliet*, written at the same time as the concerto. Never before had Prokofiev written music for the theater on such a profound and human theme, one that impels the artist so inevitably along the path of realistic philosophical art.

The composer's former opponents, who regarded him merely as a crude violator of respectable æsthetic standards, would never have believed Prokofiev capable of writing the music for such a subject. Kolomytsev, the critic, had written of the *Scythian Suite*: "To one it is given to sing of the love of Romeo and Juliet, to another to depict the wild screams and absurd contortions of monkeys" (*Den*, January 19, 1916). And now twenty years later the impossible had happened: the rude Prokofiev had sung tenderly of the love of Romeo and Juliet.

It is instructive to compare the conception of the ballet with Prokofiev's former ballet works. What Paris had demanded primarily of a new ballet was brief action and good dancing; profound ideas were not wanted. Diaghilev and Stravinsky had sought in ballet an escape from the trials and tribulations of everyday life, regarding it as the freshest and most naïve — in other words, the most irrational — of the theatrical arts. The

---

[1] In the foreign period the broken-up suite constructions predominated (*Divertissement*, Quintet, piano cycles of Op. 59 and 62); in preference to the sonata Prokofiev cultivated the sonatina (Op. 54 and 59), or variation forms (Second Symphony, Quintet), and he very often deliberately violated the sonata cycle (two-movement Second Symphony, three-movement Quartet with slow finale, etc.).

ballet *Sur le Borysthène* was a typical example of this deliberate avoidance of ideas in ballet music; it was the composer's job to write thirty minutes of lyrico-dramatic music to fill in one third of a program (in Paris it was the custom to present two or three short ballets in one evening).

Romeo and Juliet, as distinct from Prokofiev's Paris ballets, was conceived as a large choreographic tragedy, with all the psychological complexities of the heroes, clear-cut musical character portraits, and realistic theatrical depiction of scenes. Prokofiev came out with flying colors from the difficult contest with the classics (Bellini, Gounod, Berlioz, Tchaikovsky) who had used the plot of *Romeo and Juliet* before him. He had succeeded in finding his own independent approach to this grand theme.

In the foreground of Prokofiev's music for this ballet we find a group of images depicting the love of the tragic couple and their sad fate. The love motiv is utterly devoid of sensuousness, however; it is tinged with a gentle, restrained sadness, with

15. *Romeo and Juliet*, love theme.

quiet, hidden emotions, transparent and silvery tones predominating (solo flute, *concertante* violin).[2] Developing the methods outlined in *L'Enfant prodigue*, the composer em-

---

[2] The effects are admirably suited to Romeo's words in Act II, Scene ii:
> How silver-sweet sound lovers' tongues by night,
> Like softest music to attending ears!

ploys the most expressive melodic images with extreme economy of timbral and harmonic embellishment. It is no wonder that after the passionate chromatic sensuousness of Wagner's love themes Prokofiev's lyricism, with its cautious linear construction reduced at times to a mere two or three voices and its simple chord accompaniment (long, soft, monotonous harmonic backgrounds), may sometimes seem a shade too passionless. It is not until one grows accustomed to this music that its amazing purity of emotion and power of conviction can be appreciated to the full. Shakespeare is given not with the ardent passion of nineteenth-century romanticism, but in the refined adolescent spirit of early Renaissance art.

But while Prokofiev's lyricism was new and not altogether comprehensible at first, in the concrete images of *Romeo and Juliet* we at once recognize the familiar hand of the master painter, with his ability to sketch the human profile in a few bold strokes of the brush. The sunny, merry little Juliet, the gay, light-hearted Mercutio, the wise and gentle Laurence, the haughty Montagues and Capulets, the proud and vindictive Tybalt — these figures are so vividly drawn by Prokofiev that one can clearly visualize them, their movements and gestures by merely listening to the music.

The dramatic intensity that distinguished so many dynamic images in the early Prokofiev (from *Études*, Op. 2, to the *Diabolic Suggestions*) made itself most powerfully felt in the culminating scenes of the tragedy (duel and death of Tybalt). Prokofiev's fondness for contrasts, which had all but disappeared in most of his latter compositions, was revived here with new force: the merry pranks of Mercutio, the fun and laughter of the youthful Juliet, on the one hand, and the mortal combats between the hostile camps, the grief and despair of the doomed lovers, on the other.

Last, but not least, *Romeo and Juliet* saw the awakening of Prokofiev's old passion for the dance in its most diverse manifestations (the precipitate "Folk Dance" in the tarantella style, the crude rustic "Dance with Mandolins," the slow

graceful "Dance of the Young Antillean Girls," the stately old-
fashioned minuet); it is no accident that at the end of the second act the composer introduced his D-major Gavotte from
the *Classical Symphony*, in a slightly new version, as if to em-
phasize his deliberate return to his former neo-classical tendencies.[3]

From the point of view of drama, however, the ballet was
open to criticism. It lacked a broad symphonic development,
the same themes were rather mechanically shifted from one
scene to another, and in the last scenes there were practically
no new themes at all. All this may have been the result of certain abstract rationalistic tendencies that had appeared previously in the music of *L'Enfant prodigue* and other of Prokofiev's recent compositions for the stage.

Prokofiev's new opera, *Betrothal in a Convent*, is evidently
a continuation of the lyrical and romantic trend outlined in
the Violin Concerto and *Romeo and Juliet*. Here, as in the
latter ballet, tender love lyrics, the poetry of hidden passions,
and the bright dreams of youth are in the foreground, with the
gaiety of masquerade revels, and merry, good-natured buffoonery forming the contrast. Although the Sheridan text affords
rich material for musical satire and grotesque in the comical
old men — Don Jerome, the cantankerous father, and the fish
merchant Mendoza, Louisa's wealthy suitor, in the drunken
monks Father Chartreuse and Father Benedectine — and in
the wily Duenna, the composer has shifted the emphasis to
the lyrical episodes of the comedy, the story of the love of two
young couples, Antonio and Louisa and Ferdinand and Clara.
The very fact that Prokofiev has chosen the genre of lyrical
comedy, a genre untouched by opera since the days of Verdi's
Falstaff, is highly symptomatic.

No small part in his search for new simplicity and clarity of

---

[3] This leaning toward the dance runs all through Prokofiev's work, embracing a number of youthful pianoforte pieces (gavottes in Op. 12 and 32,
rigaudon, minuet, mazurka), the tarantella rhythms of the sinfonietta in the
First Concerto, Overture, Op. 42, the rude primitive dances in the *Andantino*
of the Fifth Sonata, the finale of the Second Violin Concerto, etc.

graphic outline was played by the composer's interest in music for children. Here an absolute clarity of musical thought was essential, for a juvenile audience will never accept anything forced and unnatural.

Prokofiev has also written a whole series of excellent pianoforte landscape sketches executed with amazing simplicity (Op. 65). After the abstract outlines of *Landscape*, Op. 59, the vibrant poetry of the calm Russian twilights and radiant summer mornings sounded a welcome new note in Prokofiev's music. His landscape is realistic almost to the point of tangibility (*Rain and Rainbow*). A similar concreteness of ideas and ability to depict nature with a keen and original pen are to be found also in the music of *Peter and the Wolf*, in which melodic ingenuity and clever character-portrayal are combined with true virtuosity in the use of tone color.

Romeo and Juliet, the Violin Concerto, and the children's music have proved beyond all shadow of doubt that Prokofiev has taken the path of reproducing living nature. Prokofiev painter and dramatist, the observer of life as it is, has unceremoniously ousted Prokofiev the unfathomable dreamer, the juggler with abstract sounds.

When speaking of the new instrumental trends in Prokofiev's work (a métier that now seems to have shifted to a secondary plane as compared with his work connected with the theater), mention must be made of his Sixth Pianoforte Sonata. Once again after the Second Violin Concerto the composer has built an elaborate symphonic form. After the subdued lyricism of *Romeo and Juliet* and the Violin Concerto the sonata seems to suggest that the biting fury and audacity of Prokofiev's talent has broken loose again. Its dramatic plan is complex and serious. The long first movement (*allegro*) is a tense dramatic narrative. The magnificent virile main theme is followed by a melancholy, songlike subordinate theme; in the intricate development both themes clash in a rising tempest of sound. In this music we recognize the full demoniacal power of Prokofiev's *feroce*. The two subsequent movements

16. Sixth Piano Sonata, 1st movement, main theme.

supply the lyrical relief after the fury of the *Allegro*: the second movement is in the spirit of a graceful, faintly ironic dance (akin to the gavottes and some of the dances in *Romeo and Juliet*), while the third movement, in slow waltz time, is a delightful nocturne that seems to be filled with the echoes of clandestine trysts and lovers' sighs. This last is similar to the lyrical passages of *Romeo and Juliet* and *Betrothal in a Convent*. And lastly, in the finale we meet again with pleasant surprise the familiar mischievous grin of the young Prokofiev, author of the Second Sonata, with his delightful pranks on the keyboard.[4] At the end of the sonata, however, the composer

---

[4] In this part the undoubted affinity between Prokofiev's images and the characteristic images of Shostakovich's pianoforte music is striking. For example, the G-sharp minor episode in the middle of the finale is extremely close to the main theme of the finale of Shostakovich's piano concerto; and vice versa, in the same finale of Shostakovich it is not diffcult to discover a connection in both image and pattern with Prokofiev's Second Sonata (Scherzo and finale).

returns to the initial material of the *Allegro*, treated in the form of serious reminiscence, thus completing the circle of development and achieving unity of statement.

The Sixth Sonata is one of the few monumental and philosophically profound works for the piano written in recent years. Such harshness as may occur in the writing (jarring contrapuntal effects and crude harmonic blotches pounded out *con pugno* in the development of the first movement; bold polytonal twists in the finale) is no longer an end in itself; it is clearly subordinated to the aims of artistic expression. Of interest also are the fragments of Russian national melody in a number of themes (subordinate themes in the second movement and finale). In both cases the Russian melodies are active and exuberant rather than feebly contemplative.

After the self-imposed asceticism of Prokofiev's later piano pieces the new sonata marked a revival of his characteristic full-blooded, flexible, and technically bold piano style. He resorted to a vast number of technical devices in this sonata — complicated skips in the manner of Scarlatti (used also in the Fifth Concerto), intricate finger technique (finale), and rich, meaty chords with dense figuration (third movement).

Along with the revival of theatrical and virtuoso tendencies in Prokofiev's music, the Russian national influences began to make themselves felt more and more strongly. It was not until he became conscious of himself as a Russian artist singing of the living nature and the living people of his own country that he was fully at home in his Soviet environment: the pragmatic cosmopolitanism of the foreign period had obviously had a stultifying effect on his talent.

Russian melodic idiom found expression in his first piece of music written in the Soviet Union: *Lieutenant Kije*. It occurs both in the plaintive theme of Kije, which forms the framework of the entire suite, and in the ironic stylization of the old-fashioned, "heart-rending" love-song (*The Little Blue Dove is Cooing*).

Evidence of Prokofiev's search for an original Russian style that would not be a passive imitation of the Five can be found in many mass songs to Soviet texts and in the children's music (*Evening, The Moon Goes over the Meadows*). The composer here creates original melodies in the national spirit, at times deliberately stressing his refusal to borrow. For example, he wrote an entirely new melody for Shevchenko's *Commandments*, for the Ukrainian song *All Is Ahum and Abuzz* in *Semyon Kotko*, and for the "cooing dove" song in *Lieutenant Kije*. On the other hand, however, he has increasing recourse to folklore sources, poring over volumes of Russian and Ukrainian songs before sitting down to write any music associated with national themes, and a few folklore quotations are bound to occur, especially in works like *Semyon Kotko* (central episode in Frosya's song, second theme in the wedding chorus), or the *Russian Overture*, Op. 72 (two dance melodies in the main theme).

The most eloquent testimony to Prokofiev's national aspirations was his *Russian Overture*, which is full of the healthy spirit of folk dances. In this kaleidoscope of dynamic Russian melodies, in this dizzy whirl of popular merry-making, there is something reminiscent of the decorative canvases of Malyavin, with their passionate dynamics and crude splashes of color. Extremely simple in structure (in the form of a rondo sonata), the overture, like its classical "ancestor," Glinka's *Kamarinskaya*, is built up on the simplest juxtaposition of Russian dance images and broad Russian song melodies, without any elements of drama or complicated development. True, the composer was unable to resist the temptation to indulge in a few eccentricities. The strident thunderous bellow of the brasses, for instance, which breaks now and again through the dashing movement of the dance, gives the impression of a somewhat superfluous and belated illustration of Russian bigheartedness. But the author is readily forgiven these few excesses for the gay, virile energy of the dance themes and the exuberant melodiousness of the subordinate theme in B-flat major. In this, the best theme in the overture, one hears echoes of the broad, rolling Russian peasant-girl songs like *I Was at a Feast.*[5]

If the *Russian Overture* might be called the apotheosis of the Russian dance, in *Zdravitsa* Prokofiev strove to embody the elements of Russian choral singing. The new Soviet folk-songs that form the basis of this little folk cantata demanded a maximum clarity of musical style: *Zdravitsa* is a cycle of

17. *Zdravitsa.*

choral songs merged in one rondo-like pattern. The lyrical features (*Lullaby, Song of the Old Woman* who dreams of meeting Stalin [6]) give way to episodes of landscape depiction

---

[5] Three years later another splendid sample of this type of melody was the "Farewell" episode in the cantata *Zdravitsa* (song about the shock-worker Aksinya going off to a reception in the Kremlin).

[6] The text for this episode was taken from words composed by Marfa Osyk, an aged Mari collective farmer woman:

or narrative ("Farewell") or to solemn dance tunes in the spirit of the festive choruses in Russian opera. Apart from the theme of the "Farewell," one of the finest musical images in the cantata is to be found in its principal refrain: the flowing C-major air is full of a noble optimism and an inexpressible melodic charm; the extreme simplicity of harmony and general clarity of the refrain, combined with the extremely intricate inner coloring of the C major with its various related triads, is noteworthy. *Zdravitsa* has been justly appraised as one of the best Soviet compositions singing of the love of the people for Stalin.

Prokofiev's two major works in the past years, the *Alexander Nevsky* cantata and the opera *Semyon Kotko*, are a synthesis of both trends of the Soviet period of his work: the theatrical and descriptive trend, which acquired tremendous force in these two compositions, and the national trend, likewise developed here in full measure. Both these works at the same time revealed an amazing foresight on the part of the artist. Long before the Germans attacked the U.S.S.R., and even before the war in Europe, he wrote two compositions permeated through and through with fierce hatred for German barbarism. The Teutonic knights in *Alexander Nevsky* who trample the Russian wheatfields and put Russian towns to fire and sword and the repulsive faces of the German invaders who plunder and lay waste flourishing Ukrainian villages in *Semyon Kotko* are all reproduced as graphically and convincingly as if the author had already personally witnessed the horrors of German fascist atrocities. There is no doubt that future generations will regard these works as the most striking musical chronicle of the sanguinary events that were later to take place during the Soviet-German war.

In *Alexander Nevsky* the composer wrote on a major patriotic theme for the first time in his life, bringing to it all the

> If my eyes sparkled as when I was a girl,
> If my cheeks were as red as an apple ripe,
> I would hie me to Moscow, the great city,
> And say "Thank you" to Joseph Stalin.

resources of his musical palette. Notwithstanding the historical nature of the theme, the cantata had a direct, topical appeal for Soviet Russia: it was a clarion call to self-sacrificing
defense of the homeland. Hearing *Alexander Nevsky* for the
first time, one could not but recall the weighty words uttered
by Igor Glebov so many years before with regard to the *Scythian Suite*. "It seems to me," he wrote in 1916, "that the impression first produced by the music of Borodin, with his
striking individuality, his mighty and savage impetuosity filled
with the aroma of the broad and rolling steppes, must have
been similar or equivalent to that which we now received when
listening to Prokofiev's music."

What Glebov felt at that time in the thunderous peals of
Ala and Lolli — the powerful perception of life and nature,
à la Borodin — sounded with new force in *Alexander Nevsky*.
As in the *Scythian Suite*, Prokofiev here is a brilliant landscape-
painter, the superb master of sound color. The Russian landscape forms the background of almost all the scenes in this
historical tragedy: the bleak panorama of pillaged and ravaged
Russia in the first movement; the mist of the early morning
frosts done in the style of a Surikov painting at the beginning
of the "Battle on the Ice," and the gloomy nocturnal tones of
the "Field of the Dead" scene. Against the background of this
tangible Russian landscape arise fearsome, semi-fantastic
sound pictures reminiscent of the nightmares of Goya and
Matthias Grünewald or medieval Catholic frescoes ("Crusaders in Pskov"). It is a long time since such powerful and convincing symphonic battle scenes as that of the "Battle on the
Ice," giving an almost visual portrayal of the historic episode,
have been written.

Two sharply contrasting styles are presented in the cantata:
on the one hand, there are the inhuman and barbarous themes
of the German invaders, repulsive in their hideous bestiality,
and, on the other, themes of the Russian people, now manly
and brave, now sorrowful and stern. These two ranges of images
give rise to two different styles of sound expression: complex

polytonal constructions, harsh, repellent harmonies, ugly, distorted melodies, heavy and strident instrumentation to characterize the crusaders, and Russian national melodies in clear and sober diatonic style for the depiction of the Russian warriors.[7] Prokofiev's favorite guignol, familiar to us from the music of his early piano pieces and *The Flaming Angel*, acquires in this work not only a vivid concrete shape but also a definite purpose. The horror and ugliness embodied in the repulsive images of the Livonian knights personify the bestial face of the warmongers of the present day.

Prokofiev's fine feeling for style derived from his early World of Art experiences — the ability to reproduce in his own mind images of remote antiquity without resorting to static museum forms — here stood him in good stead. The composer tells us that, when working on the depiction of the crusaders, he endeavored to study authentic Catholic hymns of the Middle Ages. But "this music was so far removed from us that it could not possibly be used. There is no doubt that the crusaders sang it with a warlike frenzy as they marched into battle; nevertheless to the modern ear it sounded too cold and indifferent. I was therefore obliged to discard it and compose for the crusaders music more suited to the modern conception" (*Pioneer*, No. 7, 1939).

And listening to the austere Catholic chorales sung by Prokofiev's crusaders, or to their menacing battle-cries, one feels that the music of the distant Middle Ages must indeed have sounded thus. While the impressive guignol scenes of the cantata ("Crusaders in Pskov," "Battle on the Ice") represented a continuation of the favorite tendencies of the early Prokofiev, the chorus episodes ("It Happened on the Neva River," "Arise, Men of Russia") gave evidence of his new quest for images

---

[7] A similar juxtaposition of two different styles (new harmonic combinations for the fantastic scenes and the ordinary major and minor for the realistic episodes) is quite frequently to be met with in nineteenth-century Russian opera (Glinka, Rimsky-Korsakov). In Prokofiev's opera music we find such contrasts as well (the world of realistic characters and the world of fantasy represented in *The Love for Three Oranges*; contrasting of lyricism and guignol in *Semyon Kotko.*

to depict the grandeur and nobility of the warrior patriots, the whole world of Russian melody embodying the heroic aspirations of the Russian people. Perhaps for the first time the composer has created broad full-blooded cantilena melodies instead of recitative music. Every passage in these songs betrays its Russian origin (specific contrasting of major and relative minor, stressed plagal cadences, the use of the seventh and third chords, and other traditional effects of the Russian school). Yet in spite of the familiar qualities of the music, the composer nevertheless succeeded with a few bold strokes in imbuing it with his own individual manner (for example, the unusual harmonic relationship between the various parts: E-flat major and B major, and E-flat major and G major in the chorus "Arise, Men of Russia").

The mastery displayed by Prokofiev in *Alexander Nevsky* deserves detailed study. The multiformity of his orchestral resources, from the subtlest impressionism of the water-color painter to the crude fresco daubs of the stage decorator, is truly amazing, as are also his bold contrapuntal dual-plane methods, by which striking cinematographic effects are transferred to the realm of symphonic music. One of many examples is the simultaneous sounding of the triumphant theme of the Russian horsemen and the distorted theme depicting the route of the Livonian knights in the "Battle on the Ice." The very genre (vocal and symphonic) of the piece, combining in one canvas broad descriptive passages with choruses of a general type and arias in the manner of opera (No. 6, "Girl's Song"), is both novel and unusual. All the more gratifying is the strong unity of form reminiscent in essence of a large sonata construction.[8] The only point on which the author has been reproached was his purely cinematographic montage of musical stills in certain parts of the cantata ("Battle on the Ice"), together with some naturalistic exaggerations in the battle episodes.

---

[8] First movement, introduction; the following three parts, exposition of the main themes; "Battle on the Ice," a tremendous development group; sixth and seventh parts, recapitulation built primarily on the main themes.

In spite of its complex construction and bold harmonic, orchestral, and polyphonic effects, *Alexander Nevsky* is entirely comprehensible to the general public. This is evidenced by the inclusion in the repertory of the Red Army Song and Dance Ensemble of the first chorus, while an arrangement of the second chorus is played by Red Army military bands. The chorus "Arise, Men of Russia," became especially popular during the war and is frequently included in radio programs along with other popular favorites.

The advent of this music has given every ground for assuming that the great Russian classic tradition, the heroic and epic traditions of Glinka, Borodin, and Rimsky-Korsakov, have reawakened in Prokofiev's music.

The opera *Semyon Kotko* was fraught with much greater difficulties for the composer than *Alexander Nevsky*. In the first place, this was Prokofiev's first attempt at a major contemporary theme depicting the heroics of the Revolutionary struggle: the plot is based on the Civil War in the Ukraine. Secondly, there was the inherent difficulty of operatic style arising from Prokofiev's attitude to opera. To many it seemed that the very task of writing an opera on a Revolutionary theme would be altogether beyond Prokofiev's powers inasmuch as he had had no practical knowledge or personal experience of the Revolution and the Civil War.

Indeed, his numerous attempts at contemporary themes had revealed the more vulnerable aspects of Prokofiev's style, those which might be called the birthmarks of modernism — the cold artificiality, eccentric leaps, *brusqueries* not always justified by the content, and, in some cases, an unnecessary aloofness and indifference to the theme. This regrettable discrepancy between the inception of the music and its means of expression had made itself most strongly felt in the greater part of *Songs of Our Days*, and particularly in the popular songs, Op. 79. At times one felt here the cold composure of the master who has not perceived the inner essence of the image he seeks to portray. In such cases it was obvious that the burden of the past, the force of tradition and habit inculcated in modernist and Western musical circles, still shackled and stifled the artist's living muse.

Fortunately, these birthmarks of Prokofiev's modernist past are affecting his latest works to an ever lesser degree.

Another serious apprehension that was felt after the first hearing of *Semyon Kotko* had a bearing on the very approach of the composer to opera in general. When he composed *The Gambler* many years ago, Prokofiev emerged as a strong opponent of the traditional operatic forms: the beautiful but static opera arias and choruses, poetical texts, all manner of conventions governing the action, were all cast aside as so much useless rubbish. Opera, he maintained, should above all be active, flexible, and absorbing. The composer was primarily interested at that time in the movement and tempo of the development and in keen character portrayal.

"Of late," he had maintained, "we have witnessed in Russian operas a decline of interest on the part of the composer in the stage aspect of opera, with the result that opera has become static, filled with a host of boring conventions. . . . In my opinion, the custom of writing operas to rhymed texts is an utterly absurd convention. The prose of Dostoyevsky is more vivid, striking, and convincing than any poetry." The composer went on to announce his rejection in principle of the conventional opera chorus, "since the chorus is neither flexible nor scenic" (*Vecherniye Birzheviye Vedomosti*, May 12, 1916).

Modern opera, Prokofiev argued, should reflect the speed and business-like pace of modern city life. "A hundred to a hundred and fifty years ago our ancestors enjoyed gay pastorales and the music of Mozart and Rameau; last century they admired slow, serious music; in our day, in music as in everything else, it is speed, energy, and push that are preferred" (Riga newspaper *Segodnya*, January 1927).

Prokofiev's opera principles, which had taken their most concrete shape in *The Gambler*, were at that time to a certain extent progressive, for they were directed mainly against the tinsel trappings and fossilized methods of the imperial grand opera. The young Prokofiev continued the opera tradition of Mussorgsky, exaggerating and emphasizing the methods outlined in the latter's *Marriage*. But these experiments of the young composer undoubtedly contained the seeds of an arbitrary rejection of the very essence of opera, for to condemn all operatic conventionality, to reduce operatic action to endless musical prose with no songs or complete melodies, would be to undermine the very foundations of operatic art. Later, in the twenties, this same tendency, extensively represented in the new urbanistic opera of the West, actually did lead operatic art to an impasse.

When he sat down to write a new opera in 1939, after an interval of twelve years since *The Flaming Angel*, Prokofiev was still burdened by these former principles. And whereas in *The Gambler* a demonstrative rejection of operatic conventionality was to a certain extent justified, in the Soviet opera conceived on the plane of national musical drama this nihilism could only have played a negative role.

What, then, are the contradictions that were revealed in *Semyon Kotko*? On the one hand, the opera marked a definite approach on the composer's part to the realistic portrayal of life, to modern topical themes. Again, as in *Romeo and Juliet*, a gallery of living human portraits arose before the listener, drawn with an inimitable, individual touch. It is worthy of note that the more successful of these were images that were brutal and ugly (Tkachenko the kulak, the Germans) or tensely expressive (the mad Lyuba), or gay, carefree, mischievous (Frosya, Mikola, Tsarev) — that is, the types in which Prokofiev had always excelled. In the macabre, tragic scenes (Act III, scenes of the fire and execution, Act IV, funeral scene) and, on the other hand, in the merry, semi-ironic episodes (beginning of Act I) we recognize the favorite Prokofiev images in a new setting. *Semyon Kotko*, however, brought out new qualities in Prokofiev's music as well. First, there is the poetic world of love lyrics, more real than in *Romeo and Juliet* (unforgettable scene of the nocturnal idyll at the beginning of Act III, the tryst of Semyon and Sophia in Act I, etc.). Second, there is the Ukrainian national coloring, conveyed in an ex-

18. *Semyon Kotko*, Introduction to Act III.

tremely original, if perhaps disputable, manner in the choral episodes (wedding chorus in Act II, *Commandments*) and some solo character portraits (Tkachenko, Semyon, and Frosya). Extremely interesting is Prokofiev's technique of musical dramaturgy: complex and imposing leitmotiv development, pointed, natural declamatory effects, laconic and poster-like directness of symphonic characterization. As for the leading idea of the opera, mention should be made of the exceptional power and dramatic force of the episodes depicting the brutality of the German invaders; these episodes evoke a fierce hatred for the enemy in the manner of the best specimens of revolutionary satire.

An important defect of the opera is the inadequacy of positive characters to counteract the world of violence and oppression. Neither Semyon Kotko nor the Bolshevik Remenyuk have the resolution and selfless heroism of true revolutionary fighters. In this respect a good measure of the blame is due to the libretto, whose author (Valentin Katayev) has laid too much emphasis on prosaic, mundane details and failed to rise to the heights of lofty generalization. The unwarranted intrusion of local slang and the abundance of naturalistic detail diverted the composer's attention away from the need to romanticize the basic images and situations of the opera. The fine melodic seeds scattered generously throughout the score almost never develop into full aria forms. All this makes the opera difficult for the average listener to follow, and inevitably lowers it to the level of a commonplace prosaic presentation. The views on opera propounded by Prokofiev as far back as *The Gambler* made themselves felt in all this.

It is gratifying to note, however, that in his subsequent work for the musical theater Prokofiev is endeavoring to overcome his modernist principles. His opera *Betrothal in a Convent* contains a number of rounded-out vocal numbers (arias, ariettas, duets, a quintet with chorus, etc.). A similar reversion to the finished classical forms, the use of traditional variations, *adagios*, *grands pas*, etc., is also to be observed in his ballet *Cinderella*.

The above criticism of *Semyon Kotko* is by no means intended to minimize the excellent artistic qualities of the opera, its inner poetic wealth and superlative skill in the development of expressive musical detail. This is not merely an important landmark in Prokofiev's career; it is to a no lesser degree a substantial step forward in the development of Soviet opera in general.

11 : The War Years

And Legend marches in step with him. She grows
And ever walks beside him, singing and beating
the earth with her gun-stock.
Her glance is no longer childlike as she speeds the
avenger forward.

ANTOKOLSKY: *Ballad of the Unknown Boy*

IN THE summer of 1942 Prokofiev changed his residence from Tbilisi to Alma-Ata, the capital of Kazakhstan, whither the production base of the Soviet film industry had been evacuated from Moscow. There Sergei Eisenstein, the admirer and friend with whom Prokofiev had worked so harmoniously on *Alexander Nevsky*, invited him to work with him on his new film, *Ivan the Terrible*. Parallel with the preparation of this score, Prokofiev wrote music for three other films in production at the Alma-Ata and Stalinabad studios: *Lermontov, Tonya, Kotovsky*. Worth particular remark in the *Lermontov* score are several period dances, which were later included in piano arrangement in a collection of piano pieces, Op. 96. There are interesting bitter musical caricatures of German militarists in the scores of *Tonya* and *Kotovsky*.

This film work did not upset Prokofiev's basic creative plans. During the summer of 1942 he completed the piano score of *War and Peace* and worked on the orchestration of the opera. New chamber works were composed: the Seventh Piano Sonata, Op. 83, begun two and a half years earlier and completed in May 1942 in Tbilisi; [1] a Sonata in four movements for flute and piano (D major, Op. 94); two series of new piano pieces, Op. 95 and 96. And Prokofiev finished the sketches for *The Ballad of the Unknown Boy*.

The *Ballad* was based on the anti-fascist verses of the Soviet

---

[1] This sonata is in three movements: first, in a rather impetuous tempo (*allegro inquieto*), second, a lyrical *Andante*, alternately tender and tense, and a finale, rhythmically whimsical (in $\frac{7}{8}$ time).

poet P. Antokolsky, which Prokofiev used for the creation of a sharply dramatic vocal narrative directed against German barbarism. The hero of the ballad, "a merry boy in a gray cap," apparently attracted the composer by something more than chance: boyish images, naïve and teasing, had interested Prokofiev for a long time, in instrumental music, opera, and ballet. But this time the fascinating child character, a close relative to Peter of the well-known symphonic fairy-tale, is lifted into an entirely different atmosphere, a mood of engrossing tragedy.

Spreading death and horror as they come, the German invaders enter a small town. They shoot the mother and sisters of our "unknown boy." The young hero takes a fierce revenge, throwing a grenade into a staff car, blowing to bits the fascist generals in it. The *Ballad* is written in Prokofiev's characteristic manner of free declamation, and is scored for dramatic soprano, dramatic tenor, chorus, and full symphony.

After an absence of one and a half years Prokofiev returned in December 1942 to Moscow, where he introduced his most important works composed in the south: the piano score of *War and Peace* and the Seventh Sonata.

The year 1943 opened for Prokofiev with deserved success. The new Seventh Sonata was splendidly performed by the young pianist Svyatoslav Richter, and this most "Left" of all his sonatas was, unexpectedly for many, enthusiastically received. And in March 1943 the work brought to its composer the highest award to which a Soviet artist may aspire — the Stalin prize. They were correct who sensed in the tempestuous, precipitate rhythms of the first movement, in its menacing "percussive" harmonies, in the Cyclopean might of its finale — music of gigantic, thundering tension, as if overturning everything in its path — a reflection of the shattering events endured by the Soviet Union in these years. The sonata has no program, but the storms of the war years are surely reflected in its general emotional tonality.[2] For a brief moment at the

---

[2] Felix Borowski, the music critic of the *Chicago Sun*, wrote very convincingly on the ideological connection between the Seventh Sonata and the

beginning of the second movement the nervous dynamics give way to the charm of a love-lyrical minuet theme. But soon this oasis of pure lyricism is engulfed by the steely pressure of the B-flat major finale, courageously uniting in itself the Russian monumentalism of Borodin with sharp modern "machine" rhythms.

The prevailing interest of the composer, however, was still in the theater rather than in instrumental music. In the summer of 1943 Prokofiev temporarily interrupted his work on *Ivan the Terrible* in Alma-Ata in order to visit the city of Molotov, in the Urals, whither the Leningrad Kirov Theater of Opera and Ballet [3] had been evacuated at the beginning of the war. This best of all Soviet ballet troupes, with which Prokofiev had prepared the first production of his *Romeo and Juliet*, had encouraged him to complete the ballet *Cinderella*, on which he had been working when war came. Now, in close contact with K. Sergeyev, the choreographer, and N. Volkov, the librettist, Prokofiev enthusiastically completed the ballet, the three creators discussing each detail of music and staging, thus guaranteeing an inseparable linking of the elements of music and drama.

In addition to the Seventh Sonata 1943 also heard other new works by Prokofiev, such as the new Flute Sonata in D major, Op. 94.[4] After the stark and furious images of the Seventh Sonata, the Second Quartet, and *The Ballad of the Unknown Boy*, Prokofiev was obliged to find an outlet for the pure lyrical feeling that had accumulated in him. He had experienced such lyrical intervals before: the *Classical Symphony* and *Fugitive Visions* had followed *The Gambler*; *The Prodigal Son* and the Fourth Symphony had followed the Second Sym-

---

war: "Something in the inexorable rhythm of the finale also gives a suggestion of the heroic inflexibility of a people who are not to know defeat."

[3] The former Imperial Maryinsky Theater. It was at this theater that Prokofiev's two most important theatrical works had been staged: *The Love for Three Oranges* in 1927, the ballet *Romeo and Juliet* in 1940.

[4] A later version of this sonata, arranged for violin and piano, was performed with success by David Oistrakh in Moscow by Josef Szigeti in New York.

phony and *The Flaming Angel*. The direct charm of the classic line, the original Russian Mozartism within a strictly modern concept, colored with characteristic Prokofievian irony — as in the *Sinfonietta* and the *Classical Symphony* — all this again appeared in the elegant and fragile piece for flute. The transparent "white" color of the flute, used so often by Prokofiev to paint lyrical feminine themes and images, suited perfectly the gentle, half-childlike lyricism of this sonata, with its rather toylike Scherzo (the second movement), and the playful dancing finale.

Along with his completion of *Cinderella*, Prokofiev also finished his orchestration of *War and Peace* and prepared the piano score for lithographic printing in two volumes by the Music Foundation of the U.S.S.R. These publishers also issued the piano score of *Betrothal in a Convent* as well as a collection of piano pieces — transcriptions from *Cinderella* and separate choruses and arias from *War and Peace*.

In the fall of 1943, because of the Red Army's advance toward the West, the majority of the evacuated musical institutions as well as the entire mass of Moscow musicians, returned to the capital according to plan. Liberated from dangerous proximity to the front, Moscow resumed its busy artistic life. Prokofiev returned in October, and the concert seasons of 1943–4 and especially that of 1944–5 gave prominent place to his symphonic and chamber compositions. Thus, in February 1944 his *Ballad* was given its first performance, with the participation of soloists from the Bolshoi Opera, N. Schpiller and F. Fedotov, the Leningrad Cappella Chorus, and the State Symphonic Orchestra of the U.S.S.R. under the leadership of Alexander Gauk.

The slightly cumbersome and over-kaleidoscopic music of the cantata, unsupported by clear, memorable melody and repetitions, did not produce a very great effect. And old tendency of Prokofiev's had reappeared. Several times before in his vocal music the chorus and singers had been disproportionately overweighed by the textual material, usually a heavy and unmelodious narrative forcing the music to struggle in order to keep up with it, without ever revealing its significance.[5] The cantata composed on the occasion of the twentieth anniversary of the October Revolution had suffered in the same way, never achieving its purpose because of clumsiness, melodic sogginess, and abundance of prosaic detail.

Meeting at the end of March 1944 in Moscow, the organizing committee of the Composers' Union took the form of an All-Union Congress of Soviet Composers, at which a special report was presented on the work of Sergei Prokofiev during the war years. Prokofiev himself made an important address at one of the plenary sessions, calling his fellow workers in art to improve their craftsmanship.

In 1944 Prokofiev was again honored by the Soviet Government. Along with a group of other prominent musicians of the older generation — Miaskovsky, Vassilenko, Anatoli Alexandrov — Prokofiev was awarded the order of the Red Banner of Labor for outstanding services in the development of Soviet music. At the same time the title of Honorary Worker in Art was bestowed on him.

After a year's interruption Prokofiev returned with great enthusiasm to the score of Eisenstein's *Ivan the Terrible,* Part I of which was approaching completion in the Mosfilm studios. In the international history of the art of the sound film there is no closer creative friendship between director and composer than that between Eisenstein and Prokofiev. The two artists discussed each sequence of the film before the musical passage was written and the sequence finally edited. Prokofiev was thrilled by Eisenstein's temperament and taste and by his graphic skill in directly or paradoxically formulating his

---

[5] The *Ballad* was given a critical evaluation by Shostakovich in his report to the organization committee of the Union of Soviet Composers on March 28, 1944: "In the *Ballad* the music is deprived of a solid, constructive base. I sense it as a series of separate, unconnected musical cadres. To me it seems impossible to create a work of the largest dimensions by a method of this sort." (Printed in *Literatura i Iskusstvo,* April 1, 1944.)

"orders" to the composer: "At this point the music must sound like a mother tearing her own child to pieces," or "Do it so that it sounds like a cork rubbed down a pane of glass." [6] In his turn Eisenstein more than once listened profitably to the keen comments of Prokofiev.

The historical film about Ivan the Terrible had to upset the traditional portrayals of this Moscow monarch — contemporary of Elizabeth of England and Philip II of Spain — in order to find the real man behind the former simplified representation of him as a raging, bloody despot. In the new film the authors aimed to show Ivan the Terrible as a courageous unifier of the Russian state and as a clever warrior who made his empire's power firm despite the personal greed of the reactionary boyars. A grandiose epic in three parts was planned, the first to be completed in the fall of 1944. As in *Alexander Nevsky*, the music was to occupy the role of an active participant in the drama, and was not only to accompany the more important episodes in the film, but also to fill it with a parallel, developing action of emotional sound.

One of the most fruitful periods in the creative work of Prokofiev was the summer of 1944, which he spent in the composers' rest-home at a picturesque Russian village near Ivanovo. He composed during this summer two monumental instrumental works: his Eighth Piano Sonata and his Fifth Symphony, Op. 100.

This Ivanovo rest-home, given by the government to the Composers' Union, made it possible in the difficult years of the war for composers to live at the expense of the government in the conditions of a first-class *pension* and to create without the disturbing cares of city life in war-time. During the summer of 1944 Prokofiev, Shostakovich, Miaskovsky, Khachaturian, and Kabalevsky lived and worked there, rivaling each other in creative productivity. During two months

---

[6] Prokofiev quoted these remarks in his article "My Work on the Film *Ivan the Terrible*" in VOKS *Musical Chronicle*, October 1944.

were born the most brilliant new musical works of the following season: the Second Quartet and Piano Trio by Shostakovich, the Eighth Sonata and Fifth Symphony by Prokofiev.

The Eighth Sonata is the third in the group of three sonatas begun as early as 1939. Thus the work on this cycle of
sonatas, Op. 82, 83, 84, had been stretched over a period of
five years, to flower in a display of Prokofiev's monumental
pianism. The novelty and unusual freshness of thematic material, combined with the sparkle and technical complexity of
the piano medium, again, as in the Seventh Sonata, amazed its
auditors. If the most impressive movement of the Seventh
Sonata was its tempestuously rushing finale in 7/8, then the
real surprise in the Eighth was the soothing theme of the first
movement (*andante dolce*), music that reveals shining bal-
ance and quiet wisdom. This sonata immediately interested
the young virtuoso Emil Hillels, famous for his victories in the
international piano contests in Vienna and Brussels, and the
Eighth Sonata was triumphantly introduced by him in his
concert of September 29, 1944.

During that autumn musical Moscow was also introduced
to the *War and Peace*, performed in excerpts with piano accompaniment by the opera ensemble of the All-Russian Theatrical Association in October. Somewhat later these excerpts
were performed with the State Symphonic Orchestra, conducted by Samuel Samosud. Controversial moments of the
opera, even before its full theatrical presentation, aroused critical comment in the Soviet press; for example, Visarion Shebhalin, director of the Moscow Conservatory, wrote a severe
article in *Literatura i Iskusstvo* (October 1944). This has been
the fate of most of Prokofiev's theatrical works: their appearance inevitably arouses keen disputes and discussions of the
most cardinal points of musical dramaturgy.

The season of 1944–5 brought one more important victory
to Prokofiev: his artistic adaptation of ten Russian folk-songs,
collected originally by the distinguished folk-lorist Yevgeni
Hippius. The best of these concert arrangements — *Fly, Hazel-*

berry, and *The Green Grove* (for solo voice and piano) — received the first and second prizes at the song contest of the All-Russian Concert Tour Association.[7]

In January 1945 Prokofiev's name twice claimed the full attention of Soviet musical circles: his Fifth Symphony was given its *première* at the composer's concert on January 13, 1945 in the Grand Hall of the Moscow Conservatory; *Ivan the Terrible* (Part I) was released throughout the Union.

The performance of the Fifth Symphony had special significance: as Prokofiev's Opus 100, it was a sort of jubilee composition in his career. The idea of the symphony had long been ripening in the consciousness of the composer, filling his notebooks with its accumulating themes. The new symphony had also a doctrinal function: it had to refute the idea that the medium of pure philosophic symphonism is alien to Prokofiev. It is true that much of his symphonic work had been born of theatrical images (the *Scythian Suite,* the Third and Fourth Symphonies, the *Alexander Nevsky* cantata, the suites from *Romeo and Juliet, The Buffoon,* and *Lieutenant Kije*) or had been determined by descriptive or stylized motives. Now Prokofiev for the first time declared his right to evolve a symphonic concept that had not been forged in pictorially descriptive problems. According to the unanimous opinion of musicians, he achieved his aim. The fifth Symphony was pronounced not only a genuine Prokofiev symphony, fully comprehending the philosophic purpose of the medium, but also one of the most important phenomena of twentieth-century Russian symphonism. Approaching in manner the objective epic symphonism of the Borodin-Glazunov line rather than the lyrical dramatic symphonism of Tchaikovsky and Shostakovich, it captured the auditors with its healthy mood of affirmation. In the heroic, manly images of the first movement, in the holiday jubilation of the finale, the auditors sensed a living transmutation of that popular emotional surge, of that bright faith in a joyous fu-

---

[7] Earlier, in May 1944, Prokofiev had arranged and orchestrated an English folk-song, *Oh, No, John!*

ture, which we felt in those days of victories over Nazi Germany. A detail: at the moment when the first chords of the symphony sounded in the Grand Hall of the Conservatory, we also heard the powerful cannon saluting the heroes of the crossing of the Vistula. This coincidence seemed a striking symbol of the topical social significance of Prokofiev's new composition.

No less contemporary were the musical images of *Ivan the Terrible*: themes of supreme Russian valor (episode of the siege of Kazan), themes of firm Russian statesmanship (the Overture), the virile and impulsive people's choruses (especially the splendid chorus of Gunners). The bright pictorial quality, the graphic perception, the almost material tangibility of separate episodes, as in *Alexander Nevsky*, were amazing: the heavily crawling passages for trumpets and tympani for the transport of the Tsar's cannon; or the musical portrayal of the tortures of the captured Tatars (with shrieking *fioriture* of screaming brass and harsh rolls of the percussion). However, the central place in the music is taken by the profoundly human, many-sided image of Ivan, his youthful love (the wedding choruses), his maturing wisdom, and the nervously tragic ecstasy of his agony (unforgettable sobs of the celli, capturing the very reality of straining human grief). For the first time in his life Prokofiev had turned seriously toward the ecclesiastical music of ancient Russia, re-creating, in a series of church choruses, the triumphant exultation and funeral ceremonies of the Orthodox Church.

After the completion of all three parts of *Ivan the Terrible*, Prokofiev will undoubtedly reshape its music into a vocal symphonic work — or perhaps into an opera.

Prokofiev's capacity for creative work appears unlimited. While these lines are being written the composer is working on a new Violin Sonata, Op. 80 (originally sketched in 1939), he is developing sketches for a Sixth Symphony and a Ninth Piano Sonata (the latter having been outlined in the summer of 1944), and he is revising the score of his Fourth Symphony.

Waiting in line also is a new comic opera, of life in Kazakh-stan, but the composer intends to turn to it only after his several recent theatrical works have been produced.

What are the new features of Prokofiev's works in the 1940's — these years of world-shaking military events? It cannot be said that the war lessened his energy; on the contrary, it seems to have intensified his creative impetus. More than a dozen new opus numbers in less than four years — including a monumental opera, a symphony, three sonatas, the major part of a ballet, a quartet, a cantata, several songs, marches and piano pieces, music for four films — this is sufficient evidence of Prokofiev's amazingly prolific skill during the war years. The patriotic surge of all Soviet people during this period inevitably sharpened the composer's own patriotic and social tendency. Thus, after *Alexander Nevsky*, there rise huge musical canvases of Russian history — *War and Peace, Ivan the Terrible* — glorifying the valor and invincibility of the people. Thus also are born more urgent, timely works, musical posters directly reflecting the theme of the patriotic war — the suite *1941*, songs, *The Ballad of the Unknown Boy*. Alongside Prokofiev's predilection for the acid and the picturesque, there has been a search in his music for a positive social hero — missing in his previous compositions, particularly in those of his youth. Now we have Kutuzov, Ivan the Terrible, the leading images of the Fifth Symphony, the fighting, grieving, angry, and joyful people in the mass scenes of *War and Peace*. This circumstance has increased the role of the chorus in Prokofiev's music; the chorus now functions as a living, active, human collective, as a bearer of the people's song.

The 1940's also display a new rise in the theatrical development of Prokofiev's talent. This can be seen in three scores, all of great interest, and each totally different from the others: *Betrothal in a Convent* (which appeared on the very eve of war), *Cinderella*, and *War and Peace*. Studying these works, one notes a new enrichment of thematic material in Prokofiev's music for opera and ballet, as well as the marked growth

173

of a specific gravity of melody, as an organizing, image-forming element. After the uncompromising declamatory flow of *The Gambler*, after the broken and kaleidoscopic quality of *The Love for Three Oranges*, one senses a tendency in these latest operas toward rounded, singing melodic constructions, toward frank ariosos and ensembles, toward a more living and natural song in general. This tendency is more noticeable in *Betrothal* than in *War and Peace*. A comparable process is shown in *Cinderella* as well: moving away from continuous pantomime toward classically rounded ballet numbers. This naturally does not indicate a mechanical return to the doctrinal routine of academic opera, in the denial of which Prokofiev strengthened his dramatic talent, showing his powerful qualities as an innovator: flexibility and freedom of form, living impulsive tempos, acute and unexpectedly contrasting juxtapositions — these are still the specifics of his dramatic style.

We consider the sparkling *Duenna*, by Richard Brinsley Sheridan, given modern musical life by Prokofiev, as the most vital of his operatic creations. *Betrothal in a Convent* has the least of those nihilistic twists peculiar to the composer's previous operas, but has, instead, firmly constructed comedy intrigue and witty character portraits, all fruitful soil for natural musical expression. The Soviet theater audience, surrounded as it is by new interpretations of the classic comedies of the seventeenth and eighteenth centuries — the comedies of Shakespeare, Lope de Vega, Beaumarchais, Sheridan, and Goldoni — would not find a Sheridan-Prokofiev work in the least out of place. Without making any major change in the original text and lyrics, Prokofiev created a true modern *opera buffa*. In each of the opera's nine scenes there is a dominant, clear musical image or a chain of images. These are more or less broad ariosos for the leading figures, or polished opera ensembles (such as the beautiful quartet at the end of Scene v and the love-duet in Scene ii), or music functioning as a backdrop of sound (the carnival dances and choruses in Scenes i and and ix, the chorus of women venders in Scene iii, the minuet in the music-making episode of Scene vi). These rounded constructions are usually at the same time leitmotivs for certain characters or situations and are repeated or developed in later episodes. Thus the opera contains, at several points, the theme of growling Don Jerome (his arioso "If a daughter you have"), the mocking musical caricature of Mendoza ("Mendoza is a cunning rogue"), the amorous melodies of the lovers (Antonio's serenade), the languishing, seductive theme for the Duenna, and the youthful, carefree musical images of feasting and fun. Interesting also is the method of Prokofiev's musical image-formation, defined not so much in the inner structure of a traditional arioso scheme as in changing situations. From this method comes the organically mature rondo in the music-making episode (the whole of Scene vi), the three-part love aria of Antonio, interrupted by the pranking masks, and similar examples. The opera's humor often evolves not only from the wit of the text but also from the comedy of the musical situations, as in the comical trio of music-making friends (clarinet, cornet, and bass drum), or the grotesque *ostinato* of the drunkard continuing under the dignified chorus of monks. Prokofiev's fantasy in this direction has no limits as he invents new, witty orchestral effects (the comic chamber ensemble in Scene vi, the guitar and individual groups of strings backstage in Scene i, and even the playing on glasses in the final scene of the wedding feast).

Reviving in his opera the eternal images of classic *opera buffa* (the enamored and ugly oldster, the bad-tempered guardian, the overripe maiden in search of a fiancé, the inexhaustible soubrette), Prokofiev enriches and individualizes these traditional masque-types. As in *Romeo*, there is a genuine Renaissance feeling in this work: a blend of humor and lyricism, of everyday life and elevated ideal, of frivolous and almost indecent gesture with poetically penetrating elements. One cannot decide which to prefer — the glamorous sparkle of the carnival scenes, the good-humored mockery that never descends to vulgar grotesque, or the lyrical feeling expressed so warmly, full-bloodedly, sunnily. The satirical scene in the monastery may remind one of the pagan wickedness of the Boccaccio *novelle*, but the carnival and feasting scenes (i and ix) have the hot, epicurean pulse of Rubens. This favorite theme in Russian art, the festive jubilation — originating in Pushkin — was brought into our music by Glinka, Borodin, and Glazunov.

In *Cinderella*, however, Prokofiev, as he invariably does in his selection of themes and subjects, makes a turn of at least 180°. After the intoxicating Renaissance juiciness of *Betrothal in a Convent*, after its lusty laughter and passionate serenades, he turns to the "nursery world," toward the toylike fantasy of Perrault. Among his important theatrical works, *Cinderella* will no doubt occupy the same place that *The Nutcracker* occupies among Tchaikovsky's — that of a small, jeweled *chef d'œuvre* that loses none of its charm by its proximity to *The Queen of Spades* or the Pathetic Symphony.

This is not to say that the world of images embodied in *Cinderella* is limited by the world of dolls and toys. Cinderella herself, our familiar childhood heroine, is endowed with deeply human feelings: she has a naturally quiet, melting sadness, the tender, transparent first love of a girl's heart. She is the heiress of Rimsky-Korsakov's Snow-Maiden, and among Prokofiev's feminine characters she is akin to Beautiful Maiden in *The Prodigal Son*, and, especially, to Juliet. Cinderella's orchestral leitmotiv, which is followed through with classical order, and her love-duets with the Prince are filled with true romantic charm. It is only when this love palpitation gives way to a more active, dancing quality that we see a charming doll, a toy, come to life, recalling the three Princesses in the *Three Oranges*.

The score of *Cinderella* again displays, on a grand scale, the dances of the seventeenth and eighteenth centuries, so beloved by Prokofiev and so often cultivated by him since the period of his piano pieces, Op. 12, and his *Classical Symphony*. Here we have a Gavotte (his *fifth* gavotte), a Passepied, a Court Dance full of a slightly heavy grace, a Bourrée, and a faintly caricatured Minuet. These dances all contain at least a particle of good-humored irony. Smiling slyly, the composer draws amusing portraits of the old fairy-tale's figures: the pompous guests, the impoverished cavaliers, Cinderella's envious sisters. Those who are puffed-up with bourgeois pride set off the others, scrawny and rachitic, and the effect of clumsy grandeur acts as a spur to the irony of Prokofiev's neo-classicism.[8]

Other dances in *Cinderella* sound more modern and are treated more seriously: waltzes, mazurkas, lyric solos, duets. Prokofiev's broad use of the waltz, in its passion and exciting sensualism, is an interesting novelty in his music. The series of waltzes from *Cinderella* (a grand waltz, a slow waltz, a waltz coda), together with a whole waltz scene from *War and Peace* (Scene iii), and the Mephisto-Waltz from *Lermontov*, show that the form holds a new attraction for the composer. This tendency is definitely connected with the general revival of waltz rhythms in the Soviet musical milieu in recent years, in mass songs and occasionally in instrumental works such as the second quartet and ballet suite of Shostakovich.

There is one more interesting indication in the *Cinderella* score: for the first time since the *Three Oranges* and *The Flaming Angel* Prokofiev returns to purely picturesque, graphic fantasy. The impressionist fairy portraits (the fairies of Spring, Summer, Autumn, and Winter), the magic transformation scenes, the fairy-tale images of tap-dancing dwarfs, of grasshoppers and dragon-flies, of midnight chimes — all these visual theatrical effects required the use of a generous and decorative palette. In such episodes as the dances of the four fairies — especially those of the Autumn and Winter fairies — there is a typically impressionist approach to sound-production: an extended play of spicy, colorful harmonies, vividly pictorial pas-

---

[8] There are clues to this irony in the original source of the ballet in Charles Perrault's *Cendrillon*: "They had gone without food almost two days, they were so overjoyed. They broke more than a dozen laces in the effort to make their waists look more slender and they passed the entire time before their mirror."

sages, and a domination of harmonic means over melodic-constructive ones.[9] A similar inclination toward coloristic sound-production can be seen also in Prokofiev's suddenly fired interest in Eastern music. The Oriental dances in *Cinderella* and in *Betrothal in a Convent*, the wild Tatar strains in *Ivan the Terrible*, and finally an entire string quartet on Kabardinian themes — all this makes an interesting Oriental page in Prokofiev's latest work. He treats this Eastern thematic material in his own way, each time emphasizing the wiryness in it, its severe archaism of consonance, its awkward melodic line, its obstinacy that permits no sensual flabbiness, and finally its wild fantasy of harmonic color (for example, the Lydian mode used in the "Orientalia" of *Cinderella*).

There is a compelling blend of fantasy and irony, of boyish lightness and dreamy lyricism, that relates *Cinderella* to *The Love for Three Oranges*. Like an unexpected eyewitness to this fact, we suddenly hear in the second scene of *Cinderella*, just as Cinderella offers oranges to her guests, the familiar music of the March from the *Three Oranges*.[10] It is as if a living musical thread had tied together Prokofiev's two fairy-tales across the twenty-five years that separate them.

The most controversial and complex of Prokofiev's last three musical works for the theater is his *War and Peace*. The very intention of the composer to create an opera on Tolstoy's huge historical epic was recognized as extremely precarious. Repeated attempts by Soviet playwrights to dramatize the all-embracing epics of Tolstoy had rarely had even partial success, often resulting in no more than talented illustrations of Tolstoy or clumsy dramatizations that over-simplified and distorted their sources (such as the Maly Theater's 1812, an attempt to dramatize *War and Peace*). Is it really possible to

---

[9] This pictorial-impressionist admiration for colorful consonance can be noticed in some episodes of the Eighth Piano Sonata, particularly in the transitional passages of the first movement.

[10] There are plenty of precedents for such a device, the most famous of which is Mozart's quotation from *The Marriage of Figaro* in the finale of *Don Giovanni*.

cram into a three-hour spectacle the greatest chronicle of the life and struggle of an entire nation that we know in the history of literature? Fully aware of the scale and significance of *War and Peace*, Prokofiev did not pause before this apparently insuperable difficulty. For several years the idea of a musical embodiment of *War and Peace* had been in the composer's consciousness. The year of 1941, when the memory of the people went back with special vividness to Napoleon's invasion of 1812, gave him the impetus to realize his intention. The speed with which the opera was created, the dimensions and forms of its execution, are among the most amazing phenomena of Prokofiev's entire creative career.

Once more, as in *The Gambler* and in *Semyon Kotko*, Prokofiev wrote an opera almost exclusively on a prose text, refusing on principle to employ verse. This method of operatic prose, of giving musical form to everyday speech, which had been used for the first time by Mussorgsky in *Marriage*, is Prokofiev's main operatic method. Here, in practice, comes to life Vladimir Stasov's prophecy if fifty years ago: "The time will come for the overthrow of the prejudice that 'verse texts' are inevitable for the opera libretto — when opera, in the hands of those future followers of Mussorgsky, will grow increasingly realistic." [11] Actually, nearly the entire libretto of *War and Peace*, with the exception of choral episodes, is drawn from Tolstoy's original prose text, the scenes only occasionally abridged or slightly transformed. The poetic charm of the musical characterization of the main roles, primarily the roles of Natasha Rostova and Andrei Bolkonsky, depends on the fascination of Tolstoy's prose, its sincerity, humanness, and maximum laconicism. Natural vocal declamation does not in the least suffer in these instances from the absence of rhyme and poetic meter. But there are passages in which the libret-

[11] From Vladimir Karenin's biography of Stasov, Vol. II (Leningrad, 1927). Karenin (the pen-name of Stasov's niece, Varvara Komarova) comments on this: "Reading these lines now . . . when Prokofiev has already realized *The Gambler* and *The Ugly Duckling*, makes one involuntarily exclaim: 'Stasov the prophet again!'"

tists' abuse of wordiness and complicated verbal constructions make the declamation clumsy and difficult to accept, edging as it does toward blank verse without, however, taking the final step. In such cases the laws of operatic form revenge themselves on the composer for his neglect, the opera being stripped of the most necessary musical thematic freighting.

The construction of the entire work is extremely complicated and original: there are eleven episodes and over sixty characters, the majority of whom appear only episodically, usually only once during the course of the work. Alongside intimate "lyrical scenes" portraying the personal experiences of the leading characters, there are grand and somewhat kaleidoscopic mass scenes presenting a multi-colored picture of various events and situations. Since Mussorgsky's *Khovanshchina* Russian opera has not known a monumental historical narrative that so freely and broadly develops mass-scenes of the people, saturated with genre naturalness and acute dynamism. However, the dramaturgy of the opera, in spite of its originality and freedom, has some basic defects: an abundance of cast-off, undeveloped characters and dramatic lines, and the presence of personages who reason but have not the "dominating passion" so necessary to the characterization of genuine opera heroes (Pierre Bezukhov himself turns out to be such a "needless link" in the opera), and also a prolixity of separate scenes that caused the composer himself to note in the published piano score a series of possible cuts. The lyrical love thread (the themes of Natasha and Andrei) is developed from act to act through the familiar channel of true operatic "central activity," but the same cannot be said of the themes of war and the people's calamities. These do not receive a similar natural development, and therefore the division of the spectacle into scenes of "peace" (Acts I and II) and of "war" (Acts III–V) is sensed as something mechanical and unsymphonic.

Three basic strata of musical characteristics form the sonorous sphere of *War and Peace*: first, the lyrical images revealing the personal emotional world of the chief heroes; second, the images of the people who rise against the aggressors; and third, genre-descriptive and naturalistic episodes, providing an illustrative, decorative sound background for the spectacle. The first of these three lines is the most profoundly and organically developed in a whole series of heightened emotional leitmotivs of Natasha's and Andrei's love, music whose sincere breath of youth is truly captivating. The scenes in which Natasha participates — the spring nocturne of the Otradnoye garden (Scene i), the intoxicatingly tempting scene of the ball (Scene iii), the scene at Akhrosimova's, culminating in almost tragic ecstasy, and the unforgettably expressive scene of Andrei's delirium (Scene x) — are among the best episodes in the opera. Each of these is grouped around its own circle of musical images, themes of bright hopes or of forebodings: the sinful, sensual impulses of the first scene; the wonderful waltz motivs that provide an uninterrupted emotional background to the ball scene, and the themes of sickening nightmare and the premonition of approaching death in the shattering scene of delirium.

Much more variegated and diverse is the musical sphere that characterizes the feelings and thoughts of the fighting people. Among the ten mass choral episodes concentrated in Scenes vii, ix, and xi we encounter several accomplished song constructions approaching the traditional type of song in couplets, such as the slightly archaic, purposely primitive soldiers' chorus, "As of old, as in Suvorov's time," or the splendidly audacious Cossack chorus in ¾ time, or the artful song of the women partisans, "Ah, you pretty ones," in the finale of Scene ix. Besides such "inserted" choral numbers, there are broad presentations of more developed symphonic choral episodes. In these an interwoven style of orchestral accompaniment and choral texture gives the music a more instrumental character. Occasionally, symphonic leitmotivs are directly transposed into the choral parts. Often the specific choral singing elements are integrated into the whole system of emotional means. Primarily this complex of means rightly belongs to the developed symphonic principle combined with a greater saturation of the spectator's impressions in the stage action. Among these vocal symphonic mass scenes are the tragically expressive chorus of refugees from Smolensk (based on the ominous leitmotiv of the people's calamaties), the martial chorus of the people's army, "How our Kutuzov came to the people," and the Funeral March in the finale of Scene vii, the Moscow procession with the bodies of the executed heroes.

The manly, sagaciously majestic leitmotiv of Kutuzov and the broadly singing leitmotiv of victory — these bright and noble Russian melodies are heard frequently in the opera and they also characterize a series of the most important choral scenes.

The third circle, of genre-descriptive images, again shows the qualities of Prokofiev as dramatist, hitting the bull's-eye each time with his keen observation. Here he seems to have turned realistic portraitist, with a flexible brush and a rich palette. In economical, sure strokes he paints such episodic characters as the old grumbler, Prince Bolkonsky, the fearless coachman, Balaga, the gypsy Matriosha, the landowner Akhrosimova. Prokofiev's irresistible finality is most expressively shown in the scene of the Battle of Borodino from Napoleon's viewpoint on the Shevardin redoubt. Rejecting any portrait details of Bonaparte, the composer expresses only the general feeling of the scene — the mad hazard of a gambler, shown in rushing *ostinato* rhythms.

Among the orchestral-pictorial episodes must be mentioned the landscape of ruined Moscow (at the opening of Scene ix), the huge symphonic picture of burning Moscow, and the dynamic battle-painting of the fight between the partisans and the retreating French (in Scene xi).

The Overture to *War and Peace* is the most developed and thematically saturated of all of Prokofiev's opera overtures. It is based on the juxtaposition of two of the above image-spheres: on one side the images of the people's liberating surge (themes of the partisans and Kutuzov), and on the other side the lyricism of personal emotion (themes of Natasha and Andrei and the theme of Pierre).

War and Peace can be discussed from many angles. Compared with *Betrothal* and *Cinderella*, the specific gravity of its music as an organizing image-forming element is evidently lowered. This is apparent not only in a certain underestimation by Prokofiev of the vocal medium and a certain overabundance of prose declamation, occasionally descending to *Sprechstimme*, but also in the presence of whole episodes that are deprived of their rightful melodic fullness. This fault also appears in the clumsy and inorganic quality of the whole dramatic plan. It is quite possible, however, that in the process of theatrical production these impressions, received from a study of the piano score, will be smoothed out. But there is one thing that is unquestionable: in spite of the many nihilistic exaggerations natural to this opera, its best pages capture one with their profound veracity and their seizure of real life. One feels sure that these best pages of *War and Peace* will embellish Russian operatic classicism of the twentieth century.

Surveying Prokofiev's works of the 1940's one notes with satisfaction another achievement: the richest flowering of his instrumentalism, ever acquiring more obviously the character of an accomplished and mature symphonic style. The three piano sonatas, the Quartet on native North Caucasian themes, and the Flute Sonata, Op. 94, were steps toward the wonderful Fifth Symphony, a milestone in Prokofiev's creative work, summing up his searches of many years in the medium of pure, generalized, and philosophic instrumental thought. The three sonatas make one speak not only of some new flowering of Prokofiev's instrumentation, but also of a new quality of crystallization in his thematic material. Compared with the youthful pianism of Prokofiev these sonatas disclosed a greater breadth and freedom of intention, a might of imagery that fits only with difficulty into the chamber frame of the sonata. Evidently the thematic quality and imagery of the new Prokofiev so-

natas reflects the composer's long experience in the realm of
theater music. The concrete images of his operas and ballets,
transplanted into the world of instrumental music, crystallize
into these unusual and surprising sonata themes. Rushed in-
tonations, turns, and rhythms born from the words, gestures,
and actions of stage situations break into the fenced-in sphere
of pure instrumentalism. In the same way Mussorgsky's living
reproduction of real nature brought his inventive pianism into
being. Today Prokofiev fills the old wineskins of classic sonata
form with unaccustomed content, upsetting traditional limits
in the selection of thematic means, in character of melody, in
methods of textural exposition. We therefore encounter in his
instrumental works either reflections of operatic recitative (itself rising from musical prose rather than from traditional
vocal cantilena) or self-sufficient lyrical melody barely supported by harmonic fullness, or strangely whimsical machine-
like throbbing rhythms that might have been summoned to
reveal the dynamic core of some tense scenic situation, or
captivating and playful dance episodes full of delicate, smiling grace. One finds the most unexpected images in his new
instrumental works. Such are the emotional declamation in
the supplementary movements of the Sixth and Eighth Sonatas; the irresistibly powerful throbs in the finales of the
Seventh and Eighth Sonatas, with their fantastic asymmetric
rhythms; the slow openings of the Eighth Sonata and the Fifth
Symphony, seeming to reveal the very process of the author's
deepening thought, and the willful, carved, and obstinately repeated "formulas of appeal" that open the first movements of
the Sixth Sonata and the Second Quartet. We need not em-
phasize Prokofiev's beloved scherzo quality, so long familiar
to us, and maintained in the middle movements of all three
piano sonatas, the Flute Sonata, and the Fifth Symphony.
But one must note especially the original treatment of the
folk material in the Quartet on Kabardinian themes: the national themes are not merely "adapted" by the composer; they
are forced to surrender completely to his commanding creative

personality, dissolving in Prokofiev's specific sound-sphere, and existing in complete harmony with his most individual rhythm, with his free polyphonic manner, and even with his tonic thought, with his long familiar tart diatonic "white notes" (the supplementary part of the first movement).[12]

Interesting, too, is Prokofiev's stubborn aspiration toward a more integrated and fused sonata form, toward instrumental poetry, and toward the obliteration of thematic disunion between the separate movements. I have in mind the underlined reminiscences of images from the first movements in the finales of the Sixth and Eighth Sonatas and the Fifth Symphony. As in an organically dramatic narration, the leading image of the drama reappears before the conclusion, demonstrating the general logic of the dramatic plan. This detail clearly proves the adult content and philosophic growth of Prokofiev's new instrumentalism. In the process of enriching the inner content of his sonatas the composer has not in the least rejected the complex and effective advantage of instrumental exposition. The rich piano technique of his three latest piano sonatas revives the best parts of his youthful virtuosity, amazing in its athletic technical strength and in the controlled "sporting" audacity of certain passages, leaps and crossings. As for orchestral exposition, the Fifth Symphony embodies the highest achievements of Prokofiev the orchestrator, uniting an intoxicating many-colored palette with a clean discipline of orchestral development.

In general, listening to the Fifth Symphony, one accepts it as the most important summing-up of the composer's searches of many years in the domain of pure symphonic form. As rivers and streams flow into the ocean, so do the many previous compositions of Prokofiev — his sonatas, suites, and, in part, his operas — all nourish the imagery and thematic rich-

---

[12] An analogy to this may be found in an earlier work, his *Overture on Hebrew Themes*, Op. 34. There also the composer did not in the least subordinate his individuality to the folk material, but, on the contrary, collected and employed material deriving exclusively from his own tastes and preferences.

ness of the Fifth Symphony, flowing into it through dozens of living waters.

We may well imagine that the serious and heroic thematic material of the symphony's first movement, its noble, elevated tone, its epic Russian heroism and severely weighed logic of form, could have been inspired by the musical images of Kutuzov, Andrei Bolkonsky, Ivan the Terrible, warrior and citizen, and the legendary warriors of *Alexander Nevsky*. The originality of this movement is in its slow singing strata, in the domination of elevated thought over concrete, living action, in the very method of its development — slowly built layers of self-sufficient melodic lines and instrumental dialogues.[13] One hears in this profound meditation the artist's thoughts about the fate of his native land, an expression of his inextinguishable faith in the spiritual triumph and moral power of the conquering people.

Listening to the second movement of the symphony, one recalls the entrancing scherzo moods of Prokofiev's lyrical comedies and the enchanting atmosphere of light, youthful pranks in which his theater heroes meet and fall in love. Outstanding in one's memory are the night revels of *Romeo* and *Betrothal*, in which carnival masks enjoy playful extravagances, the half-ironical Mozartean style of the *Classical Symphony* and the Flute Sonata, the smiling, dancing second movements of the Sixth, Seventh, and Eighth Sonatas. The colors are as transparent as those of a fine, rare lace. Half-way through this semi-fantastic Scherzo appears, for just a moment, a clear and naïve song like that from some piece of children's music by Prokofiev; it suddenly discloses a fragment of reality as concrete and familiar as if lit by living sunbeams. And then everything is turned upside down: the jolly masks become menacing jesters, the orchestral timbres are painted over with oily and uncouth brush-strokes, choked with mocking and quacking

---

[13] These peculiarities of development contradict the apparent similarity between the themes in the first movement of this symphony and characteristic symphonic themes of Glazunov, usually treated elastically and step by step.

sounds. Wicked freaks and monsters launch into an evil dance, laughing and sneering at the world of rainbow hopes.

After this queer nocturnal spectacle the third movement enters with a special power of bright lyricism, ripe, healthy, and life-affirming. Analogies with Prokofiev's opera-images again appear, primarily with the lyricism of Andrei Bolkonsky, whose life-wisdom was not enough to shield his faith in ideal love. But the song-element soon gives way to dramatic declamation, ever more inspired, reaching climactic points saturated with funereal tragedy. And then again appears the light of calm, noble meditation.

Reminiscences from the first movement, opening the path toward the final movement, again establish the basic philosophical direction taken by the whole composition, the idea of the triumphing, courageous, and mature spirit. And then unrolls a colorful and festive *panneau* and an incessant flood of brilliant carnival activity. The richness and tumult of color again summon up analogies with the intoxicating fruitiness of Flemish painting. This carnival festivity had been heard more than once in previous symphonic works by Prokofiev, not to mention in actual "ballet music"; but this time the whirling mass dance is often interrupted by profound lyrical meditations, epic extended melodies in the spirit of Mussorgsky (lines from the first and third movements). And toward the end the contagious merriment of the festivity again triumphs, echoing with living peals of healthy, human laughter.

In the clear optimistic tone of the Fifth Symphony are embraced a firm faith in life and an elemental hymning of life's great joys. Prokofiev's inherent "feeling of a healthy country and the energies and forces hidden in it" are expressed in the thoughts and moods of the symphony. Here in these images is hidden a living prescience of the hard-won morrow of the Soviet Union.

Sergei Prokofiev is now at the height of his powers. Having written some one hundred numbered works of various genres, including operas, ballets, symphonies, cantatas, piano and violin concertos, piano sonatas, many orchestral suites, overtures, and chamber pieces, some fifty songs and lyrics, and nearly one hundred piano pieces, he is by no means content to rest on his achievements. A host of ideas for new major instrumental compositions are awaiting fulfillment, and Prokofiev is nursing many an interesting plan in the field of opera. After *Zdravitsa, Semyon Kotko,* and *War and Peace,* new achievements with Soviet subject matter may be expected from him as well.

Prokofiev's music may not always be wholly comprehensible to the average concert-goer. An outstanding artist and an inveterate innovator, he continues stubbornly to blaze paths into the future. In our days his experiments in harmony, intonation, and orchestration, subordinated as they are to the leading idea, have acquired a new meaning and purpose. And what may not be fully comprehended by everyone today will, with the growth of our general musical culture, be universally accepted tomorrow.

We have every reason to be proud of the fact that we have in our midst today a master whose work is flourishing along with Soviet music as a whole, consolidating its prominent position in the world of art.

Catalogue of Prokofiev's Works

Giving for Prokofiev's first one hundred opera the opus number, title, date of composition (date of original form), and — when possible — first publisher and date and place of first performance.

Op. 1. First Sonata for piano, F minor. 1909 (1907). Jurgenson. February 21, 1910, Moscow.

Op. 2. Four *Études* for piano: D minor, E minor, C minor, C minor. 1909. Jurgenson. February 21, 1910, Moscow.

Op. 3. Four Pieces for piano: *Story, Badinage, March, Phantom.* 1911 (1907–8). Jurgenson. March 28, 1911, St. Petersburg.

Op. 4. Four Pieces for piano: *Reminiscence, Élan, Despair, Diabolic Suggestions.* 1910–12 (sketches, 1908). Jurgenson. December 18, 1908, St. Petersburg.

Op. 5. Sinfonietta for orchestra, A major, in five movements. 1909–14. Gutheil. October 24, 1915, St. Petersburg.

Op. 6. *Dreams,* symphonic picture for orchestra. 1910. MS. November 22, 1910, St. Petersburg.

Op. 7. *Swan* and *Wave,* two female choruses with orchestra to Balmont's words. 1910. MS.

Op. 8. *Autumnal Sketch* for orchestra. 1910. MS. July 19, 1911, Moscow.

Op. 9. Two Poems for voice and piano. 1910–11. Gutheil.

Op. 10. First Concerto for piano and orchestra, D-flat major. 1911. Jurgenson. July 25, 1912, Moscow.

Op. 11. *Toccata* for piano. 1912. Jurgenson. December 10, 1916, St. Petersburg.

Op. 12. Ten Pieces for piano: *March, Gavotte, Rigaudon, Mazurka, Caprice, Legend, Prelude, Allemande, Scherzo humoristique, Scherzo.*

1913 (sketches, 1906–12). Jurgenson. Orchestral transcription of No. 9, *Scherzo for Four Bassoons.* Jurgenson.

Op. 13. *Magdalene,* opera in one act to Lieven's text. 1913 (1911). MS.

Op. 14. Second Sonata for piano, D minor, in four movements. 1912. Jurgenson. January 23, 1914, Moscow.

Op. 15. *Ballad* for cello and piano. 1912. Jurgenson. January 23, 1914, Moscow.

Op. 16. Second Concerto for piano and orchestra, G minor, in four movements. 1913. Gutheil. August 23, 1913, Pavlovsk.

Op. 17. *Sarcasms,* piano cycle. 1912–14. Jurgenson. December 10, 1916, St. Petersburg.

Op. 18. *The Ugly Duckling* (based on Andersen's fairy-tale) for voice and piano. 1914. Gutheil. January 17, 1915, St. Petersburg. There is also a manuscript version for voice and orchestra.

Op. 19. First Concerto for violin and orchestra, D major, in three movements. 1916–17. Gutheil. October 18, 1923, Paris.

Op. 20. *Scythian Suite (Ala and Lolli),* in four movements. 1914. Gutheil. January 16, 1916, St. Petersburg.

Op. 21. *The Buffoon (Chout),* ballet in six scenes. 1920 (1915). Gutheil. May 17, 1921, Paris.

Op. 21–A. *The Buffoon,* symphonic suite in twelve movements. Gutheil.

Op. 22. *Fugitive Visions,* twenty

pieces for piano. 1915–17. Gutheil. April 15, 1918, St. Petersburg.

Op. 23. Five Poems for voice and piano: *Under the Roof, Gray Dress, Trust Me, In My Garden, Wizard.* 1915. Gutheil.

Op. 24. *The Gambler,* opera in four acts, based on Dostoyevsky. 1927, (1915–16). Gutheil. April 29, 1929, Brussels.

Op. 25. *Classical Symphony,* D major. 1917. Gutheil. April 21, 1918, St. Petersburg.

Op. 26. Third Concerto for piano and orchestra, C major. 1921 (1917). Gutheil. December 16, 1921, Chicago.

Op. 27. Five Songs to the words of Anna Akhmatova: *The Sun Fills My Room, True Tenderness, In Remembrance of the Sun, Good Morning, The Gray-Eyed King.* 1916. Gutheil. February 5, 1917, Moscow.

Op. 28. Third Sonata for piano, A minor. 1917 (1907). Gutheil. April 15, 1918, St. Petersburg.

Op. 29. Fourth Sonata for piano, C minor. 1917 (1908). Gutheil. April 17, 1918, St. Petersburg.

Op. 29–A. *Andante* from the Fourth Sonata, transcribed by the author for symphony orchestra. MS.

Op. 30. *Seven, They Are Seven* for solo tenor, chorus, and orchestra, to Balmont's text. 1917. Gutheil. May 29, 1924, Paris.

Op. 31. *Tales of the Old Grandmother,* four pieces for piano. 1918. Gutheil. January 7, 1919, New York.

Op. 32. Four Pieces for piano: *Dance, Minuet, Gavotte, Waltz.* 1918. Gutheil.

Op. 33. *The Love for Three Oranges,* opera in four acts, based on Carlo Gozzi. 1919. Gutheil. December 30, 1921, Chicago.

Op. 33–A. *The Love for Three Oranges,* symphonic suite in six movements. 1924 (1919). Gutheil. November 29, 1925, Paris.

Op. 33–B. March and Scherzo from *The Love for Three Oranges,* transcription for piano.

Op. 34. *Overture on Hebrew Themes,* for clarinet, piano, and string quartet (two violins, viola, and cello). 1919. Gutheil. January 26, 1920, New York.

Op. 34–A. *Overture on Hebrew Themes,* for symphony orchestra. 1932 (1919). Gutheil. Moscow.

Op. 35. Five Melodies without Words, for voice and piano. 1920. Gutheil. March 27, 1921, New York.

Op. 35–A. Five Melodies, for violin and piano. 1925 (1920). Gutheil.

Op. 36. Five Songs, for voice and piano, to Balmont's words. 1921. Gutheil.

Op. 37. *The Flaming Angel,* opera in five acts, based on Bryusov. 1919–27. MS.

Op. 38. Fifth Sonata for piano, C major, in three movements. 1923. Gutheil. March 9, 1924, Paris.

Op. 39. Quintet for wind and strings in six movements. 1924. Gutheil. February 1927, Moscow.

Op. 40. Second Symphony for large orchestra, D minor, in two movements. 1924. Gutheil. June 6, 1925, Paris.

Op. 41. *Le Pas d'acier,* ballet in two scenes, libretto by Yakulov. 1924. Gutheil. June 2, 1927, Paris.

Op. 41–A. *Le Pas d'acier,* symphonic suite. 1926 (1925). Paris.

Op. 42. Overture for seventeen performers, B-flat major. 1926. MS. February 7, 1927, Moscow.

Op. 42–A. Overture for large orchestra, B-flat major. 1928. (1926).

Op. 43. Divertissement for orchestra in four movements. 1925–9. Gutheil. December 22, 1929, Paris.

Op. 43–A. Divertissement, author's transcription for piano. 1938 (1925). Gutheil.

Op. 44. Third Symphony for large orchestra, in four movements.

1928. Gutheil. May 17, 1929, Paris.

Op. 45. *Things in Themselves*, two pieces for piano. 1928. Gutheil.

Op. 46. *L'Enfant prodigue*, ballet in two scenes. 1928. Gutheil. May 21, 1929, Paris.

Op. 46–A. Symphonic Suite based on *L'Enfant prodigue*. 1929. MS.

Op. 47. Fourth Symphony, C major, in four movements. 1930. MS. November 14, 1930, Boston.

Op. 48. Sinfonietta for little symphony orchestra, A major (version of Op. 5). 1929. Gutheil. December 22, 1929, Paris.

Op. 49. Four Portraits from *The Gambler*, suite for large orchestra, in five movements. 1930–1. Gutheil. March 12, 1932, Paris.

Op. 50. First String Quartet, B minor, in three movements. 1930. Gutheil. April 25, 1931, Washington.

Op. 51. *Sur le Borysthène*, ballet in two scenes. 1930. Gutheil. December 16, 1932, Paris.

Op. 51–A. *Sur le Borysthène*, symphonic suite. 1933 (1930).

Op. 52. Six Transcriptions for piano: *Intermezzo, Rondo, Étude, Scherzino, Andante, Scherzo*, 1931. Gutheil.

Op. 53. Fourth Concerto for piano, left hand, in four movements. 1931. MS.

Op. 54. Two Sonatinas for piano, E minor and G major. 1931–2. Gutheil.

Op. 55. Fifth Concerto for piano and orchestra, G major, in five movements. 1932. Gutheil. October 31, 1932, Berlin.

Op. 56. Sonata for two violins, C minor. 1932. Gutheil. December 16, 1932, Paris.

Op. 57. Symphonic Song, for orchestra. 1933. MS. April 14, 1934, Moscow.

Op. 58. Concerto for cello and orchestra, C minor. 1933–8. MS.

Op. 59. Three Piano Pieces: *Prom-*

enade, Landscape, Pastoral Sonatina. 1934. Gutheil.

Op. 60. *Lieutenant Kije*, symphonic suite based on music for film, in five movements: *Birth of Kije, Romance, Marriage of Kije, Troika, Burial of Kije*. 1933–4. Gutheil.

Op. 60–A. Two Songs for voice and piano from *Lieutenant Kije*.

Op. 61. *Egyptian Nights*, symphonic suite based on music for play, in seven parts: "Night in Egypt," "Cæsar," "The Sphinx and Cleopatra," "Alarm," "Dances," "Antony," "Eclipse of Cleopatra," "Roma Militaris." 1934. Gutheil. 1938, Moscow.

Op. 62. *Thoughts*, three pieces for piano. 1933–4. Gutheil. September 1940, Moscow.

Op. 63. Second Concerto for violin and orchestra, G minor. 1935. Gutheil. December 1, 1935, Madrid.

Op. 64. *Romeo and Juliet*, ballet in four acts. 1935. MS. 1938, Brno.

Op. 64–A. *Romeo and Juliet*, suite for orchestra in seven movements. 1936 (1935). State Music Publishing House. June 24, 1936, Moscow.

Op. 64–B. Second suite from *Romeo and Juliet*, in seven movements. 1936 (1935). State Music Publishing House.

Op. 65. *Children's Music*, twelve pieces for piano: "Morning," "The Walk," "Fairy-tale," "Tarantella," "Repentance," "Waltz," "Grasshoppers' Parade," "Rain and Rainbow," "Touch and Run," "March," "Evening," "The Moon Goes over the Meadows." 1935. Gutheil.

Op. 65–A. *Summer Day*, symphonic suite for children (Nos. 1, 5, 6, 9, 10, 11, 12 from *Children's Music*). 1941 (1935). MS.

Op. 66. Six Popular Songs: *Partisan Zheleznyak, Anyutka, My Coun-*

PROKOFIEV'S WORKS

try is Growing, etc. 1935. State Music Publishing House.

Op. 67. *Peter and the Wolf*, symphonic tale to author's text. 1936. State Music Publishing House. May 2, 1936, Moscow.

Op. 68. Three Pieces for Children: *Chatterbox, Sweet Melody, Little Pigs.* 1936–9. State Music Publishing House.

Op. 69. Four Marches for brass band. 1936–7. State Music Publishing House.

Op. 70. *The Queen of Spades*, music for film; *Boris Godunov*, music for play. 1936. MSS.

Op. 71. *Yevgeny Onyegin*, music for play. 1936. MS.

Op. 72. *Russian Overture*, for orchestra, C major. 1936. Gutheil. October 29, 1936, Moscow.

Op. 73. Three Songs to Pushkin's words: *Pine Trees, Roseate Dawn, In Your Chamber.* 1936. State Music Publishing House.

Op. 74. *Cantata for the Twentieth Anniversary of the October Revolution*, to the words of Lenin, Stalin, and Marx, for symphony orchestra, military band, accordions, percussion, and two choruses, in ten movements, 1936–7. MS.

Op. 75. *Romeo and Juliet*, ten pieces for piano. 1937 (1935). Iskusstvo Publishing House.

Op. 76. *Songs for Our Days*, for chorus and orchestra: Orchestral Introduction, *Over the Bridge, Be Well, Golden Ukraine, Brother for Brother, Girls, The Twenty-Year-Old, Lullaby, From End to End.* 1937. State Music Publishing House. November 1938, Moscow.

Op. 77. Music to *Hamlet.* 1938. MS.

Op. 77–A. Gavotte No. 4, E-flat major, from music to *Hamlet.* 1938. Gutheil.

Op. 78. *Alexander Nevsky*, cantata for solo, chorus, and orchestra, in seven movements: "Russia under

the Mongol Yoke," "Song about Alexander Nevsky," "Crusaders in Pskov," "Field of the Dead," "Arise, Men of Russia," "Battle on the Ice," "Entry of Alexander into Pskov." 1939. State Music Publishing House. April 1939, Moscow.

Op. 78–A. Three Songs from *Alexander Nevsky*, for voice and piano. State Music Publishing House.

Op. 79. Seven Popular Songs: *Song of the Homeland, Stakhanovite Woman, Over the Polar Sea, Send-Off, Bravely Forward, A Cossack Came Through the Village, Down the Road.* 1939. State Music Publishing House.

Op. 80. Sonata for violin and piano, C major.

Op. 81. *Semyon Kotko*, opera in five acts, libretto by V. Katayev. 1939. MS. June 1940, Moscow.

Op. 81–A. *Semyon Kotko*, symphonic suite in eight movements. December 23, 1943, Moscow.

Op. 82. Sixth Sonata for piano, A major, in four movements. 1939–40. State Music Publishing House. February 1940, Moscow.

Op. 83. Seventh Sonata for piano, in three movements. 1942 (1939). January 18, 1943, Moscow.

Op. 84. Eighth Sonata for piano, B-flat major, in three movements. 1939–44. MS.

Op. 85. *Zdravitsa*, cantata for Stalin's sixtieth birthday, to folk texts. 1939. December 1, 1939, Moscow.

Op. 86. *Betrothal in a Convent*, opera in four acts, based on Sheridan's *Duenna.* 1940. MS.

Op. 87. *Cinderella*, ballet in three acts, libretto by N. Volkov.

Op. 88. *Symphonic March.* July 1941. MS.

Op. 89. Seven Mass Songs on War Themes; March, A-flat major, for military band. 1941–2.

Op. 90. "*1941*," symphonic suite in three movements: "In Battle," "At Night," "For the Brotherhood of

Nations." 1941. MS. January 21, 1943, Sverdlovsk.

Op. 91. *War and Peace*, opera in eleven scenes, based on Tolstoy, libretto by the composer and Myra Mendelssohn. 1941–2.

Op. 92. Second String Quartet, F major, in three movements (based on Kabardinian and Balkarian themes). 1942. Muzghiz. April 7, 1942, Moscow.

Op. 93. *The Ballad of the Unknown Boy*, cantata in one movement, for soprano, tenor, chorus, and orchestra, to Antokolsky's words. MS. 1942–3. March 21, 1944, Moscow.

Op. 94. Sonata for flute and piano, D major, in four movements. MS. 1942–3. December 7, 1943, Moscow.

Op. 94 bis. Violin and piano version of the Sonata above. MS. 1944.

Op. 95. Three Pieces for piano, from *Cinderella*. 1942. Muzghiz.

Op. 96. Three Pieces for piano, transcriptions from the opera *War and Peace* and the music for the film *Lermontov*. 1942. Muzghiz.

Op. 97. Ten Pieces for piano, from the ballet *Cinderella*. 1943. MS.

Op. 97 bis. Adagio for cello and piano, from *Cinderella*. 1944. MS. April 19, 1944. Muzghiz.

Op. 98. Two Songs offered in the contest (1943) for a new national anthem.

Op. 99. March for band.

Op. 100. Fifth Symphony, B-flat major.

Index

i

INDEX

INDEX

INDEX

INDEX

INDEX

Index of Compositions by Prokofiev Referred to in the Text

x

INDEX

INDEX

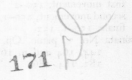

xiv